Skillstreaming the Adolescent

REVISED EDITION

New Strategies and Perspectives for Teaching Prosocial Skills

Arnold P. Goldstein
Ellen McGinnis

Research Press • 2612 North Mattis Avenue • Champaign, Illinois 61822

5 4 3 2 98 99 00 01

Copies of this book may be ordered from the publisher at the address given on the title page.

Cover design by Linda Brown, Positive I.D. Graphic Design Inc.
Printed by McNaughton & Gunn

ISBN 0–87822–369–X

Library of Congress Catalog Number 97–67001

CONTENTS

Figures and Tables

FIGURES

TABLES

PREFACE

Skillstreaming is now over 20 years old. Starting with its introduction in 1973 as one of the very first social skills training approaches, it has been widely used in the United States and beyond, and is now in place in hundreds of schools, agencies, and institutions serving youth. What lessons have we learned? What do we now know that will maximize the program's skills-training effectiveness?

This book is both a summing up and a looking ahead. We seek in it to share our own experiences and training recommendations, as well as those provided by many of the hundreds of teachers, administrators, youth care workers, and other practitioners who have employed this method—usually productively but certainly not always—with adolescents lacking or weak in prosocial behaviors. Our debt to them for their efforts, their energy, and their creativity as trainers is considerable.

We begin our examination of Skillstreaming today by placing it in both past and present contexts. Although the procedure is appropriate for diverse types of interpersonally skill deficient youths, in actual practice its primary target has been chronically aggressive adolescents, as well as those seemingly on their way to becoming so. Thus, chapter 1 fully examines the nature and impact of such youngsters as they currently exist in our primary and secondary schools. In addition, this chapter makes explicit the teaching of alternative, prosocial behaviors as Skillstreaming's central goal. Chapter 2 follows with a comprehensive review of the program's history and development. Though almost all of the other social skills training approaches following ours grew from social learning theory, Skillstreaming had a largely different origin. We describe it here both as relevant historical fact and for its implications for current and future practice.

Successful use of Skillstreaming requires more than skilled management of actual training sessions by teachers or other practitioners. Program implementation begins with awareness of and responsiveness to district and school needs. It depends on competent and motivated trainers, as well as on appropriately selected and grouped trainees. And successful programs are those that deal effectively with the mundane but oh-so-consequential details of where, when, how long, and so forth. These several concerns are the focus of chapter 3.

In a user-friendly manner, chapter 4 provides an up-to-date description of the "how-to" details of procedures necessary to conduct a Skillstreaming group. Step by step, we move from skill introduction to skill modeling by trainers, role-playing by trainees, feedback by participants, and assigned homework outside the group. A transcript of a group session illustrating these procedures constitutes chapter 5.

Skillstreaming's skills for adolescents are provided in chapter 6. We include the behavioral steps making up each of the 50 skills, trainer notes further concretizing these steps, and suggested situations for modeling displays. Real-world use of this skill curriculum, especially in the face of difficult and challenging interpersonal circumstances, will require that trainees be skilled in employing skill sequences and combinations. Chapter 7 describes and illustrates such "advanced Skillstreaming."

Even when the program is competently initiated and energetically maintained, the decision to target "problem youth" will inevitably result in occasional (and sometimes substantial) problems within the group, problems reflecting deficient trainee motivation and heightened trainee resistance. That, as they say, is the bad news. The good news is that the experience gained in now thousands of Skillstreaming sessions has yielded readily employed motivation-enhancing and resistance-reducing procedures, which chapter 8 describes in detail.

Chapter 9 turns to the serious problem and challenge of skill generalization. Decades of social skills training research and practice have made all too clear that, although trainees learn new skill behaviors relatively easily, their successful use in the often difficult real-life environments in which such youths function is usually much less frequent. Newly learned skills, in other words, often fail to generalize. Over this same time period, however, a substantial technology of generalization enhancement has emerged, some of it contributed by our own evaluation research. This valuable technology, again described in a manner directly useful to the practicing trainer, forms the substance of chapter 9.

As chapter 9 makes clear, interventions are never offered in isolation. Their ultimate effectiveness is influenced by environments beyond the training setting. One such environment, especially important and therefore singled out for special consideration, is the school. Chapter 10 considers the school's social and physical ecology. Here we address the person and place qualities of the school context in which Skillstreaming may be offered and share what is known about social and physical characteristics that may influence Skillstreaming outcomes for the better.

In the book's last chapter, we take the opportunity to reemphasize what the past 20 years of Skillstreaming use has already shown—it is an intervention always in transition. Chapters 1 through 10 describe where Skillstreaming has been and what it has become; chapter 11 speculates on where it might profitably be heading. This is, admittedly, our brainstorming chapter for the next 20 years of Skillstreaming.

Finally, three appendixes, new in this volume, respectively present an annotated bibliography of Skillstreaming research, copies of the Skillstreaming checklists and grouping chart, and a complete description of supplementary Skillstreaming components. A fourth appendix lists Skillstreaming program materials available for other instructional levels.

ACKNOWLEDGMENTS

Skillstreaming is the shared product of the energies and creativity of many people—colleagues, trainers, trainees, and others. Three persons, in particular, share major responsibility for bringing it into existence and nurturing its development over these many years. Robert P. Sprafkin and N. Jane Gershaw co-developed it with us originally and were prime contributors to enhancing both its early application and its initial evaluation. Barry Glick fully shared the effort to expand its boundaries to include especially difficult-to-reach adolescents. These colleagues well deserve special thanks and appreciation.

In trainer-training workshops, graduate student class lectures, and other venues, we have benefited greatly from the questions, challenges, and insights of a great many teachers, teachers-to-be, youth care workers, and other frontline personnel working with challenging youngsters. We have easily learned as much as we have taught and have sought to reflect these much appreciated lessons throughout this book.

An applied text such as this is no better than its utility in the real world of aggressive youngsters. In many of the hundreds of Skillstreaming sessions conducted with such adolescent trainees, they have held our feet to the fire, challenging the relevance, usefulness, and appropriateness of what we were teaching. We are greatly in debt to them for their confrontations and suggestions. Skillstreaming is undoubtedly a better approach because of their efforts and insights.

CHAPTER 1

Introduction: Aggression in America's Schools

This book is a journey to the world of people skills. It is a trainer preparation manual written in how-to detail for teachers and other professionals concerned with changing the behavior of aggressive adolescents for the better. As the real-life incidents next described illustrate, aggressive youngsters are often proficient in antisocial ways of responding to real or imagined provocations but weak in carrying out various prosocially constructive alternative behaviors.* It is a curriculum of just such positive alternatives that the Skillstreaming method is designed to teach.

Skill 12: Following Instructions

L. was told several times by several different staff members to take off his hat. He ignored all requests. He would touch his hat each time but not take it off (as if he was taunting us). He began to walk into the office (without permission). I told him that if he didn't take his hat off, I would. He didn't, and I did. He followed me out of the office and down the hall, leaning on me all the way. I told him to back off. He did not. He then said, "Give me my fucking hat." He then pushed me. I began to escort him to the office.

*The events described are drawn from a pool of 1,000 teacher-reported incidents gathered for our book *Break It Up: A Teacher's Guide to Managing Student Aggression* (Goldstein, Palumbo, Striepling, & Voutsinas, 1995).

He started to wrestle with me by grabbing my legs and pulling me up. We both fell to the floor. He did not release from me until he was pulled away from me. After he was pulled away from me, he slapped me across the face. (p. 27)

Skill 26: Using Self-Control

O. was rude and disrespectful to me and given a warning. She also refused to do her work. [Two days later] I gave her yet another warning because she wasn't doing any work, was mimicking my instructions and disrupting those who were working. Today O. came into class blowing bubbles, so I asked her to throw the gum away. She did so after telling me not to "get her going." Immediately, she popped another piece of gum into her mouth, and when I asked her to remove it she called me a "bitch." Her behavior is hampering the learning process of others. (p. 45)

Skill 28: Responding to Teasing

Shortly after my class began, two students (boys) verbally began arguing over the detention and referral one of them had received. The referral occurred in the previous class. One student was making fun of the other's troubles.

A fight broke out. Tables and chairs were being pushed around the room. I tried to get between [the students]. They were not hearing me. I then told the others in [the] classroom to move out of the way. I told one student to push the buzzer to the office and say "fight." We didn't need to say anything—they could hear. Other teachers came over to see if I needed help. Some students from another class had to be told to go back. I let [the boys] fight until the principal and assistant arrived.

Both boys were bleeding from the nose. One's face was swollen. When they realized the principal was in the room, they broke themselves up.

Each was suspended for 3 days. (p. 89)

Skill 30: Keeping Out of Fights

> The episode that I want to talk about happened in a high school cafeteria. I was on lunch duty and standing near the lunch lines as the students were lining up to get in. The line had just been allowed to go in so that it was moving up rather rapidly to file through the area where you pick up your food. . . . Two ninth-grade girls . . . had a confrontation, and there was a lot of shouting and screaming going on behind me, and as I turned around the first punch was landed. And I was standing behind . . . the puncher, and before she could land another one, I grabbed her arm and tried to keep her away from the other girl. As soon as I grabbed her arm and held her, that was a sign for the other girl to start beating on her. There were no other adults around. What I had to do was to let the one go that I had and try to get in the middle. . . . Another teacher arrived, and actually a couple more arrived, and one girl was grabbed and subdued by one of the male teachers, and I took the one that was nearer to me. . . . I grabbed her by the left arm, and she hit me three times in the face with the right arm. (pp. 86–87)

Facts and Figures

For most of America's approximately 51 million schoolchildren, the school day unfolds with no threats to safety and security—no fights, no weapons, no bullying, no theft. So let us begin our consideration of the school violence problem by keeping it in perspective: Yes, violence is a real and growing concern, a concern demanding effective solutions; however, for most of our children, it is still irrelevant to their school experience.

In American public education for the many decades preceding the 20th century, school-based aggression apparently was infrequent, low in intensity, and—at least in retrospect—almost quaint in character. "Misbehavior," "poor comportment," "bad conduct" and the like in the form of getting out of one's seat, insubordination, throwing a spitball, sticking a pigtail in an inkwell, or even the rare breaking of a window are the events of another era, events so mild in comparison to today's aggression that it is difficult to conceptualize them as the extremes of a shared continuum. Commenting on the nature of urban school violence for the years 1870 through 1950, Bayh (1975), observes, "If, however, the system has never been totally immune from incidents of student misbehavior, such problems have historically been viewed as a relatively minor concern seldom involving more than a few sporadic and isolated incidents" (p. 3).

The years prior to the 1960s may indeed appropriately be called the "preescalation period" in American school violence. Consistent with Bayh's observations, a 1956 National Education Association survey reported that two-thirds of the 4,270 teachers sampled from across the United States reported that fewer than 1 percent of their students caused disruption or disturbance and "95 percent [of the responding teachers] described the boys and girls they taught as either exceptionally well behaved, or reasonably well behaved" (National Education Association, 1956, p. 17).

In 1975, the Bayh Senatorial Subcommittee issued its Safe School Report. This survey of 750 school districts indicated that in America's schools between 1970 and 1973, homicides increased by 18.5 percent, rapes and attempted rapes increased by 40.1 percent, robberies increased by 36.7 percent, assaults on students increased by 85.3 percent, assaults on teachers increased by 77.4 percent, burglaries in school increased by 11.8 percent, drug and alcohol offenses increased by 37.5 percent, and the number of weapons confiscated by school personnel (pistols, knives, chukka sticks, even sawed-off shotguns) increased by 54.4 percent. The National Association of School Security Directors (1975) reported that, in 1974, there were 204,000 assaults and 9,000 rapes in American schools. Plainly, matters had gone a long way from spitballs and pigtails. There were 18,000 assaults on teachers in 1955, 41,000 in 1971, and 63,000 in 1975. By 1979, the number of such attacks had risen to 110,000 (Goldstein, Harootunian, & Conoley, 1994). The situation did not improve in the subsequent decade.

In the 1988–1989 school year, compared to the preceding year, school crime increased 5 percent and in-school weapons possession rose 21 percent in California's public schools (California Department of Education, 1990). In a similar comparison, the New York City public school system reported a 35 percent increase in assaults on students and school staff, a 16 percent increase in harassment, a 24 percent increase in larceny, and an overall crime rate increase of 25 percent.

Noteworthy is the fact that the greatest increase in crime rate occurred at the elementary school level (U.S. Department of Justice, 1993).

Assaults on Teachers

The level of assaults on teachers in America's public schools is sufficiently high that the vocabulary of aggression has been expanded to include what Block (1977) has called the "battered teacher syndrome": a combination of stress reactions including anxiety, depression, disturbed sleep, headaches, elevated blood pressure, and eating disorders. The National Center for Education Statistics reported in 1991 that nearly one out of five U. S. school teachers had been verbally abused by students, 8 percent had been physically threatened, and 2 percent had been attacked during the previous year. A 1993 Metropolitan Life survey indicated that 11 percent of American teachers had been assaulted at school—in 95 percent of the instances by students. Eleven percent of the 2.56 million teachers in the United States is 270,000 individuals!

Assaults on Students

The seriousness of attacks on teachers notwithstanding, it must be remembered that most aggression in America's schools is directed toward students. Victimization data from 26 major American cities surveyed in 1974 and 1975 indicated that 78 percent of personal victimizations in schools (rapes, robberies, assaults, larcenies) were directed toward students (McDermott, 1979). Ban and Ciminillo (1977) reported that in a national survey the percent of principals who observed "unorganized fighting" between students had increased from 2.8 percent in 1961 to 18 percent in 1974. Examining much of the data on correlates of aggression toward students, Ianni (1978) reported that seventh graders were most likely to be attacked, twelfth graders the least likely; at about age 13 the risks of physical attack tended to be greatest. Fifty-eight percent of such attacks involved victims and offenders of the same race; 42 percent were interracial. It has also been demonstrated that the smaller the size of a minority group in school, the more likely its members will be victimized by members of other racial groups.

The 1989 annual school crime report from the School Safety Council indicated that almost 3 million students, faculty, staff, and visitors were crime victims in American schools in 1987. Two and a half million of these crimes were thefts. During the first half of 1990, approximately 9 percent of all students ages 12 to 19 were crime victims in the United States—2 percent of violent crimes, 7 percent of property crimes. Fifteen percent said their schools had gangs. Sixteen percent claimed their schools had experienced an actual or threatened attack on a teacher (Goldstein, 1992). Siegel and Senna (1991) add that "although teenagers spend only 25 percent of their time in school, 40 percent of the robberies and 36 percent of the physical attacks involving this age group occur in school" (p. 217).

A report aptly titled *Caught in the Crossfire* (Center to Prevent Handgun Violence, 1990) fully captures the central role of firearms in the recent surge of school violence. From 1986 to 1990, 71 people (65 students and 6 employees) were killed by guns in American schools. Another 201 were seriously wounded, and 242 were held hostage at gunpoint. Older adolescents were most frequently perpetrators as well as victims. Such gun violence in schools grew from gang or drug disputes (18 percent), longstanding arguments (15 percent), romantic disagreements (12 percent), fights over possessions (10 percent), and accidents (13 percent). An estimated 270,000 students carried handguns to school one or more times each year. The American School Health Association (1989) estimates that 7 percent of boys and 2 percent of girls carry a knife to school every day.

During the 1991–1992 school year, 14.4 percent of New York City middle school children reported being threatened by another student at least once each month, and 7.7 percent of them were in an actual fight (Goldstein et al., 1994). In 1992, a California survey of fifth to twelfth graders revealed that in the month prior to the survey, a third of them had had personal property stolen, been grabbed or shoved, or seen a weapon at school (Goldstein et al., 1994). Two-thirds reported being put down or cursed at by a fellow student. A recent National Crime Survey (U. S. Department of Justice, 1993) reported nearly 3 million crimes per year on or near American school campuses—16,000 per school day.

Aggression toward Property

We have portrayed the escalating trends in aggression against teachers and fellow students in America's schools. Much the same appears to be true for aggression toward property. Numerous survey and anecdotal reports during the past 25 years support the contention that school vandalism levels are both absolutely high and still growing in the United States (Bradley, 1967; Casserly, Bass, & Garrett, 1980; Goldstein et al., 1994; Rubel, 1977; Tygart, 1988), regularly costing over 600 million dollars each year.

Such costs are due to damage and destruction of school property, as well as to theft. In 1991, for example, one of eight teachers and one of nine students reported incidents of stealing within any given month (Miller & Prinz, 1991).

Vandalism not only costs money, it typically has social costs as well. As Vestermark and Blauvelt (1978) suggest, the social cost of vandalism is the sum of three components: (a) impact on the school's educational program, (b) psychological impact on both students and adults, and (c) degree of disruptiveness of group or intergroup relations. In terms of the breadth and depth of disruptiveness upon the primary educational functions of the school, the social costs of an act of vandalism actually may far exceed its monetary impact. One social cost, in particular, may be very high—namely, the arousal of fear among students and staff.

Violence toward persons and property in America's schools is substantial and apparently growing. Students, teachers, and staff are its targets; physical, emotional, and fiscal injury are its costs. The negative impact of violence on the core educational purpose of our schools is great, both for those subjected directly to such aggression and for the majority who are not. The injured student, the battered teacher, the violence-preoccupied principal, the fearful parent—these are its victims. Subsequent sections of this chapter examine certain sources of student aggression, propose reasons such behavior is typically so difficult to change, and introduce the Skillstreaming method as one effective intervention for reducing aggression.

Aggression as Learned Behavior

Aggression is primarily learned behavior. True, for genetic, biochemical, or hormonal reasons we are not all equally predisposed to learn it. But learn it we do, typically starting at a very early age. For the chronically aggressive youngster, the regular contributor to disruption in school (as well as home, street, and other settings), such learning is often rooted in a developmental sequence that begins with coercive parenting. As Patterson, Reid, Jones, and Conger (1975) describe this course of development (see Figure 1), in the first years of life the aggressor-to-be is the target of parenting that is often hostile, threatening, irritated, and inconsistent. Both very tight and very lax supervision occur in an unpredictable manner. Yelling is frequent and corporal punishment not infrequent. The coerciveness and abusiveness just described also finds expression in the interactions between the parents.

One consequence of such a child-rearing style is that, sometimes, the child complies. The coercion "works." Such a successful outcome serves as a reward to the coercive parent, making it more likely that

FIGURE 1 Development of Aggression in Childhood

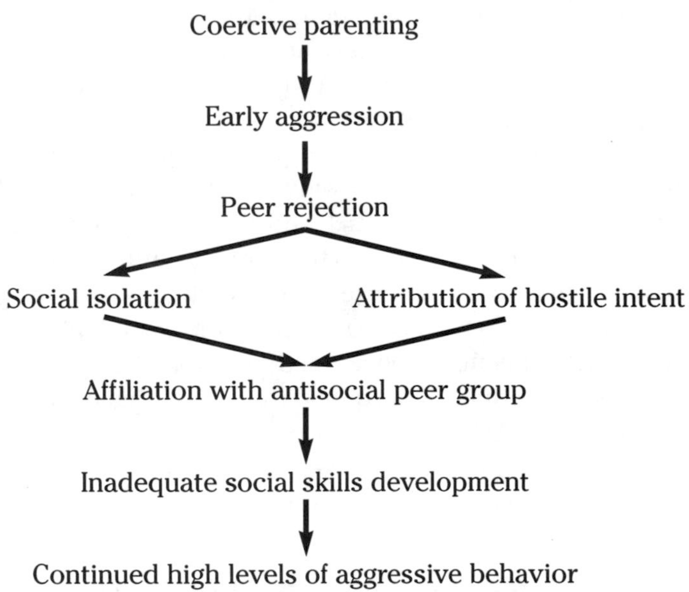

Note. From *A Social Learning Approach to Family Intervention* (Vol. 1), by G.R. Patterson, J.B. Reid, R.R. Jones, and R.E. Conger, 1975, Eugene, OR: Castalia. Copyright 1975 by Castalia. Adapted by permission.

such parenting behavior will continue. A second frequent consequence is that rather than comply, the child begins to act coercively in turn. After all, his or her parents have served as powerful models: It works for them—why not for me? While the learning-by-modeling process is not entirely conscious, it proceeds nonetheless. The toddler responds to coercive parenting with coercion of his or her own—yelling, threatening, hitting, kicking, tantrums, and more. And it, too, succeeds often enough that the likelihood of a continuation of such early aggression grows. Probably at that age, if we chose to label such a youngster, we would call him or her "temperamental."

As the child grows to 3, 4, and 5, he or she becomes an increasingly social being, seeking out other children with whom to play. Yet in these peer relations, too, early learning of successful coercion serves the child poorly. He or she takes Johnny's tricycle and rides off, grabs and kicks Keisha's soccer ball, crashes into the line of other children waiting to use the slide. The other children—or their parents—respond by turning the child away. Thus, the positive models, the youngsters whose prosocial play behavior might serve as at least a partial learning counterweight to what the youngster has already begun to learn from his or her coercive parents, are unavailable. The youngster, who if relabeled now would probably be called "oppositional," begins to experience both a sense of social isolation and a growing tendency to see others as threatening, challenging, or hostile, even when they are not.

The child's need to affiliate and have friends continues, as does his or her growing level of antisocial and perhaps even violent behavior. In school now, age 6 or 7, he or she seeks out (and is sought out by) other youths caught up in a similar developmental pattern. Antisocial skills are learned and refined, but opportunities to acquire prosocial alternative ways of dealing with others are far less frequent—not at home, not at play, not at school. Often the youngster receives an actual, formal label at this point in his or her development—namely, "conduct disordered."

The pattern persists and perhaps even escalates through the youngster's elementary school years into secondary school. Inadequate development of social skills and high levels of aggressive behaviors are its main characteristics. For far too many such youngsters, such actions lead to an eventual relabeling as "juvenile delinquent" or even, in this era of our criminal justice system's tendency to treat juvenile felons as adults, "juvenile offender."

Aggression as Addiction

Aggression is a remarkably stable behavior. Several longitudinal studies make it quite clear that very often, the chronically aggressive child will still be so in adolescence and adulthood. Aggressive, antisocial behaviors, once learned and working, in a sense take on a life of their own—eliciting, fostering, and producing more of the same, as a cycle of aggression and the rewards aggression brings spins on and on in the absence of the learning and use of prosocial alternative behaviors.

In fact, sometimes, for some youths, the resistance to changing a longstanding pattern of aggressive behavior seems so great that we have begun to wonder whether there are those for whom aggression may be tantamount to an addiction. If one examines what is known about the more traditionally addictive behaviors—concerned with drugs, gambling, smoking, eating—a lengthy list of characteristics may be gathered that also are commonly true for aggression (see Table 1). For some youngsters, aggression may indeed be an addiction. Addictions persist for two primary reasons. First, they "work"—they yield reward in the form of positive feelings, material goods, relationships, or other. Second, alternative means for succeeding in such ways do not seem to be available. For the chronically aggressive youngster, whether in school or other settings, aggression is *the* alternative available. He or she has never learned to listen openly to complaints, respond constructively to accusations, react in a reparative manner to failure, resist negative peer pressure, deal with rejection, negotiate differences, walk away from perceived challenges, resolve conflict with words and not fists, or use the many, many other skills that constitute a nonaggressive yet interpersonally satisfying and effective lifestyle. In 1973, our first version of Skillstreaming was developed to promote just such learning.

Table 1 Aggression as Addiction

- A long-term, stable behavior, repetitively enacted
- Subjective compulsion to use it
- Reduced ability to control or reduce it, in frequency or intensity
- Frequent relapses associated with:

  Negative emotional states

  Interpersonal conflicts

  Situations where used before
- Initiated and sustained by both person and environment
- Yields short-term pleasure despite long-term negative effects
- Used in response to, and to relieve, stress, negative mood, general arousal
- Often encouraged and rewarded by (peer, family) "enablers"
- Often experienced with a "rush" of pleasure/excitement
- Frequently accompanied by denial (e.g., attribution of blame)
- Preoccupation with others' use of the behavior (e.g., excessive viewing of violence on television)
- High rate of health risk, injury, death
- Taught, encouraged, rewarded by larger society

CHAPTER 2

Skillstreaming: History and Development

Until the early 1970s, three major psychological approaches existed to alter the behavior of aggressive, unhappy, ineffective, or disturbed individuals—psychodynamic/psychoanalytic, humanistic/nondirective, and behavior modification. Although each differed from the others in major respects, one significant commonality was the assumption that the client had somewhere within himself or herself, as yet unexpressed, the effective, satisfying, or healthy behaviors whose expression was among the goals of the therapy. Such latent potentials, in all three approaches, would be realized by the client if the therapist was sufficiently skilled in reducing or removing obstacles to such realization. The psychoanalyst sought to do so by calling forth and interpreting unconscious, material blocking, progress relevant awareness. The nondirectivist, who believed that the potential for change resided within the client, sought to free this potential by providing a warm, empathic, maximally accepting therapeutic environment. And the behavior modifier, by means of one or more contingency management procedures, attempted to see to it that when the latent desirable behaviors or approximations thereto did occur, the client received contingent reinforcement, thus increasing the probability that these behaviors would recur. Therefore, whether sought by means of interpretation, therapeutic climate, or contingent rewards, all three approaches assumed that somewhere within the individual's repertoire resided the desired, effective goal behaviors.

In the early 1970s, an important new intervention approach began to emerge—psychological skills training, an approach resting upon rather different assumptions. Viewing the helpee more in educational, pedagogic terms than as a client in need of therapy, the psychological skills trainer assumed the individual was deficient, or at best weak, in the skills necessary for effective and satisfying daily living. The task of the skills trainer therefore became not interpretation, reflection, or reinforcement, but the active and deliberate teaching of desirable behaviors. Rather than an intervention called *psychotherapy,* between a patient and a psychotherapist, what emerged was *training,* between a trainee and a psychological skills trainer.

The roots of the psychological skills training movement lie within both education and psychology. The notion of teaching desirable behaviors has often, if sporadically, been a significant goal of the American educational establishment. The Character Education movement of the 1920s and more contemporary Moral Education and Values Clarification programs are but a few examples. Add to this institutionalized educational interest in skills training the hundreds of interpersonal and planning skills courses taught in America's more than 2,000 community colleges, and the hundreds of self-help books oriented toward similar skill-enhancement goals, and it becomes clear that the formal and informal educational establishment in America provided fertile soil and explicit stimulation within which the psychological skills training movement could grow.

Much the same can be said for American psychology, as it, too, laid the groundwork by its prevailing philosophy and interests in the development of this new movement. The learning process has above all else been the central theoretical and investigative concern of American psychology since the late 19th century. This focal interest also assumed major therapeutic form in the 1950s, as psychotherapeutic practitioners and researchers alike came to view psychotherapeutic treatment more and more in learning terms. The still-expanding field of behavior modification grew from this joint learning-clinical focus and may be viewed appropriately as the immediately preceding context in which psychological skills training came to be developed.

Perhaps psychology's most direct contribution to psychological skills training came from social learning theory—in particular, work conducted and stimulated by Albert Bandura. Based upon the same broad array of modeling, behavioral rehearsal, and social reinforcement investigations which in part helped stimulate and direct the development of our Skillstreaming approach, Bandura (1973) commented as follows:

> The method that has yielded the most impressive results with diverse problems contains three major components. First, alternative modes of response are repeatedly modeled, preferably by several people who demonstrate how the new style of behavior can be used in dealing with a variety of . . . situations. Second, learners are provided with necessary guidance and ample opportunities to practice the modeled behavior under favorable conditions until they perform it skillfully and spontaneously. The latter procedures are ideally suited for developing new social skills, but they are unlikely to be adopted unless they produce rewarding consequences. Arrangement of success experiences, particularly for initial efforts at behaving differently, constitute the third component in this powerful composite method. . . . Given adequate demonstration, guided practice, and success experiences, this method is almost certain to produce favorable results. (p. 253)

Other events of the 1970s provided still further impetus for the growth of the skills training movement. The inadequacy of prompting, shaping, and related operant procedures for adding new behaviors to individuals' behavioral repertoires was increasingly apparent. The widespread reliance upon deinstitutionalization, which lay at the heart of the community mental health movement, resulted in the discharge from America's public mental hospitals of approximately 400,000 persons, the majority of whom were deficient in important daily functioning skills. And, especially to us, it had grown clear that what the American mental health movement had available to offer clients of lower socioeconomic status was grossly inadequate to meet their psychotherapeutic needs. Relevant supportive research, the incompleteness of operant approaches, large populations of grossly skill deficient individuals, and the paucity of useful interventions for a large segment of society—all in the context of support from both education and psychology—came together in our thinking and that of others as demanding a new intervention, something prescriptively responsive to these needs. Psychological skills training was the answer, and a movement was launched. Our involvement in this movement, a psychological skills training approach that we first termed *Structured Learning,* and later renamed

Skillstreaming, began in the early 1970s. In developing and evaluating its constituent procedures, we sought to avoid the "one-true-light assumption" that had guided so much intervention work up to that time and, instead, to build an approach that prescriptively sought to respond to significant qualities of the persons whose skill levels we wished to change.

Our first major trainee target group, vastly underserved in terms of mental health and psychoeducational needs, were persons from low-income families. Interventions, whether psychotherapeutic or psychoeducational, are basically interpersonal learning experiences. Thus, how persons most effectively learn is a major consideration—in fact, the major consideration—in determining the optimal form of the intervention. Developmental psychological research amply demonstrates that prototypical socialization practices in socioeconomically middle class and lower class U.S. homes are substantially different (Davis, 1967; Hess & Shipman, 1965; Jensen, 1967). As Figure 2 summarizes, the middle class child is repeatedly taught, both explicitly and implicitly, to look inward and consider the causes or antecedents of his or her behavior (motivation); to look outward and sensitively and accurately decipher the feelings of others with whom he or she is interacting (empathy); and to muster and employ restraint, regulation, and other expressions of self-management (self-control).

FIGURE 2 Social Class and Learning Style

Middle Class	Lower Class	Skillstreaming Procedures
Motivation	Consequences	Modeling
Empathy	Action	Role-playing
Self-control	External authority	Performance feedback
		Generalization training

In contrast, it is much more common in the child-rearing of low-income homes to find a focus on the outcome or results of enacted behavior (consequences); a direct, concrete, behavioral response to such perceived consequences (action); and a heavy reliance on the urgings, directives, or commands of others rather than on self-control (external authority). Thus, the middle class adolescent male caught pulling his sister's hair is likely to be asked why he did so (motivation) and how he thinks such behavior made his sister feel (empathy), and be reminded that he is old enough to be able to squelch the urge to engage in such behaviors (self-control). The more action-oriented, consequence-oriented, external authority, low-income parent is more likely to respond to such a transgression by slapping the child, without urging motivational introspection, feelings inspection, or heightened self-control.

What are the intervention-relevant consequences of these two contrasting child-rearing experiences? Outcome statistics for middle class clients participating in verbal, insight-oriented psychotherapy or counseling consistently indicate that approximately two-thirds improve (Bergin & Lambert, 1978; Rachman & Wilson, 1980; Smith & Glass, 1977). We believe that such a felicitous result is at least in part a result of the high degree of correspondence between the learning style such clients bring with them to treatment (focus on motivation, feelings, self-control, etc.) and the client qualities optimal for that treatment to succeed. Low-income clients, with their contrasting learning style, do much less well in response to such an approach (Goldstein, 1973; Schofield, 1964; Yamamoto & Goin, 1965) but might do very well indeed if one followed a prescriptive strategy and offered an intervention tailored to this learning style.

This is precisely what we sought to accomplish with the initial development of Skillstreaming (Goldstein, 1973). Its constituent procedures are modeling, role-playing, performance feedback, and generalization training. As depicted in Figure 2, each of these procedures prescriptively follows from a major feature of a low-income person's characteristic learning style.

In the years following its initial development as an intervention prescriptively targeted to low-income, socially skill deficient adults, the growth of applications of Skillstreaming to other populations has been substantial. These programs have included young children (preschool and elementary age), elderly adults, child-abusing parents, industrial managers, police officers, and others. Applications of

Skillstreaming to skill-deficient adolescents, the concern of the present book, appeared early in this course of expansion and dissemination. Over the more than 20 years during which these applied efforts were initiated and spread to large numbers of schools, agencies, and institutions, a considerable amount of evaluation research was conducted and reported, by ourselves and by numerous other investigators. These studies collectively represent an especially healthy dimension in the development of Skillstreaming, as their results have been employed not only as overall tests of the method's efficacy but also as guidelines for improving the program's procedures and materials. An annotated bibliography describing these several strands of Skillstreaming research is presented as Appendix A in this book.

This chapter has, we hope, conveyed a sense of the history and development of Skillstreaming and pointed to its firm foundation in an extended series of research evaluations. The chapters that follow will present in detail all the "how-to" information necessary to carry out the effective formation, management, and dissemination of Skillstreaming programs.

CHAPTER 3
Facilitative Skillstreaming Arrangements

The preceding two chapters have sought to place Skillstreaming in historical and contemporary context by examining both its course of development and current utility with aggressive and other prosocially skill deficient youngsters. Before turning in chapter 4 to a detailed description of the training procedures involved in conducting a Skillstreaming group, we first need to present the several arrangements we recommend that trainers carry out in order to set the stage for effective use of these training procedures. Thus, in the present chapter we consider such matters as trainer and trainee selection, preparation, and motivation; trainer-trainee cultural compatibility; the group's physical and curricular placement; the number, length, and spacing of sessions; needed materials; development of a positive group culture; skill selection and negotiation; and the monitoring, supervision, and assessment of trainer performance and program effectiveness. These matters, if dealt with in an attentive and skilled manner, will facilitate a positive Skillstreaming outcome.

TRAINER SELECTION, PREPARATION, AND MOTIVATION

Who is the ideal Skillstreaming trainer? In the decades since Skillstreaming began, hundreds of persons with a wide variety of backgrounds and credentials have served as effective trainers. Teachers, counselors, and psychologists in school settings; youth care workers in delinquency centers; social workers in mental health and other community agencies; and correctional officers in prisons are the primary examples of such personnel. Three related qualities seem to characterize effective trainers. First, they are at ease with adolescents and comfortable working with groups of them—whether doing Skillstreaming or another activity. The concerns youngsters share, even their musings, are taken seriously, listened to respectfully, never looked down upon. In short, whether dealing with youngsters individually or as a group, skilled trainers show sensitive awareness of the fact that adolescence is a stormy time of life composed of unpredictable expressions of both adult and childlike behaviors.

At times this mix of youthful qualities causes problems, problems manifested in Skillstreaming groups in a wide variety of aggressive, resistive, or otherwise difficult behaviors. When these behaviors occur, the skilled trainer is able to respond effectively. Chapter 8 presents techniques for moderating, reducing, and even eliminating such problem behaviors. Effective trainers are competent in the use of these techniques, consequate problematic deeds without demeaning the doer, and are able to maintain the skills training agenda of the group.

The third quality of effective Skillstreaming trainers is that they deliver the skills training agenda well. They are highly competent teachers, whether or not they possess formal teaching credentials. Their teaching styles are alive, energetic, and responsive to diverse learning styles. The contents of their skill lessons, such as the modeling displays they enact, are clear and relevant to trainees' real-world needs and aspirations. They are able to work with individual trainees during group sessions without losing the group-oriented focus of Skillstreaming. There is little "down time," transitions are made easily, and in a variety of ways the trainer communicates to the participating youths a "can do" sense of positive expectancy.

The preparation of trainers for the role of effective leader of Skillstreaming groups optimally will follow what may be called an *apprenticeship training sequence.* Such high quality personnel as just described must first familiarize themselves with the actual procedures and contents of the Skillstreaming method. Reading the present book is a good first step, as it comprehensively describes the Skillstreaming background, methods, and materials necessary to initiate and sustain high levels of trainee skill acquisition and performance. *The Skillstreaming Video* (Goldstein & McGinnis, 1988) is helpful as an adjunct training tool. We also provide regular trainer preparation workshops at various sites, which developing trainers may attend to augment such materials. At this stage in the dissemination of Skillstreaming, a great many competent and experienced trainers exist and are regularly employing the method in diverse schools and other locations in the United States and beyond.

A good next step in trainer preparation, following the imparting of information from text, video, and/or workshop, is the opportunity to participate in a mock Skillstreaming group led by experienced trainers and made up of trainers-to-be pretending to be adolescent trainees. After one or more such role-play training opportunities, the trainer-to-be can observe one or more experienced trainers actually lead a group of adolescent trainees, then co-lead such a group with the experienced trainer, and, finally, lead the group alone (or better, as part of a pair of apprentice trainers) while the experienced trainer observes. This incremental training sequence, each of its steps adjustable in duration, has proven to be a most satisfactory means for training Skillstreaming group leaders.

What is the best way to motivate trainers to participate in this training effort? After all, most teachers and other professionals working with unskilled and often aggressive adolescents are frequently overworked, underpaid, and the target of a barrage of other interventions they are urged to implement. It is the rare school or other institution that is able or willing to pay its staff for participation in activities such as Skillstreaming. Other forms of external reward or recognition, such as titles, perks, awards, or even compensatory time or relief from other duties, are similarly uncommon. In the final analysis, volunteering to learn and offer this approach is most typically motivated by the trainer-to-be's wish to enhance his or her own level of competence and by the desire to be that much more helpful to the adolescents for whom he or she is responsible. External rewards are rarely forthcoming. It is these internal goals and satisfactions that usually drive the trainer's decision to participate.

TRAINEE SELECTION, PREPARATION, AND MOTIVATION

Skillstreaming is a technique for teaching an extended curriculum of interpersonal, aggression management, and related skills to youngsters who are weak or lacking in these competencies. Although in the present book we place special emphasis on its use with youngsters who frequently employ aggressive behaviors, in actual practice in schools and elsewhere Skillstreaming has frequently been offered successfully to other types of skill-deficient adolescents. Included here are shy or withdrawn teenagers, those who are immature, those who have developmental delays, and still others perhaps harder to categorize but who display nonaggressive inadequacies in their interpersonal skill attempts. The core assessment task in screening adolescents for participation is determining their degree of skill proficiency and deficiency. Those already relatively competent in the skill curriculum are excluded; those proving deficient in what Skillstreaming is prepared to teach are included. This selection process, at least theoretically, may make use of a number of assessment techniques—interviews, sociometric procedures, skill games, trial groups, direct observation, and skill checklists.

We have found it most useful to rely primarily on direct observation and skill checklists. Direct observation is especially valuable if the persons planning to serve as the group's trainers (teachers, youth care workers, etc.) are the same persons who are with the youngsters all day and routinely see them in interaction with others. In such circumstances, the needed observations of behavior can be frequent, take place in the youngster's natural environment, and, since skill deficiencies are often situation specific, reflect each youth's skill competence across diverse peers, adults, challenges, times, and physical conditions. In other words, when the Skillstreaming trainer is also the behavioral assessment observer, a valuable sample of observational opportunities becomes available.

Adequate assessment is, in addition, both multimodal and multisource. *Multimodal* means that more than one type of assessment approach (such as observation) is employed in order to minimize assessment biases associated with the type of measure being administered. Our choice in this regard is the Skillstreaming Checklist, in versions for teacher, parent, and student (see Appendix B). This checklist is a straightforward screening and selection device, on which all 50 Skillstreaming skills are listed and defined. It is a frequency-of-use response format, on which the rater simply circles a number corresponding to "almost never," "seldom," "sometimes," "often," or "almost always."

Multisource assessment means that more than one type of person is asked to complete a checklist for each youth, in order to minimize assessment biases associated with the source of the measures being administered. In most Skillstreaming programs, such assessment has typically involved each youth's teacher and parent, as well as the youth himself or herself. In some instances, siblings, peers, or other significant adults have been queried. In carrying out multisource assessments, it is common for persons such as teachers and parents to report considerably more skill deficiency for the youth (in number and frequency) than does the youth. Teacher and mom or dad may circle "almost never" or "seldom" for 25 skills when the youth does so for only 6 or 7. Whether such a discrepancy reflects overconfidence, denial, blaming others, or some other process in the youth's self-perception, it nonetheless is *very* important to assess the skill deficiency perspective of each youth because, as will be seen in later discussion (see chapter 8), teaching trainees the skills in which *they* feel they are deficient has proven to be a successful motivational tactic.

Once selected for program participation, how are youngsters to be grouped? We have relied most heavily on two grouping criteria. The first is *shared skill deficiency.* We urge that trainers place in the same group those trainees who share highly similar skill deficiencies and skill deficiency patterns. The Skillstreaming Grouping Chart included in Appendix B—used to summarize skill scores across all Skillstreaming skills for entire classes, units, or other large sets of youngsters—can be employed to identify such shared skill deficiencies. The second grouping criterion we strive to meet is responsive to the generalization-enhancing principle of *identical elements.* This principle is discussed in depth in chapter 9, which examines an array of means for facilitating generalization. The heart of this notion, however, is that the greater the similarity between qualities of the training session and the real-world setting in which the youth can profitably use the skill, the greater the likelihood of training-to-application transfer. One means for maximizing such cross-setting identical elements is to have the same people involved. Thus, this second grouping criteria is operationalized by placing in the same Skillstreaming group adolescents from the same class, living unit, neighborhood, and the like. As we like to put it, "If they live together, hang around together, even fight together, put them in the same group together."

Once selected and grouped for training, the next tasks are jointly preparing and motivating youths for their Skillstreaming participation. Such preparation-motivation efforts are conducted first individually, then repeated as appropriate in the group context as the youngsters come together for their initial Skillstreaming group meetings. Such structuring typically includes the following components.

Purposes

A description of the purposes of the Skillstreaming group as they relate to the specific skill deficits of the youngster with whom one is meeting. For example, the trainer might say, “Remember last week, when you got into a fight with Russ, and got 2 days in-school suspension? Well, in these meetings you’ll be taught skills to help you keep out of that kind of trouble and stay out of in-school suspension.” Note how a statement such as this can serve both group preparatory and motivational purposes.

Procedures

A general description of the procedures that constitute the Skillstreaming process, and hence the sessions to come. Here, the trainer might say something like

> In order to learn how to handle such difficult situations well, we’ll first show you some good examples of the skills needed for that purpose, then you and the other members of your group will take turns trying it here. Then we’ll all let each other know how well we did in our rehearsals. Finally, you’ll have a chance to go practice each skill on your own, where and when you need it.

Such a brief structuring statement should be viewed as but an introduction to Skillstreaming’s modeling, role-play, feedback, and generalization procedures. The full nature of these techniques, and their nuances, will be much better understood by trainees once they have participated in a round or two of actual skills training.

Incentives

Explanation of the class, school, agency or institutional incentive or level system when one is in place. The tangible or token rewards that are the currency of such an economy, as well as the specific rules by which they may be gained or lost, can be introduced in meetings with individual youths and spelled out in operational detail at the first group meeting.

In addition to repetition or elaboration as appropriate of any of the above points, when the group comes together for the first session, two additional topics must be covered.

Group rules

Skillstreaming is but one of many educational and training approaches whose ultimate effectiveness depends not only on such matters as its teaching procedures or content curriculum, but also upon core qualities of the group itself. Is it a safe place, one free of put-downs, intimidation, or even subtle bullying? Are the trainers, in addition to being competent teachers, also competent protectors? Has the group come up with a useful set of operating rules, and are members functioning in accord with them? No matter how well-crafted the modeling displays, how true-to-life the role-plays, and how accurate the feedback, if the trainees feel threatened, skill learning will not go forward. It is highly desirable, as we describe more fully in chapter 8, that each group's rules be established by its own members. Ownership enhances compliance. In doing so, the trainer may wish to suggest consideration of such rule domains as attendance, participation, confidentiality, management of disagreements, and others unique to one or another particular setting.

Skill negotiation

Chapter 8 examines issues and means useful for motivating high levels of appropriate trainee participation. A great deal of experience now exists to suggest that one of the most potent of these means, of use from the very first Skillstreaming session and regularly thereafter, is negotiation of the skill curriculum. Many of the youths for whom Skillstreaming is appropriate chronically ascribe responsibility for their antisocial acts to others. They externalize; rarely is something *their* fault. As noted earlier, a teacher or parent may indicate on the Skillstreaming Checklist that the youngster seldom or almost never uses two or three *dozen* of the prosocial skills listed. Yet the youth checks but a few of the skills as deficient! However inaccurate and inadequate such a self-picture may be, knowledge by the trainer of those few, self-admitted trainee deficiencies is golden. Teaching these skills (in addition to those that are trainer selected) has proven to be an especially positive facilitator of trainee motivation. In what might be called a "consumer model," we give the "customer" what he or she feels is needed. The customer then much more eagerly returns to our store. Thus, as frequently as every other Skillstreaming session for any given group, we begin the meeting not by announcing and enacting a modeling display for a skill chosen by the trainers but, instead, with "How is it going?" or "What's been happening to you all since our last meeting?" Out of the brief discussion such openings engender often comes information about difficulties at home, in school, on the street, or elsewhere—difficulties that can be ameliorated or resolved by the Skillstreaming skill the trainers and trainees then jointly select and portray. The earlier in the group's life such negotiation of the curriculum commences the better. In fact, in the group's very first session, when open discussion of life difficulties by trainees may still be uncomfortable, the trainer can initiate such negotiation by tallying on a chalkboard the skills checked on the Skillstreaming Checklist by *all* the members of the group, without revealing who checked which ones, and then by teaching the one or ones checked most often.

TRAINER-TRAINEE CULTURAL COMPATIBILITY

Which specific behaviors optimally define a given Skillstreaming skill, which skills are optimal for use in any given setting, and the very teaching-learning processes by which such skills may best be acquired vary from culture to culture. Culture may be defined by geography, ethnicity, nationality, social class, gender, sexual orientation, age, or some combination thereof. For Skillstreaming to be meaningful, it must be viewed in a multicultural context and practiced in a manner responsive to such a context. When trainer and trainee are members of or are merely only familiar with different cultural groups, identities, definitions, and prescriptions may conflict. Training goals may fail to be met. Cartledge and Johnson (1997) state it well when they assert:

> Cultural differences may cause children from diverse backgrounds to respond to environmental events in different or nonproductive ways and cause their actions to be misperceived by peers and adults who do not

> share the same cultural orientation. School personnel are challenged to interpret accurately the behaviors of culturally different learners, to distinguish social skill differences from deficits, and to employ instructional strategies effective in helping those learners maximize their schooling experiences. (p. 407)

Skillstreaming will be most effective when it is delivered in a manner appreciative of and responsive to such culturally relevant notions as skill strengths and differences versus skill deficits, differential or tailored training strategies and instructional tactics, trainee channels of accessibility and communication styles, stereotyping of and by culturally different trainee populations, and culturally associated qualities of the particular trainees one is seeking to assist. Trainer knowledge, skill, and sensitivity will be required if such assistance is to be provided.

SUPPORT STAFF PREPARATION

Skillstreaming training never goes forward in isolation: Trainers, and their training groups, are part of a school, a delinquency center, a residential facility, or some other institution peopled by both youths and by staff—teachers, youth care workers, and so forth. We have already suggested means for preparing those staff members who will serve as Skillstreaming trainers. What about the rest of the staff? Do they have a meaningful role to play in the youth skill-enhancement effort, even though they won't be serving as group trainers? Indeed they do!

Programs that try to change the behavior of aggressive adolescents often succeed only at a certain time and in a certain place. That is, the program works, but only at or shortly after the time it occurred and only in the same place where it occurred. Thus, a program may make a youth behave more prosocially during and immediately after the weeks it is going on and in the school where it took place. But a few weeks later or when in the schoolyard, out on a field trip, home visit, or elsewhere outside the school, the youth may be as aggressive and prosocially unskilled as ever. This temporary success followed by a relapse to old, negative ways of behaving is a failure of generalization. Generalization failures are much more the rule than the exception with aggressive youth. During Skillstreaming, adolescents receive a great deal of support, enthusiasm, encouragement, and reward for their efforts. Between sessions, or after the program terminates, many of them may receive very little support, reward, or other positive response.

The common failure of generalization should not surprise us. Yet this outcome can be minimized. Newly learned and thus fragile constructive skills need not fade away after Skillstreaming. If attempts by adolescents to use such skills in the real world are met with success—support, enthusiasm, encouragement, reward—skill use will be considerably more likely to continue. Research has shown that teachers, school staff, community workers, parents, friends, peers, and employers are in an ideal position to provide support and reward. In the following ways, these individuals can serve in the powerful role of *transfer coach*, helping make sure that the curriculum of skills practiced in Skillstreaming turns into long-term or even permanent learning.

Prompting

Under the pressure of real-life situations both in and out of school, adolescents may forget all or part of the Skillstreaming skills they learned earlier. If their anxiety isn't too great or their forgetting too complete, all that may be needed for them to perform the skill correctly is some prompting. Prompting is reminding the person such things as *what* to do (the skill), *how* to do it (the steps), *when* to do it (now or the next time the situation occurs), *where* to do it (and where not to), and/or *why* to use the skill here and now (describing the positive outcomes expected).

Encouraging

Offering encouragements to adolescents to use a given skill assumes they know it well enough (thus, they do not need prompting) but are reluctant to use it. Encouragement may be necessary, therefore, when the problem is lack of motivation rather than lack of knowledge. Encouragement can often best be given by gently urging youths to try using what they know, by showing enthusiasm for the skill being used, and by communicating optimism about the likely positive outcome of skill use.

Reassuring

For particularly anxious youths, skill use attempts will be more likely to occur if the threat of failure is reduced. Reassurance is often an effective threat-reduction technique: "You can do it," "I'll be there to help if you need it," and "You've used the other skills well, so I think you'll do fine with this one, too" are examples of the kinds of reassuring statements the transfer coach can fruitfully provide.

Rewarding

The most important contribution by far that the transfer coach can make is to provide (or help someone else provide) rewards for using a skill correctly. Rewards may take the form of approval, praise, or compliments, or they may consist of special privileges, points, tokens, recognition, or other reinforcers built into a school's behavior management system. All of these rewards will increase the likelihood of continued skill use in new settings and at later times. The most powerful reward that can be offered, however, is the success of the skill itself. If a youth prepares for a stressful conversation and the conversation then goes well, that reward (the successful conversation itself) will help the skill transfer more than any external reward can. The same conclusion—that success increases transfer—applies to all of the Skillstreaming skills. Thus, whenever you have or can create the opportunity, reward a youth's skill use by helping the skill work. Respond positively to a complaint if it is reasonable and try to have others also respond positively. Try to react with whatever behaviors on your part signal your awareness of effective and appropriate skill use. If you do so and encourage other important people in the adolescent's environment to do so also, fragile skills will become lasting skills, and Skillstreaming will have been successful.

Let us assume that trainers, trainees, and support staff are optimally prepared and motivated to begin a Skillstreaming program. Yet the participation of one more professional person is highly desirable if success is to be facilitated. Many effective Skillstreaming programs include in their staff cadre a master trainer. It is far too common in schools and other settings for intervention programs to begin with appropriate organization, good intentions, and adequate enthusiasm but wind up in shambles just a few months later for want of a coordinating, overseeing figure to keep the program on track and rolling. The veritable barrage of other responsibilities often placed upon teachers and other frontline staff makes such programs' collapse, if not inevitable, certainly more likely in the absence of a guiding overseer.

The master trainer should be well versed in both Skillstreaming and program management. Her or his Skillstreaming responsibilities may include trainer training, session observation, monitoring of progress, and trainer supervision. Program management tasks in past uses of such leadership personnel have been many and varied, and operated at district, school, class, and group levels. Included have been "selling" the program to administration as well as participants; arranging for and at times conducting assessment for trainee selection and grouping; mounting a motivational campaign throughout the district or building (memos, posters, lectures, etc.) to build interest in the program; and the mundane but vital chores of scheduling, materials acquisition, arranging to fill in for absent trainers, and handling a myriad of other sustaining details.

PEOPLE, PLACES, AND PLACEMENT

Finally, the following "nuts and bolts" issues—essentially the mechanics of the Skillstreaming group—deserve consideration.

Number of trainers

Though a great many Skillstreaming groups have been effectively and productively led by one trainer alone, we strongly recommend that, where possible, two trainers work together. Skill-deficient adolescents are often quite proficient in generating the behavior management problems that make successful training difficult. To arrange and conduct a role-play between two youths while at the same time overseeing the attention of a half-dozen easily distractable others is a daunting challenge for even the most experienced teacher or trainer. A much better arrangement involves the use of two trainers, one in front of the group, leading the role-play, the second sitting in the group, preferably next to the youth or youths judged most likely from past experience to behave disruptively. In those school settings in which two teachers are not available for group co-leadership, the effective use of teacher aides, parents, volunteers, or other adults has been reported. Use of two trainers may be particularly valuable in the early sessions of a Skillstreaming group. As the trainees become more familiar with the group's required activities, conducting sessions with one leader may become more feasible.

Number of trainees

Typically, the Skillstreaming session lasts a class period or its equivalent—perhaps 45 to 50 minutes. It is quite common that a modeling display by the trainers and role-plays by most or all of the six to eight group members can be accomplished within that time period. Though this is our usual recommended group size, smaller numbers (as low as two) may be necessary and desirable, such as when the youths involved are very aggressive and out of control. Here, one would start with a smaller group size and slowly increase membership—perhaps at the rate of one new trainee per week—as the group comes under control and a positive group culture begins to build. At other times, the opposite challenge has emerged—namely, the successful management of larger groups. If one's class or unit consists of a dozen or so youths, one might conduct a group of six to eight trainees while another group of similar size observes, "fishbowl style." The following week, they reverse. But what if it is a class or unit of 20 to 25 or more youths? Here the problem is greater. Trainers should avoid putting on modeling enactments to groups this large without providing following role-play opportunities. Skillstreaming is an experiential activity; the rehearsal of the role-playing is vital. To accomplish this task in large groups, some trainers have constituted subgroups of five or six trainees and had each subgroup role-play simultaneously as the two teachers rotated from subgroup to subgroup. Others have gotten additional trainer help for this purpose—two aides, two parent volunteers, and so forth. Yet others have tried with some success to work with the larger group as a whole, using the standard Skillstreaming procedures but seeing to it that all or almost all of the youngsters in the group have some role in the process. This may be attempted by using several trainees as co-actors in the role-play; by instructing trainees who are not role-playing to watch for and give feedback on the actor's performance of specific skill steps; and/or by assigning other helper roles to trainees (e.g., pointing to skill steps on the chalkboard as the role-play unfolds, helping arrange "props" to make the role-play more realistic). Still other trainers, making essentially a triage decision, have provided Skillstreaming for only the half dozen or so most skill-deficient youngsters in the larger class or unit. Skillstreaming, like so much else in schools and other institutions, often is the doing of the possible.

Frequency of sessions

For Skillstreaming sessions to be more than an in-school exercise, trainees must have the time and opportunity to try out in their out-of-group lives the skills they have role-played in the group. These practice or homework attempts are more likely to occur if ample time is provided between sessions. We have, therefore, found a schedule of two sessions per week to be optimal.

Physical arrangements

Figure 3 depicts a common horseshoe-shaped room and furniture arrangement often employed for conducting Skillstreaming sessions.

Duration of program

Skillstreaming programs have lasted as briefly as 2 days, as long as 3 years, and just about all lengths in between. The 2-day programs are in in-school detention centers in which detained students are taught a single skill during their brief stay. Three-year and other lengthy programs are open Skillstreaming groups, adding new members one at a time as older members "graduate," drop out, or otherwise leave. A more typical program duration is the school year.

A second way of defining duration of program, beyond days or months of meetings, concerns the number of skills taught. The goal of Skillstreaming is the teaching of prosocial skills in such a manner that the skills are not only learned (acquired), but also used by the trainee (performed) in an effective manner, in a variety of settings, for an enduring period of time. It most definitely is not a curriculum to charge through in order to get to its end. Although the full curriculum contains 50 skills, there is no expectation that all will be taught to any given Skillstreaming group. Because the goal is to teach only those skills in which group members are deficient and that would be useful in their daily lives, a full curriculum for some groups may be only a few skills. For other groups, it may be several skills.

Whether few or several members are involved, trainers should not move on to a second skill until the first is well learned (as evidenced by successful role-play within the group) and regularly performed (as evidenced by successful homework outside the group). These training goals will usually require that the same skill be taught (modeling, role-playing, etc.) for more than one session. Even at the price of group members' boredom with skill repetition, skills should be taught until they are nearly automatic or "overlearned"—a process we will describe in more detail in chapter 9, dealing with generalization.

FIGURE 3 A Functional Room Arrangement for Skillstreaming

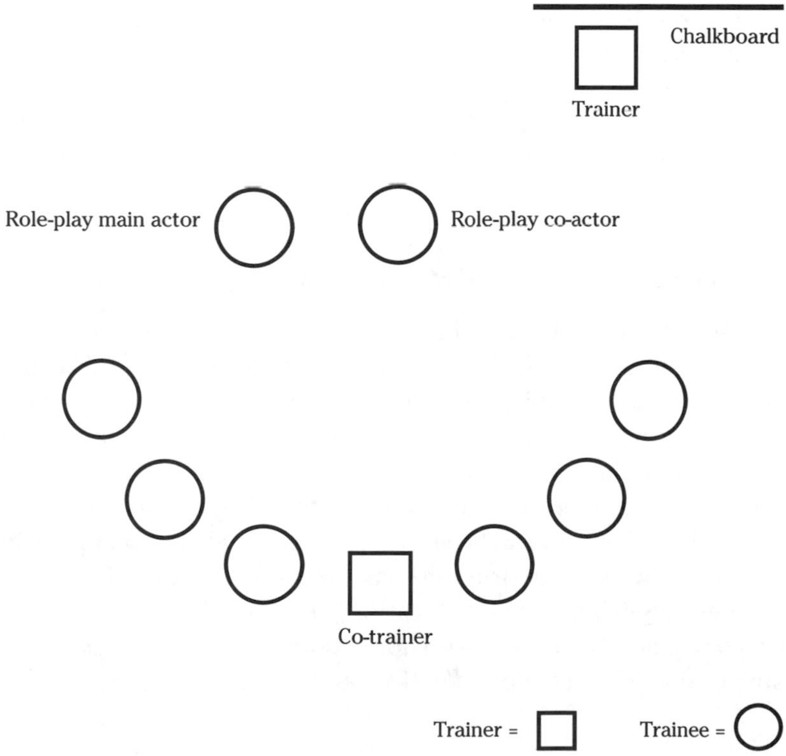

Materials needed

Other than the substantial cost of staff time, Skillstreaming is not an expensive program to implement. A chalkboard or easel pad, Skill Cards listing the skill steps, and skill step posters to hang in the classroom and school are the core materials needed. Skill Cards may be of the preprinted variety available with the program (see the example in Figure 4); trainers (or trainees) may also make these cards themselves.

In addition to these materials, two booklets augment the basic Skillstreaming procedures and enhance their effectiveness. The first is the Skillstreaming *Student Manual.* This manual for adolescents orients participants to Skillstreaming. In language appropriate for typical group members, it is designed to supplement and reaffirm trainers' verbal structuring of the Skillstreaming group's purpose and goals. Specifically, the manual introduces trainees to the Skillstreaming procedures of modeling, role-playing, performance feedback, and transfer training (homework). The *Program Forms* booklet compiles essential program forms, checklists, and charts in a reproducible 8½ × 11–inch format. We recommend that trainers use the *Student Manual* and *Program Forms* booklet in their effort to create and carry out effective Skillstreaming groups. These resources and other supplementary Skillstreaming materials are fully described in Appendix C.

Placement in the school curriculum

As noted earlier, mounting an intervention program in a school or other setting is most often the doing of the possible. All sorts of class schedule, administrative, and personnel realities must be taken into account and accommodated. These facts of institutional life have resulted in Skillstreaming's being placed in a wide variety of times and locations—from homeroom at the beginning of the day to after-school detention at its end, and just about every other possible time in between. The program has been incorporated into social studies, English, physical education, and life skills classes. Other frequent placements have been homeroom, resource room, in-school suspension, after-school detention, and more.

FIGURE 4 Sample Skill Card

Listening

1. Look at the person who is talking.
2. Think about what is being said.
3. Wait your turn to talk.
4. Say what you want to say.

SKILL 1

Labeling the group

What shall the Skillstreaming group be called? Most often, it is just called "Skillstreaming." But matters are not that simple. There has been much written in the educational (especially special educational) literature on the negative effects of labeling children and adolescents. Such effects may occur when youngsters are selected for even benignly titled interventions such as Skillstreaming. Some users have sought (we think usually unsuccessfully) to avoid the labeling problem by renaming Skillstreaming something even more positive (e.g., Positive Skillbuilding Group, Fantastics, etc.). This may help, but it is certainly not a solution, as the rest of the youth's peer group (skill-proficient classmates) see those selected as being singled out for deficit remediation. We have no solution except what we have done a number of times at the elementary and preschool levels, where Skillstreaming has been used more as a preventive than a rehabilitative intervention—namely, to include *all* members of a given class or unit in the training so that no one is singled out.

CHAPTER 4
Skillstreaming Training Procedures

The four core training procedures that constitute Skillstreaming include modeling, role-playing, performance feedback, and generalization training. In order to carry out these procedures, trainers lead the group through the nine steps listed in Table 2.

STEP 1: DEFINE THE SKILL

This session-opening activity is a brief, trainer-led group discussion of the skill to be taught that meeting. Whether the skill was selected by the trainers, or via periodic curriculum negotiation between trainers and trainees, which we urge be conducted in all Skillstreaming groups, this activity is a necessary training starter. Its purpose is

TABLE 2 Skillstreaming Training Steps

1. Define the skill
2. Model the skill
3. Establish trainee skill need
4. Select role-player
5. Set up the role play
6. Conduct the role-play
7. Provide performance feedback
8. Assign skill homework
9. Select next role-player

orientation; its contents are both the abstract meaning and concrete examples of the chosen skill. The training goal here is to make more certain that the group members have begun to understand specifically which skill is about to be taught. This goal can typically be met quite rapidly—in perhaps a few minutes—thus avoiding either a long lecture by the trainers or a protracted group discussion over definitional minutae.

Trainer: Okay, let's get started. Today's skill is a quite important one, one that lots of people have trouble doing well—or even at all. It's called Expressing Affection. Can anyone tell me what you think Expressing Affection means? Latoya? Yes, what do you think?

Trainee 1: Like, when you love somebody.

Trainer: Good, a good part of it. Anyone else? Chico, you had your hand up.

Trainee 2: Kissing, hugging.

Trainer: Okay again. Those are two ways of doing it. Good examples. What is the general idea of what expressing affection means, its definition? Emily?

Trainee 3: Letting someone know how you feel about them, when you feel really good about them.

Trainer: Agree. You've given good definitions, all of you. That's the skill we're going to learn today. Ann [second trainer], would you mind giving out the Skill Cards as I write the skill steps on the board?

STEP 2: MODEL THE SKILL

Definition

Modeling is defined as learning by imitation. Imitation has been examined in a great deal of research and under many names: copying, empathic learning, observational learning, identification, vicarious learning, matched-dependent behavior, and, most frequently, modeling. This research has consistently shown that modeling is an effective and reliable technique for both the rapid learning of new behaviors and the strengthening or weakening of previously learned behaviors. Three types of learning by modeling have been identified.

Observational learning refers to the learning of new behaviors that the person has never performed before. Adolescents are great imitators. Almost weekly, new idioms, new clothing styles, and new ways of walking, dancing, and doing emerge and take hold in the world of adolescence. Many of these events are clear examples of observational learning effects.

Inhibitory and *disinhibitory effects* involve the strengthening or weakening of behaviors previously performed only rarely by the person due to a history of punishment or other negative reactions. Modeling offered by peers is, again, a major source of inhibitory and disinhibitory effects. Youngsters who know how to be altruistic, sharing, caring, and the like may inhibit such behaviors in the presence of models who are behaving more egocentrically and being rewarded for their egocentric behavior. Aggressive models may also have a disinhibitory effect and cause observing youngsters to engage in aggressive behavior. Later in this book, when such skills as Dealing with Group Pressure (Skill 42) are discussed, ways of teaching youngsters how to avoid such disinhibitory effects will be explored.

Behavioral facilitation refers to the performance of previously learned behaviors that are neither new nor a source of potential negative reactions from others. One person buys something he seems to enjoy, so a friend buys one, too. A child deals with a recurring household matter in an effective manner, so a sibling imitates her behavior. A classmate tries talking over a class problem with her teacher; when she succeeds, a second student decides to approach the teacher in a similar way. These are all examples of behavioral facilitation effects.

Research has demonstrated that a wide variety of behaviors can be learned, strengthened, weakened, or facilitated through modeling. These include acting aggressively, helping others, behaving independently, planning careers, becoming emotionally aroused, interacting socially, displaying dependency, exhibiting certain speech patterns, behaving empathically, self-disclosing, and many more. It is clear from such research that modeling can be an important tool in teaching new behaviors.

Yet it is also true that most people observe dozens and perhaps hundreds of behaviors every day that they do not imitate. Television, radio, magazines, and newspapers expose people to very polished, professional modeling displays of someone's buying one product or another, but these observers do not later buy the product. And many people observe expensively produced and expertly acted instructional films, but they remain uninstructed. Apparently, people learn by modeling under some circumstances but not others.

Modeling Enhancers

Laboratory research on modeling has successfully identified what we have called *modeling enhancers,* a number of circumstances that increase the degree to which learning by imitation occurs. These modeling enhancers are characteristics of the model, the modeling display, or the observer (the trainee).

Model characteristics. More effective modeling will occur when the model (the person to be imitated) (a) seems to be highly skilled or expert; (b) is of high status; (c) controls rewards desired by the trainee; (d) is of the same sex, approximate age, and social status as the trainee; (e) is friendly and helpful; and, of particular importance, (f) is rewarded for the given behaviors. That is, we are all more likely to imitate expert or powerful yet pleasant people who receive rewards for what they are doing, especially when the particular rewards involved are something that we too desire.

Modeling display characteristics. More effective modeling will occur when the modeling display shows the behaviors to be imitated (a) in a clear and detailed manner; (b) in the order from least to most difficult behaviors; (c) with enough repetition to make overlearning likely; (d) with as little irrelevant (not to be learned) detail as possible; and (e) performed by several different models, rather than a single model.

Observer (trainee) characteristics. More effective modeling will occur when the person observing the model is (a) told to imitate the model; (b) similar to the model in background or in attitude toward the skill; (c) friendly toward or likes the model; and, most important, (d) rewarded for performing the modeled behaviors.

Stages of Modeling

The effects of these modeling enhancers, as well as of modeling itself, can be better understood by examining the three stages of learning by modeling.

Attention. Trainees cannot learn from watching a model unless they pay attention to the modeling display and, in particular, to the specific behaviors being modeled. Such attention is maximized by eliminating irrelevant detail in the modeling display, minimizing the complexity of the modeled material, making the display vivid, and implementing the modeling enhancers previously described.

Retention. In order to later reproduce the behaviors he or she has observed, the trainee must remember or retain them. Because the behaviors of the modeling display itself are no longer present, retention must occur by memory. Memory is aided if the behaviors displayed are classified or coded by the observer. Another name for such coding is covert rehearsal (i.e., reviewing in one's mind the performance of the displayed behaviors). Research has shown, however, that an even more important aid to retention is overt, or behavioral, rehearsal. Such practice of the specific behavioral steps is crucial for learning and, indeed, is the second major procedure of Skillstreaming. This is role-playing, a procedure that will be examined in depth shortly. It should be noted at this point, however, that the likelihood of retention via either covert or overt rehearsal is greatly aided by rewards provided to both the model and/or the trainee.

Reproduction. Researchers interested in human learning have typically distinguished between learning (acquiring or gaining knowledge about how to do something) and performance (doing it). If a person has paid attention and remembered the behaviors shown during the modeling display, it may be said that the person has learned. The main interest, however, is not so much in whether the person can reproduce the behaviors that have been seen, but in whether he or she does produce them. As with retention, the likelihood that a person will actually perform a behavior that has been learned will depend mostly on the expectation of a reward for doing so. Expectation of reward has been shown to be determined by the amount, consistency, recency, and frequency of the reward that the trainee has observed being provided to the model for performing the desired behavior. The crucial nature of reward for performance shall be further examined in chapter 8, on trainee motivation.

Modeling Guidelines

Guidelines to be kept in mind in developing live modeling displays are as follows:

1. Use at least two examples for each demonstration of a skill. If a skill is used in more than one class meeting, develop two more new modeling displays.
2. Select situations that are relevant to the trainees' real-life circumstances.
3. The main actor (i.e., the person enacting the behavioral steps of the skill) should be portrayed as a youngster reasonably similar in age, socioeconomic background, verbal ability, and other characteristics salient to the youngsters in the group.
4. All displays should depict positive outcomes. There should always be reinforcement to the model who is using the skill well.
5. All modeling displays should depict all the behavioral steps of the skill being modeled, in the correct sequence.
6. Modeling displays should depict only one skill at a time. All extraneous content should be eliminated.

In order to help trainees attend to the skill enactments, Skill Cards, which contain the name of the skill being taught and its behavioral steps, are distributed prior to the modeling displays. Trainees are told to watch and listen closely as the models portray the skill. Particular care should be given to helping trainees identify the behavioral steps as they are presented in the context of the modeling vignettes. Trainers should also remind the youngsters that in order to depict some of the behavioral steps in certain skills, the actors will "think out loud" statements that would ordinarily be thoughts to oneself and that this process is used to facilitate learning.

STEP 3: ESTABLISH TRAINEE SKILL NEED

Before the group members commence their role-playing of the skill they have seen demonstrated by the trainers, it is necessary to openly identify each trainee's current need for the skill. After all, behavioral rehearsal is the purpose of the role-play—that is, enactment of the skill as it relates to a contemporary or anticipated situation or relationship in the trainee's present life, not a fictitious situation provided by the trainers or a reenactment of a past problem or circumstances no longer relevant to the trainee. Skill need may have been established earlier as part of the selection and grouping process. Nonetheless, its open discussion in the group is needed as part of the sequence of steps necessary to establish relevant and realistic role-plays. Each trainee, therefore, is asked in turn to describe briefly where, when, and especially with whom he or she would find it useful to employ the skill just modeled.

To make effective use of such information, it is often valuable to list the names of the group members on the chalkboard or easel pad at the front of the room and to record next to each name the name of the target person(s) with whom they wish to use the skill and the theme of the role-play associated with that person. Since an ironclad rule of Skillstreaming is that every trainee must role-play every skill, with no exceptions, having such information at hand will be of considerable use should a given trainee express reluctance to participate.

STEP 4: SELECT ROLE-PLAYER

Because all members of the Skillstreaming group will be expected to role-play each skill, in most instances it is not of great concern who does so first. Typically, especially after the teaching of one or two skills has made clear that all must role-play, the selection process determining the sequence of trainee role-playing can proceed by the use of volunteers. If for any reason there are members of your group for whom the act of role-playing a particular skill (or on a particular day) seems threatening, it may be helpful not to ask them to role-play first or second. Seeing other trainees do so first can be reassuring and help ease their way into the activity. For some, reluctance may turn into outright resistance and refusal. Means for dealing with such problematic behavior are described at length in chapter 8. For the present, it is useful to indicate that, although we maintain our "no exceptions" rule, we seek to involve such youngsters in role-playing by means of support, encouragement, reassurance, and highlighting the utility of the skill for their own personal needs, rather than by making use of penalties, heavy-handed persuasion, or other authoritarian means.

STEP 5: SET UP THE ROLE-PLAY

Once a trainee has described a real-life situation in which skill use might be helpful, that trainee is designated the main actor. The main actor chooses a second trainee (the co-actor) to play the role of the significant other person (e.g., mother, peer) involved in the skill problem. The trainee should be urged to pick as a co-actor someone who resembles the real-life person in as many ways as possible. The trainer then elicits from the main actor any additional information needed to set the stage for role-playing. In order to make role-playing as realistic as possible, the trainers should obtain a description of the physical setting, the events immediately preceding the role-play, and the mood or manner the co-actor should portray, along with any other information that would enhance realism.

STEP 6: CONDUCT THE ROLE-PLAY

Before role-playing begins, trainers should remind all of the participants of their roles and responsibilities: the main actor is told to follow the behavioral steps; the co-actor, to stay in the role of the other person; and the other trainees, to watch carefully for the enactment of the behavioral steps. It is often useful to assign one behavioral step to each observing trainee and have that trainee track it during the role-play and report on its content and quality during the subsequent feedback session. For the first several role-plays, the observers can be coached as to what kinds of cues to observe (e.g., posture, tone of voice, content of speech). Then the role-players are instructed to begin. At this point it is the responsibility of the trainer to provide the main actor with whatever help or coaching he or she needs in order to keep the role-playing going according to the behavioral steps. Trainees who "break role" and begin to explain their behavior or make comments should be urged to get back into the role and explain later. If the role-play is clearly going astray from the behavioral steps, the scene can be stopped, needed instruction can be provided, and then the role-play can be restarted. One trainer should be positioned near the chalkboard or easel pad and point to each of the behavioral steps, in turn, as the role-play unfolds, thus helping the main actor (as well as the other trainees) follow each of the steps in order.

Role-playing should be continued until all trainees have had an opportunity to participate in the role of main actor at least once and, depending on the quality of the role-plays and skill homework, perhaps two or more times. Sometimes this will require two or three sessions for a given skill. We suggest that each session begin with two modeling vignettes for the chosen skill, even if the skill is not new to the group. It is important to note that, although the framework (behavioral steps) of each role-play in the series remains the same, the actual content can and should change from role-play to role-play. It is the problem as it actually occurs, or could occur, in each youngster's real-life environment that should be the content of the given role-play. When the role-play has been completed, each trainee will be better armed to act appropriately in a real situation requiring skill use.

A few further procedural matters relevant to role-playing will serve to increase its effectiveness. Role reversal is often a useful role-play procedure. A trainee role-playing a skill may on occasion have a difficult time perceiving the co-actor's viewpoint, and vice versa. Having the two exchange roles and resume the role-play can be most helpful in this regard.

On occasion the trainer can also assume the co-actor role in an effort to give youngsters the opportunity to handle types of reactions not otherwise role-played during the session. For example, it may be crucial to have a difficult adult co-actor role realistically portrayed. The trainer as co-actor may also be particularly helpful when dealing with less verbal or more hesitant trainees.

STEP 7: PROVIDE PERFORMANCE FEEDBACK

A brief feedback period follows each role-play. This helps the main actor find out how well he or she followed or departed from the behavioral steps, examines the psychological impact of the enactment on the co-actor, and provides the main actor with encouragement to try out the role-played behaviors in real life. To implement this process, the trainer should ask the main actor to wait until everyone has commented before responding.

The co-actor is asked to react first. Next, the observing trainees comment on how well the behavioral steps were followed and on other relevant aspects of the role-play. Then the trainers comment in particular on how well the behavioral steps were followed and provide social reinforcement (praise, approval, encouragement) for close following. To be most effective, trainers should follow these guidelines:

1. Provide reinforcement only after role-plays that follow the behavioral steps.
2. Provide reinforcement at the earliest appropriate opportunity after role-plays that follow the behavioral steps.
3. Always provide reinforcement to the co-actor for being helpful, cooperative, and so forth.
4. Vary the specific content of the reinforcements offered (e.g., praise particular aspects of the performance, such as tone of voice, posture, phrasing).
5. Provide enough role-playing activity for each group member to have sufficient opportunity to be reinforced.
6. Provide reinforcement in an amount consistent with the quality of the given role-play.
7. Provide no reinforcement when the role-play departs significantly from the behavioral steps (except for "trying" in the first session or two).
8. Provide reinforcement for an individual trainee's improvement over previous performances.

After hearing all the feedback, the main actor is invited to make comments regarding the role-play and the feedback of others. In this way he or she can learn to evaluate the effectiveness of skill enactment in the light of evidence from others.

In all aspects of feedback, it is crucial that the trainer maintain the behavioral focus of Skillstreaming. Trainer comments must point to the presence or absence of specific behaviors and not take the form of vague evaluative comments or broad generalities. Feedback, of course, may be positive or negative in content. A negative comment should always be followed by a constructive comment as to how a particular fault might be improved. At minimum, a "poor" performance (major departure from the behavioral steps) can be praised as "a good try" at the same time that it is being criticized for its real faults. If at all possible, youngsters failing to follow the relevant behavioral steps in their role-play should be given the opportunity to replay these same behavioral steps after receiving corrective feedback. At times, as a further feedback procedure, we have audiotaped or videotaped entire role-plays. Giving trainees opportunities to observe themselves on tape can be an effective aid, enabling them to reflect on their own verbal and nonverbal behavior.

Because a primary goal of Skillstreaming is skill flexibility, role-play enactment that departs somewhat from the behavioral steps may not be "wrong." That is, a different approach to the skill may in fact work in some situations. Trainers should stress that they are trying to teach effective alternatives and that the trainees would do well to have the behavioral steps being taught in their repertoire of skill behaviors, available to use when appropriate.

STEP 8: ASSIGN SKILL HOMEWORK

Following each successful role-play, the trainees are instructed to try in their own real-life settings the behaviors practiced during the session. The name of the person(s) with whom they will try the skill, the day, the place, and so on are all discussed and entered on the Homework Report 1 form (see Figure 5). Trainees are also urged to take notes on their first transfer attempts on this report. These latter sections of the report request information about what happened when the trainees attempted the homework assignment, how well they followed the relevant behavioral steps, the trainees' evaluation of their performance, and thoughts about what the next assignment might appropriately be.

It has often proven useful to start with relatively simple homework behaviors and, as mastery is achieved, work up to more complex and demanding assignments. This provides the trainer with an opportunity to reinforce each approximation of the more complex target behavior. Successful experiences at beginning homework attempts are crucial in encouraging the trainee to make further attempts at real-life skill use.

The first part of each Skillstreaming session is devoted to presenting and discussing these homework reports. When trainees have

FIGURE 5 Homework Report 1

Name: ______________________________ Date: __________

FILL IN DURING THIS CLASS

1. What skill will you use?

2. What are the steps for the skill?

3. Where will you try the skill?

4. With whom will you try the skill?

5. When will you try the skill?

FILL IN AFTER DOING YOUR HOMEWORK

1. What happened when you did the homework?

2. Which skill steps did you really follow?

3. How good a job did you do in using the skill? *(check one)*

   ☐ excellent ☐ good ☐ fair ☐ poor

4. What do you think should be your next homework assignment?

made an effort to complete their homework assignments, trainers should provide social reinforcement. Failure to do homework should be met with the trainers' disappointment. It cannot be stressed too strongly that without these or similar attempts to maximize transfer, the value of the entire training session is in severe jeopardy.

When most of the group's trainees are demonstrating skill proficiency by their successful role-plays of the skill in the group and their successful use of it in carrying out homework assignments outside of the group, it is time for the group as a whole to move on to another skill. But what of the trainees not yet up to speed, not yet competent in the skill most have mastered? While moving them on with the rest of the group to the new skill, we ask them to continue their homework efforts on the old skill. Homework Report 2 (Figure 6) is used for this purpose. Trainees submit these reports to the trainers, who either briefly react verbally or jot a feedback notation on the form—in either case using little or no group time in the process. By the time a Skillstreaming group is a few months into its program, all its members will be doing homework on whatever new skill is being addressed, but most will also be on one or another skill they have yet to master. A Skill Contract like the one shown in Figure 7 may help trainees, either individually or as a group, follow through with skill practice.

Trainers can encourage independent skill practice by distributing Skill Sheets like the one shown in Figure 8 and asking trainees to copy the steps of any skill or skills they intend to practice in the future. Self-recording forms like the ones illustrated in Figures 9 and 10 can also facilitate continued skill use. Self-Recording Form 1 is intended as a record of individual skill use; Self-Recording Form 2 documents the results of trainees' use of skill combinations.

STEP 9: SELECT NEXT ROLE-PLAYER

The next trainee is selected to serve as main actor, and the training sequence just described is repeated until all members of the Skillstreaming group are reliably demonstrating in-group and out-of-group proficiency in using the skill.

Figure 6 Homework Report 2

Name: ______________________________ Date: ____________

FILL IN BEFORE DOING YOUR HOMEWORK

1. What skill will you use?

2. What are the steps for the skill?

3. Where will you try the skill?

4. With whom will you try the skill?

5. When will you try the skill?

6. If you do an excellent job, how will you reward yourself?

7. If you do a good job, how will you reward yourself?

8. If you do a fair job, how will you reward yourself?

FILL IN AFTER DOING YOUR HOMEWORK

1. What happened when you did the homework?

2. Which skill steps did you really follow?

3. How good a job did you do in using the skill? *(check one)*

   ☐ excellent ☐ good ☐ fair ☐ poor

4. What do you think should be your next homework assignment?

Figure 7 **Skill Contract**

Name: ____

Date(s) of contract: ______________________________

I agree to use the skill of ___________________________

when ____

____

If I do, then ______________________________________

____

Student signature: _________________________________

Teacher/staff signature: ____________________________

Review date: ______________________________________

FIGURE 8 Skill Sheet

Name: ______________________________ Date: ____________

SKILL: ____

SKILL STEPS:

NOTES:

____

____

____

____

____

____

FIGURE 9 **Self-Recording Form 1**

Name: ______________________________ Date: ____________

INSTRUCTIONS: Each time you use the skill, write down when and how well you did.

SKILL: ____

When?	**How well did you do?** *(excellent, good, fair, poor)*
1. ________________________	________________________
________________________	
2. ________________________	________________________
________________________	
3. ________________________	________________________
________________________	
4. ________________________	________________________
________________________	

Figure 10 Self-Recording Form 2

Name: ______________________________ Date: ____________

Instructions: Each time you use any of these skills (or skill combinations), write down when and how well you did.

SKILLS:

____

____

____

When?	**How well did you do?** *(excellent, good, fair, poor)*
1. ________________________	________________________
________________________	

What happened as a result of your skill use?

____

When?	**How well did you do?** *(excellent, good, fair, poor)*
2. ________________________	________________________
________________________	

What happened as a result of your skill use?

____

CHAPTER 5
A Sample Skillstreaming Session

The following edited transcript from the training resource *The Skillstreaming Video* (Goldstein & McGinnis, 1988) depicts the core Skillstreaming procedures discussed in Chapter 4. The first portion of the dialogue illustrates the way the trainer structures the first Skillstreaming group. The second portion shows how the Skillstreaming teaching procedures are applied with Skill 42, Dealing with Group Pressure.

Trainer: Welcome, all of you, to today's Skillstreaming group. I've met with all of you individually, so as you remember this is a skill learning group. When I say our purpose is learning skills, what does the word *skill* make you think of? What are examples of skills that people learn?

Larry: Riding a bike.

Beth: Playing a piano.

A.J.: Sinking a basket, in basketball.

Michelle: Cooperating, like with other people.

Trainer: Good examples. Riding a bike, playing the piano, sports skills. Those are all skills, but so is Michelle's example, cooperating. It's one kind of what might be called "people skills." There are many others, and they are the type of skills we'll be working on. Things like how to handle failure when something you try doesn't work out, responding to teasing, what do you do when another person accuses you of something that maybe you didn't do.

These are just a few examples of what's called people skills. But whether it's people skills, or cooking skills, or athletic skills, all skills are learned the same way. Let's talk for a minute about how you all are going to learn the skills that are going to be taught in this group.

Let's say that A.J. here is a good athlete, but he never played basketball and he wants to learn it. I'm the coach, and I'm going to teach him. Let's say lesson one is on shooting a foul shot. What's the first thing that happens? Who does what?

Chico: You show him. You shoot some first.

Trainer: Right, I show him. I'm the expert. He doesn't know what to do. So I ask him to watch carefully, and I go up to the foul line, stand in a certain way, I hold the ball in a certain way, bend my knees, take a breath, look at the front rim, and I shoot the ball. Because I'm the coach, it goes right in. Is that it? He watched me do it, right? Does that make A.J. ready for the NBA? No, he's got to do something then, too. What does he have to do?

Sue: He's got to try it, to try to do it like you did.

Trainer: Exactly! So he goes to the foul line. He stands in a certain way, breathes in a certain way, bends his knees, and shoots it. Too bad, he misses. I showed him the right way, and he tried, but it didn't go in. What do I have to do then?

Sue: Help him.

Trainer: Yes, I help him. I give him what's called *feedback*. I tell him what he did right, what he did wrong, and how to do it better. I say, "A.J., it was terrific the way you stood, the way you held the ball, took a nice deep breath, but you weren't quite facing the basket squarely, and you shot it too fast." I give him feedback on the parts of the skill he did right and the parts he did wrong.

I would probably show him again the right way of doing what he did wrong. Then what? There's one more step to teaching a skill. Nobody? Well, he's got to practice. Practice, practice, practice.

So, that's how you learn the skills of basketball. Someone shows you, an expert, a coach. You try it. You get feedback on how you did, and then you practice what you learned. These steps—show, try, feedback, practice—are how you learn any skill. Shooting a basket, cooperating with others, dealing with group pressure, and any other skills that involve one person with another.

Step 1: Define the Skill

Trainer: Today we're going to learn a really important people skill. It's one that several of you told me you needed—Dealing with Group Pressure. What do you all think that means?

Larry: Group pressure, like when my friends want to go cruising or something, and I don't.

Tanya: Or your family. My parents and sometimes my older sister sometimes try to make me do stuff I don't want to do.

Trainer: Again, good examples from you folks. Yes, it's when people ask you or push you to do things that maybe you don't want to do or have mixed feelings about doing. Chico, Michelle, do you get a sense of this, of what Dealing with Group Pressure means? Good.

Here are the steps that make up Dealing with Group Pressure. A. J., would you please pass these Skill Cards around? Thanks. The steps for this skill are also on this easel pad. I'd like to read them to you.

1. Think about what the group wants you to do and why.

2. Decide what you want to do.
3. Decide how to tell the group what you want to do.
4. Tell the group what you have decided.

These four steps, together and in this order, make up one good way of dealing with group pressure. Bess and Al and I are going to model it for you. Like the basketball coach, we'll show you the skill being done in an expert way. Try to pick out the steps as we do them because when we're through doing it, I'm going to ask each of you to get up and go through the same steps.

Step 2: Model the Skill

Trainer: Here's the situation. Bess and Al are my old buddies. I haven't seen them for a long time because I've been away at a delinquency center for some stuff I did and got in trouble for. Now I'm back out on the street, my first couple of days out. I'm walking down the street, and here come my two friends, tooling along in this great-looking car. They're going to pull over and urge me to get in the car and go for a ride with them. But I don't think it's their car. I don't want to get back in trouble, but I don't want to lose their friendship. That's my dilemma. So Bess and Al are going to put pressure on me to get in the car, and I'll deal with it by going through these steps.

Trainer: Hey, how are you guys doing? Good to see ya.

Bess: Hi, Arnie, how are you? Been a long time.

Trainer: I'm good. What's up?

Bess: Al got this car started, and we're going for a ride. Maybe over to the park.

Al: Get in, man. We gotta catch up with you.

Trainer: Well, that's one nice car. I gotta admit it.

Al: You getting in or what?

Trainer: *(Thinking aloud to himself)* Well, let me see what to do here *(pointing to Step 1).* They want me to get in and go for a ride with them. I guess the "why" is just because I'm an old buddy and they'd just like my company. *(Pointing to Step 2)* Decide what I want to do. I'd like to go for a ride with them. I mean, it's a nice car, and it's nice to go cruising. But I don't want to get in trouble again, and I'm kind of embarrassed to ask about the registration, but I'm 'bout sure it's not their car. No, I'm not going to do it. I've got to take a risk here and not get in. *(Pointing to Step 3)* I could lie to them and say I've got something else to do. I could just walk away and make believe I didn't hear them, but they'd think I was crazy if I did that. I think I'm just going to have to tell them straight out what's going on here and hope for the best. *(Pointing to Step 4—to Bess and Al)* Thanks for inviting me, you guys, I appreciate it. It is a neat car, but I don't know who owns it, if you know what I mean. And the food wasn't too great up at the camp, so I'm gonna have to pass. How about I head over to the park and meet you there—Lot D—in about 25 minutes. We can shoot the breeze then. OK?

Bess: Well . . . OK. If you want to walk over. Driving is a lot easier, but we'll catch you there.

Al: I don't get it, man, ain't nobody going to stop us. But, like she says, if you want to walk.

Trainer: Good, see ya there.

Step 3: Establish Trainee Skill Need

Trainer: That's our demonstration of the skill. What is an example each of you have, in your current life, of people putting pressure on you to do things you don't want to do?

Michelle: There are three kids in my math class. Whenever there's a test, they want me to give them answers. I just don't want to do that, but they really press me a lot.

Sue: Dwayne and Christy want me to go across the street, cut out of class and go behind the drugstore to smoke. It's regular cigarettes, but if I get caught I'll be in big trouble with the truancy officer. Off school grounds and smoking.

Trainer: Tammy, how about you? What would be a good example for you?

Tammy: Well, last week Marcy and Todd asked me to go somewhere with them. But I was afraid I'd be grounded, and I told them I couldn't go. They said I should tell my mom I was just going next door and that I'd be back soon, and then go with them.

Step 4: Select Role-Player

Trainer: Good examples for all of you of tough group pressure you have to deal with. Who would like to role-play this skill first? Tammy, how about you? C'mon up and let's do it.

Tammy: Okay.

Step 5: Set Up the Role-Play

Trainer: Great, let's give it a try. Could you, Tammy, tell us a little bit more about the situation so that we could help you feel that you are really actually back in the pressure situation you faced? Let's see, two of your friends, Marcy and Todd, were urging you to lie to your mom. Tell us more.

Tammy: They wanted us all to go to the campus so we could drink. My mom's really against my going there because she says it's not for high school kids. There's more. They wanted me to tell my mom we wanted to go to a movie and ask her to drive us there!

Trainer: An interesting twist. They not only wanted you to lie to her but also to have her provide the transportation! Who in the group reminds you most of Marcy, either by the way she looks, or talks, or any other important way?

Tammy: I think Sue. I'm not sure why, but probably her hair, blond also. And you're both pretty tall.

Trainer: What about Todd? Who in the group seems to be like him or remind you of him?

Tammy: Larry. Larry is closest of the males in the group. I'm not sure why, but it just feels that way.

Trainer: Sue and Larry, would you two please come up here and play the parts of Tammy's two friends? You've got a pretty good idea by now, I think, of what they were pressuring her to do. Tammy, where might you see them next?

Tammy: I don't have classes with either of them this term, but most days we meet after eighth period and walk home together. They both live near me.

Trainer: Where do you usually meet?

Tammy: In the schoolyard.

Trainer: Okay, in the schoolyard. Larry. Sue. Would you both pretend you are in the schoolyard at the end of the day. Here comes Tammy. Stick it to her! But before you start, I want to give all of you sitting and watching an assignment. I'm going to ask each one of you to watch the role-play carefully so that you can give Tammy feedback when she's done on how well she followed the steps. A.J., would you take Step 1? When the role-play is over, tell Tammy and the rest of us just what she did to act out Step 1 and how well you think she did it. Chico, would you take Step 2? Beth, Step 3? Michelle, please handle the last step. OK? Don't forget, Sue and Larry, put pressure on her to go with you just the way you think the two friends of hers, Marcy and Todd, laid it on her. Let her have it.

Step 6: Conduct the Role-Play

Sue: Hey, Tammy, me and Todd here were just talking and we decided we want to go to campus tonight and we thought you'd really want to go, too, so how about it?

Larry: Yeah, everyone will probably be there. What do you say? Don't worry about being grounded—you can lie your way out of that. So, what do you say? About 8:00?

Trainer: Good. Now hold the action. They've put real pressure on you, now it's your turn. *(Pointing to Step 1)* What did the group want you to do and why?

Tammy: They want me to go up on campus with them and go partying and hang out and drink and stuff.

Trainer: *(Pointing to Step 2)* Decide what you want to do. Before you decide, think about different choices, and then pick one.

Tammy: Well, I could figure out some lie and tell it to my mom.

Trainer: That's one alternative. What else? Before you pick one, what else?

Tammy: I could lie to them. Tell them I had something else to do.

Trainer: Lie to them.

Tammy: I could say, in my situation, that my mom would really get mad and she really wouldn't want me to be up there.

Trainer: All right *(pointing to Step 3),* why don't you go ahead and do it *(pointing to Step 4).*

Tammy: Well, you guys, I really can't go because if my mom found out that I went up there she would ground me forever. I'd be kept from going out for who knows how long, so I'm not going to go this time.

Sue: Well, you know there's lots of other people who'd like to go.

Tammy: I think I'd like to go, too, but I really can't. Sorry.

Step 7: Provide Performance Feedback

Trainer: Okay, let's get some feedback for Tammy. First you two. Sue and Larry, if you were the real Marcy and Todd, how do you think you'd respond to how Tammy handled you?

Sue: I'd probably pursue it further. Pressure her more to see if I could convince her. Or tell her to tell her mom she's spending the night at my house, and then we'd go to campus.

Larry: Yeah, and remind her again that other people will be there.

Trainer: In other words, both of you would put still more pressure on her. She'd have to keep resisting if she wanted to not do it. Okay, A.J., what did Tammy do for Step 1, and how well did you think she did it?

A.J.: Go to campus and get drunk. That was pretty clear.

Trainer: Okay, how about Step 2? Chico?

Chico: She thought about lying. To her mom or her two friends. Or just telling them no, I ain't going.

Trainer: Beth?

Beth: She picked the last one, to tell them her mom wouldn't really want her to do that and that she'd be grounded to the next century if her mom found out.

Trainer: All right, Step 4. Michelle, you had that one: Tell the group what you have decided. How'd that come out?

Michelle: She told them what she decided, what she wanted to. They put more pressure on her, but she stuck with what she decided.

Step 8: Assign Skill Homework

Trainer: There's your feedback, Tammy. They all seem to be saying you did a good job, and I think you did also. I know that this isn't just play acting for you, that it's a situation you probably will have to face again soon. What do you think, are you up to doing this with the real Marcy and the real Todd?

Tammy: I think so. I think I could do it.

Trainer: Good. Take this homework form. Fill out the top half right now—it's your promise that you'll try the skill where and when it's needed. Fill out the bottom half right after you try the skill—the bottom half is your chance to put down how well your try went. And then we'll talk about everyone's homework at the beginning of our next meeting. Tammy, you did a good job. Good luck using the skill.

Step 9: Select Next Role-Player

Trainer: Who is next? Who would like to role-play next?

CHAPTER 6
Skills for Adolescents

Our presentation thus far has sought to make clear how Skillstreaming groups are planned, organized, and conducted. The present chapter focuses instead on the Skillstreaming curriculum (i.e., the specific skills taught in the Skillstreaming group). The 50 Skillstreaming skills, falling into six content areas, come from a number of sources. Some derive from our extensive examination of relevant research—diverse educational and psychological studies yielding information on which behaviors constitute successful adolescent functioning in school, at home, with peers, and so forth. Our own direct observation of youngsters in various classroom and other real-life settings is a second source. The trainers and trainees in the many Skillstreaming groups conducted have been a particularly valuable fund of skill information.

The 50 Skillstreaming skills are listed in Table 3 in the order they will be presented in this chapter. Their order does not necessarily imply a sequence in which they should be taught. Trainer decisions regarding which skills should be taught to whom should largely be a function of each youth's skill deficiencies (teach what he or she is weak or lacking in) and each youth's own perspective on which ones he or she would like to learn (teach those for which trainee motivation is high). Note that skills are divided into six groups or skill families: Group I: Beginning Social Skills; Group II: Advanced Social Skills, Group III: Skills for Dealing with Feelings; Group IV: Skill Alternatives to Aggression; Group V: Skills for Dealing with Stress, and Group VI: Planning Skills.

The following pages set forth the behavioral steps that constitute each skill. These steps are the framework for the vignettes or stories modeled by trainers and then role-played by trainees, and they are central to the portrayal. Trainer notes (tips that we have found facilitate skill training), suggested content for modeling displays, and further comments are also given.

Table 3 The Skillstreaming Curriculum for Adolescents

Group I: Beginning Social Skills

1. Listening
2. Starting a Conversation
3. Having a Conversation
4. Asking a Question
5. Saying Thank You
6. Introducing Yourself
7. Introducing Other People
8. Giving a Compliment

Group II: Advanced Social Skills

9. Asking for Help
10. Joining In
11. Giving Instructions
12. Following Instructions
13. Apologizing
14. Convincing Others

Group III: Skills for Dealing with Feelings

15. Knowing Your Feelings
16. Expressing Your Feelings
17. Understanding the Feelings of Others
18. Dealing with Someone Else's Anger
19. Expressing Affection
20. Dealing with Fear
21. Rewarding Yourself

Group IV: Skill Alternatives to Aggression

22. Asking Permission
23. Sharing Something

24. Helping Others
25. Negotiating
26. Using Self-Control
27. Standing Up for Your Rights
28. Responding to Teasing
29. Avoiding Trouble with Others
30. Keeping Out of Fights

Group V: Skills for Dealing with Stress

31. Making a Complaint
32. Answering a Complaint
33. Being a Good Sport
34. Dealing with Embarrassment
35. Dealing with Being Left Out
36. Standing Up for a Friend
37. Responding to Persuasion
38. Responding to Failure
39. Dealing with Contradictory Messages
40. Dealing with an Accusation
41. Getting Ready for a Difficult Conversation
42. Dealing with Group Pressure

Group VI: Planning Skills

43. Deciding on Something to Do
44. Deciding What Caused a Problem
45. Setting a Goal
46. Deciding on Your Abilities
47. Gathering Information
48. Arranging Problems by Importance
49. Making a Decision
50. Concentrating on a Task

Skill 1: Listening

STEPS	**TRAINER NOTES**
1. Look at the person who is talking.	Face the person; establish eye contact.
2. Think about what is being said.	Show this by nodding your head, saying "mm-hmm."
3. Wait your turn to talk.	Don't fidget; don't shuffle your feet.
4. Say what you want to say.	Ask questions; express feelings; express your ideas.

SUGGESTED CONTENT FOR MODELING DISPLAYS

School or neighborhood: Teacher explains classroom assignment to main actor.

Home: Mother feels sad, and main actor listens.

Peer group: Friend describes interesting movie to main actor.

COMMENTS

All of the beginning social skills are basic to the functioning of the group. In starting a Skillstreaming group, it is useful for trainees to have a reasonable grasp of these skills before proceeding to other skills.

Like Step 2 above, many of the behavioral steps that make up the skills described in this chapter are *thinking* steps. That is, in actual, real-world use of many skills, certain steps are private and occur only in the thinking of the skill user. When modeling or role-playing such thinking steps in Skillstreaming, however, it is crucial that the enactment be aloud. Such public display of thinking steps is a significant aid to rapid and lasting learning.

Skill 2: Starting a Conversation

STEPS	**TRAINER NOTES**
1. Greet the other person.	Say "hi"; shake hands; choose the right time and place.
2. Make small talk.	Talk about sports, the weather, school events, and so forth.
3. Decide if the other person is listening.	Check if the other person is listening: looking at you, nodding, saying "mm-hmm."
4. Bring up the main topic.	

SUGGESTED CONTENT FOR MODELING DISPLAYS

School or neighborhood: Main actor starts conversation with secretary in school office.

Home: Main actor discusses allowance and/or privileges with parent.

Peer group: Main actor suggests weekend plans to a friend.

COMMENTS

We have found that this is frequently one of the best skills to teach in the first Skillstreaming session with a new group of trainees.

Skill 3: Having a Conversation

STEPS	TRAINER NOTES
1. Say what you want to say.	
2. Ask the other person what he/she thinks.	
3. Listen to what the other person says.	Review steps for Skill 1 (Listening).
4. Say what you think.	Respond to the other person; add new information; ask questions.
5. Make a closing remark.	Discuss types of closing remarks. Steps 1–4 can be repeated many times before Step 5 is done.

SUGGESTED CONTENT FOR MODELING DISPLAYS

School or neighborhood: Main actor talks with coach about upcoming game.

Home: Main actor talks with brother or sister about school experiences.

Peer group: Main actor discusses vacation plans with friend.

COMMENTS

This skill starts where Skill 2 (Starting a Conversation) leaves off. After separate practice of each skill, trainers may want to give trainees practice in using these skills successively.

Skill 4: Asking a Question

STEPS	TRAINER NOTES
1. Decide what you'd like to know more about.	Ask about something you don't understand, something you didn't hear, or something confusing.
2. Decide whom to ask.	Think about who has the best information on a topic; consider asking several people.
3. Think about different ways to ask your question and pick one way.	Think about wording; raise your hand; ask nonchallengingly.
4. Pick the right time and place to ask your question.	Wait for a pause; wait for privacy.
5. Ask your question.	

SUGGESTED CONTENT FOR MODELING DISPLAYS

School or neighborhood: Main actor asks teacher to explain something he/she finds unclear.

Home: Main actor asks mother to explain new curfew decision.

Peer group: Main actor asks classmate about missed schoolwork.

COMMENTS

Trainers are advised to model only single, answerable questions. In role-plays, trainees should be instructed to do likewise.

Skill 5: Saying Thank You

STEPS	TRAINER NOTES
1. Decide if the other person said or did something that you want to thank him/her for.	It may be a compliment, favor, or gift.
2. Choose a good time and place to thank the other person.	This is a quiet time, a private place, or other time and place where you are sure you will have the other person's attention.
3. Thank the other person in a friendly way.	Express thanks with words, a gift, a letter, or do a return favor.
4. Tell the other person why you are thanking him/her.	

SUGGESTED CONTENT FOR MODELING DISPLAYS

School or neighborhood: Main actor thanks teacher for help on a project.

Home: Main actor thanks mother for fixing shirt.

Peer group: Main actor thanks friend for advice.

Skill 6: Introducing Yourself

STEPS	**TRAINER NOTES**
1. Choose the right time and place to introduce yourself.	
2. Greet the other person and tell your name.	Shake hands, if appropriate.
3. Ask the other person his/her name if you need to.	
4. Tell or ask the other person something to help start your conversation.	Tell something about yourself; comment on something you both have in common; ask a question.

SUGGESTED CONTENT FOR MODELING DISPLAYS

School or neighborhood: Main actor introduces self to a new neighbor.

Home: Main actor introduces self to friend of parents.

Peer group: Main actor introduces self to several classmates at start of school year.

COMMENTS

This skill and Skill 7 (Introducing Other People) are extremely important in a youngster's efforts to establish social contacts. They are not intended as lessons in "etiquette." Trainers should be attuned to choosing language appropriate to the particular interpersonal situation.

Skill 7: Introducing Other People

STEPS	TRAINER NOTES
1. Name the first person and tell him/her the name of the second person.	Speak clearly and loudly enough so that the names are heard by both people.
2. Name the second person and tell him/her the name of the first person.	
3. Say something that helps the two people get to know each other.	Mention something they have in common; invite them to talk or do something with you; say how you know each of them.

SUGGESTED CONTENT FOR MODELING DISPLAYS

School or neighborhood: Main actor introduces parent to guidance counselor or teacher.

Home: Main actor introduces new friend to parent.

Peer group: Main actor introduces new neighbor to friends.

Skill 8: Giving a Compliment

STEPS	TRAINER NOTES
1. Decide what you want to compliment about the other person.	It may be the person's appearance, behavior, or another accomplishment.
2. Decide how to give the compliment.	Consider the wording and ways to keep the other person and yourself from feeling embarrassed.
3. Choose the right time and place to say it.	It may be a private place or a time when the other person is unoccupied.
4. Give the compliment.	Be friendly and sincere.

SUGGESTED CONTENT FOR MODELING DISPLAYS

School or neighborhood: Main actor compliments neighbor on new car.

Home: Main actor compliments parent on good dinner.

Peer group: Main actor compliments friend for avoiding fight.

Skill 9: Asking for Help

STEPS	TRAINER NOTES
1. Decide what the problem is.	Be specific: Who and what are contributing to the problem; what is its effect on you?
2. Decide if you want help for the problem.	Figure out if you can solve the problem alone.
3. Think about different people who might help you and pick one.	Consider all possible helpers and choose the best one.
4. Tell the person about the problem and ask that person to help you.	If the person wants to help you but is unable to do so at the moment, ask the person when a good time would be.

SUGGESTED CONTENT FOR MODELING DISPLAYS

School or neighborhood: Main actor asks teacher for help with difficult homework problem.

Home: Main actor asks parent for help with personal problem.

Peer group: Main actor asks friend for advice with dating.

COMMENTS

The definition of *problem,* as used in this skill, is anything one needs help with, varying from problems with other people to school and other informational problems.

Skill 10: Joining In

STEPS	TRAINER NOTES
1. Decide if you want to join in an activity others are doing.	Check the advantages and disadvantages. Be sure you want to participate in and not disrupt what others are doing.
2. Decide the best way to join in.	You might ask, apply, start a conversation, or introduce yourself.
3. Choose the best time to join in.	Good times are usually during a break in the activity or before the activity gets started.
4. Join in the activity.	

SUGGESTED CONTENT FOR MODELING DISPLAYS

School or neighborhood: Main actor signs up for neighborhood sports team.

Home: Main actor joins family in recreational activity.

Peer group: Main actor joins peers in ongoing game, recreational activity, or conversation.

Skill 11: Giving Instructions

STEPS	TRAINER NOTES
1. Decide what needs to be done.	It might be a chore or a favor.
2. Think about the different people who could do it and choose one.	
3. Ask that person to do what you want done.	Tell the person how to do it when the task is complex.
4. Ask the other person if he/she understands what to do.	
5. Change or repeat your instructions if you need to.	This step is optional.

SUGGESTED CONTENT FOR MODELING DISPLAYS

School or neighborhood: Main actor divides chores for decorating gym for school party.

Home: Main actor tells younger brother how to refuse drugs if offered to him.

Peer group: Main actor instructs friends on how to care for pets.

COMMENTS

This skill often refers to the enlistment of others to carry out a task and thus requires youngsters to think about division of responsibility.

Skill 12: Following Instructions

STEPS	TRAINER NOTES
1. Listen carefully while you are being told what to do.	Take notes if necessary; nod your head; say "mm-hmm."
2. Ask questions about anything you don't understand.	The goal is making instructions more specific, more clear.
3. Decide if you want to follow the instructions and let the other person know your decision.	Think about the positive and negative consequences of following the instructions.
4. Repeat the instructions to yourself.	Do this in your own words.
5. Do what you have been asked to do.	

SUGGESTED CONTENT FOR MODELING DISPLAYS

School or neighborhood: Main actor follows classroom instructions given by teacher.

Home: Main actor follows parent's instructions on operating home appliance.

Peer group: Main actor follows friend's instructions on fixing bicycle.

COMMENTS

This skill concerns complying with the requests of another person. If the task seems unreasonable, it may be an instance in which another skill is needed (e.g., Negotiating, Making a Complaint).

Skill 13: Apologizing

STEPS	**TRAINER NOTES**
1. Decide if it would be best for you to apologize for something you did.	You might apologize for breaking something, making an error, interrupting someone, or hurting someone's feelings.
2. Think of the different ways you could apologize.	Say something; do something; write something.
3. Choose the best time and place to apologize.	Do it privately and as quickly as possible after creating the problem.
4. Make your apology.	This might include an offer to make up for what happened.

SUGGESTED CONTENT FOR MODELING DISPLAYS

School or neighborhood: Main actor apologizes to neighbor for broken window.

Home: Main actor apologizes to younger sister for picking on her.

Peer group: Main actor apologizes to friend for betraying a confidence.

Skill 14: Convincing Others

STEPS	TRAINER NOTES
1. Decide if you want to convince someone about something.	It might be doing something your way, going someplace, interpreting events, or evaluating ideas.
2. Tell the other person your idea.	Focus on both content of ideas and feelings about point of view.
3. Ask the other person what he/she thinks about it.	This requires use of Listening (Skill 1).
4. Tell why you think your idea is a good one.	Try your best to be fair; "get into the other person's shoes."
5. Ask the other person to think about what you said before making up his/her mind.	Check on the other person's decision at a later point in time.

SUGGESTED CONTENT FOR MODELING DISPLAYS

School or neighborhood: Main actor convinces storekeeper that he/she deserves job.

Home: Main actor convinces parent that he/she is responsible enough to stay out late.

Peer group: Main actor convinces friend to include new person in game.

COMMENTS

In persuading someone of something, a person needs to understand both sides of the argument. Use of this skill assumes that if the other person is asked about his/her position and there is no difference of opinion, the role-play should end at Step 3.

Skill 15: Knowing Your Feelings

STEPS	TRAINER NOTES
1. Tune in to what is going on in your body that helps you know what you are feeling.	Some cues are blushing, butterflies in your stomach, tight muscles, and so on.
2. Decide what happened to make you feel that way.	Focus on outside events such as a fight, a surprise, and so forth.
3. Decide what you could call the feeling.	Possibilities are anger, fear, embarrassment, joy, happiness, sadness, disappointment, frustration, excitement, anxiety, and so on. (Trainer should create a list of feelings and encourage trainees to contribute additional suggestions.)

SUGGESTED CONTENT FOR MODELING DISPLAYS

School or neighborhood: Main actor feels embarrassed when peers call him "chickenshit" after refusal to use drugs.

Home: Main actor is angry when unjustly accused at home.

Peer group: Main actor is happy when friend pays compliment.

COMMENTS

This has been included as a separate skill for adolescents to learn prior to practicing the expression of feelings to another person. Frequently, feelings can be confused with one another, resulting in rather vague, but strong, emotions. Once the feeling can be labeled accurately, the trainee can go on to the next skill, which involves prosocial modes of expressing the feeling.

Step 1, involving "tuning in" to body feelings, is often a new experience for many people. Spend as much time as needed in discussing, giving examples, and practicing this step before going on to subsequent steps.

Skill 16: Expressing Your Feelings

STEPS	TRAINER NOTES
1. Tune in to what is going on in your body.	
2. Decide what happened to make you feel that way.	
3. Decide what you are feeling.	Possibilities are happy, sad, in a bad mood, nervous, worried, scared, embarrassed, disappointed, frustrated, and so forth. (Trainer and trainees should develop a list of feelings.)
4. Think about the different ways to express your feeling and pick one.	Consider prosocial alternatives such as talking about a feeling, doing a physical activity, telling the object of the feeling about the feeling, walking away from emotional situations, or delaying action. Consider how, when, where, and to whom the feeling could be expressed.
5. Express your feeling.	

SUGGESTED CONTENT FOR MODELING DISPLAYS

School or neighborhood: Main actor tells teacher about feeling nervous before test.

Home: Main actor tells parent about feeling embarrassed when treated like a child.

Peer group: Main actor hugs friend when learning of friend's success.

Skill 17: Understanding the Feelings of Others

STEPS	TRAINER NOTES
1. Watch the other person.	Notice tone of voice, posture, and facial expression.
2. Listen to what the other person is saying.	Try to understand the content.
3. Figure out what the person might be feeling.	He/she may be angry, sad, anxious, and so on.
4. Think about ways to show you understand what he/she is feeling.	You might tell him/her, touch him/her, or leave the person alone.
5. Decide on the best way and do it.	

SUGGESTED CONTENT FOR MODELING DISPLAYS

School or neighborhood: Main actor brings gift to neighbor whose spouse has been ill.

Home: Main actor recognizes parent is preoccupied with financial concerns and decides to leave parent alone.

Peer group: Main actor lets friend know he/she understands friend's discomfort on meeting new people.

COMMENTS

This skill is well known by the term *empathy.* Although difficult to teach, it is most important that many trainees add it to their repertoire of skills. Also, see chapter 9 for a description of the Prepare Curriculum course on empathy training, which is an elaboration of this skill.

Skill 18: Dealing with Someone Else's Anger

STEPS	**TRAINER NOTES**
1. Listen to the person who is angry.	Don't interrupt; stay calm.
2. Try to understand what the angry person is saying and feeling.	Ask questions to get explanations of what you don't understand; restate them to yourself.
3. Decide if you can say or do something to deal with the situation.	Think about ways of dealing with the problem. This may include just listening, being empathic, doing something to correct the problem, ignoring it, or being assertive.
4. If you can, deal with the other person's anger.	

SUGGESTED CONTENT FOR MODELING DISPLAYS

School or neighborhood: Main actor responds to teacher who is angry about disruptive behavior in class by agreeing to cooperate and pay attention.

Home: Main actor responds to parent who is angry about messy house by agreeing to do a fair share of work.

Peer group: Main actor responds to admired older sibling's anger when main actor refuses to go drinking.

COMMENTS

This skill refers to anger directed at the trainee. As such, it usually requires some action on the part of the trainee to deal with the situation. Trainers should have the trainee make use of the steps for Skill 1 (Listening) when enacting the first step of this skill.

Skill 19: Expressing Affection

STEPS	TRAINER NOTES
1. Decide if you have good feelings about the other person.	
2. Decide if the other person would like to know about your feelings.	Consider the possible consequences (e.g., happiness, misinterpretation, embarrassment, encouragement of friendship).
3. Choose the best way to express your feelings.	Do something, say something, give gift, send card, telephone, offer invitation.
4. Choose the best time and place to express your feelings.	Minimize distractions and possible interruptions.
5. Express your feelings in a friendly way.	

SUGGESTED CONTENT FOR MODELING DISPLAYS

School or neighborhood: Main actor expresses positive feelings toward guidance counselor after sharing personal problem.

Home: Main actor brings small gift to parent as token of affection.

Peer group: Main actor expresses friendly feelings toward new acquaintance.

COMMENTS

Although trainees initially will associate this skill with romantic relationships, they will soon grasp the notion that affection and caring can be expressed toward a wide variety of persons.

Skill 20: Dealing with Fear

STEPS	TRAINER NOTES
1. Decide if you are feeling afraid.	Use Skill 15 (Knowing Your Feelings).
2. Think about what you might be afraid of.	Think about alternative possibilities and choose the most likely one.
3. Figure out if the fear is realistic.	Is the feared object really a threat? You may need to check this out with another person or may need more information.
4. Take steps to reduce your fear.	You might talk with someone, leave the scene, or gradually approach the frightening situation.

SUGGESTED CONTENT FOR MODELING DISPLAYS

School or neighborhood: Main actor is fearful of repercussions after breaking neighbor's window and discusses fear with parent.

Home: Main actor is afraid of being home alone and arranges to have friend visit.

Peer group: After being teased by older neighborhood youth, main actor is fearful of being beaten up and takes steps to avoid confrontation.

COMMENTS

Group discussion can be quite useful in examining how realistic particular fears are. Trainers should be sensitive to the fact that trainees may be reluctant to reveal their fears to peers. Modeling of frightening situations may help them overcome this reluctance.

Skill 21: Rewarding Yourself

STEPS	TRAINER NOTES
1. Decide if you have done something that deserves a reward.	It might be something you have succeeded at or some area of progress.
2. Decide what you could say to reward yourself.	Use praise, approval, or encouragement.
3. Decide what you could do to reward yourself.	You might buy something, go someplace, or increase or decrease an activity.
4. Reward yourself.	Say and do it.

SUGGESTED CONTENT FOR MODELING DISPLAYS

School or neighborhood: Main actor rewards self after studying hard and doing well on exam by going to movie after school.

Home: Main actor rewards self with positive self-statement after avoiding fight with older sibling.

Peer group: Main actor rewards self by buying soda after convincing peers to join neighborhood club.

COMMENTS

Be sure trainees apply the following rules, all of which increase the effectiveness of self-reward:

> Reward yourself as soon as possible after successful performance.
>
> Reward yourself only after successful performance, not before.
>
> The better your performance, the better your self-reward.

See chapter 9 for further discussion of self-reward.

Skill 22: Asking Permission

STEPS

1. Decide what you would like to do for which you need permission.
2. Decide whom you have to ask for permission.
3. Decide how to ask for permission.
4. Pick the right time and place.
5. Ask for permission.

TRAINER NOTES

Ask if you want to borrow something or request a special privilege.

Ask the owner, manager, or teacher.

Ask out loud; ask privately; ask in writing.

SUGGESTED CONTENT FOR MODELING DISPLAYS

School or neighborhood: Main actor asks shop teacher for permission to use new power tool.

Home: Main actor asks parent for permission to stay out past curfew.

Peer group: Main actor asks friend for permission to borrow sporting equipment.

COMMENTS

Prior to practicing this skill, it is frequently useful to discuss situations that require permission. Some youngsters tend to ask permission for things that could be done independently (without permission), whereas others neglect to ask permission in situations that require doing so.

Skill 23: Sharing Something

STEPS	TRAINER NOTES
1. Decide if you might like to share some of what you have.	Divide the item between yourself and the other person or allow the other to use the item.
2. Think about how the other person might feel about your sharing.	He/she might feel pleased, indifferent, suspicious, or insulted.
3. Offer to share in a direct and friendly way.	Make the offer sincere, allowing the other to decline if he/she wishes.

SUGGESTED CONTENT FOR MODELING DISPLAYS

School or neighborhood: Main actor offers to share books with classmate who has forgotten own book.

Home: Main actor offers to share candy with sibling.

Peer group: Main actor invites friend to try his new bicycle.

Skill 24: Helping Others

STEPS	**TRAINER NOTES**
1. Decide if the other person might need and want your help.	Think about the needs of the other person; observe.
2. Think of the ways you could be helpful.	
3. Ask the other person if he/she needs and wants your help.	Make the offer sincere, allowing the other to decline if he/she wishes.
4. Help the other person.	

SUGGESTED CONTENT FOR MODELING DISPLAYS

School or neighborhood: Main actor offers to help teacher arrange chairs in classroom.

Home: Main actor offers to help prepare dinner.

Peer group: Main actor offers to bring class assignments home for sick friend.

Skill 25: Negotiating

STEPS	**TRAINER NOTES**
1. Decide if you and the other person are having a difference of opinion.	Are you getting tense or arguing?
2. Tell the other person what you think about the problem.	State your own position and your perception of the other's position.
3. Ask the other person what he/she thinks about the problem.	
4. Listen openly to his/her answer.	
5. Think about why the other person might feel this way.	
6. Suggest a compromise.	Be sure the proposed compromise takes into account the opinions and feelings of both persons.

SUGGESTED CONTENT FOR MODELING DISPLAYS

School or neighborhood: Main actor negotiates with neighbor a fee for after-school chores.

Home: Main actor negotiates with parent about curfew or chores.

Peer group: Main actor negotiates with friend about recreational activity in which to participate.

COMMENTS

Negotiating is a skill that presupposes mastery of Understanding the Feelings of Others (Skill 17). We suggest that Skill 17 be reviewed prior to teaching Negotiating. Negotiating is also similar in some respects to Skill 14 (Convincing Others). Negotiating, however, introduces the concept of compromise, a concept that is often worth discussing before role-playing this skill.

Skill 26: Using Self-Control

STEPS	**TRAINER NOTES**
1. Tune in to what it is going on in your body that helps you know you are about to lose control of yourself.	Are you getting tense, angry, hot, fidgety?
2. Decide what happened to make you feel this way.	Consider both outside events and "internal" events (thoughts).
3. Think about ways in which you might control yourself.	Slow down; count to 10; breathe deeply; assert yourself; leave; do something else.
4. Choose the best way to control yourself and do it.	

SUGGESTED CONTENT FOR MODELING DISPLAYS

School or neighborhood: Main actor keeps from yelling at teacher when teacher criticizes harshly.

Home: Main actor controls self when parent forbids desired activity.

Peer group: Main actor controls self when friend takes something without asking permission.

COMMENTS

It is often helpful to discuss various ways of controlling oneself before role-playing the skill. The list of self-control techniques can be written on the chalkboard or easel pad and used to generate alternative tactics youngsters can use in a variety of situations.

Skill 27: Standing Up for Your Rights

STEPS	**TRAINER NOTES**
1. Pay attention to what is going on in your body that helps you know that you are dissatisfied and would like to stand up for yourself.	Some cues are tight muscles, butterflies in your stomach, and so forth.
2. Decide what happened to make you feel dissatisfied.	Are you being taken advantage of, ignored, mistreated, or teased?
3. Think about ways in which you might stand up for yourself and choose one.	Seek help; say what is on your mind; get a majority opinion; choose the right time and place.
4. Stand up for yourself in a direct and reasonable way.	

SUGGESTED CONTENT FOR MODELING DISPLAYS

School or neighborhood: Main actor approaches teacher after being disciplined unfairly.

Home: Main actor talks with parent about need for more privacy.

Peer group: Main actor talks with peer after not being chosen for the club (team).

COMMENTS

Also known as *assertiveness,* this skill is particularly important for withdrawn or shy trainees, as well as for trainees whose typical responses are inappropriately aggressive.

Skill 28: Responding to Teasing

STEPS	**TRAINER NOTES**
1. Decide if you are being teased.	Are others making jokes or whispering?
2. Think about ways to deal with the teasing.	Gracefully accept it; make a joke of it; ignore it.
3. Choose the best way and do it.	When possible, avoid alternatives that foster aggression, malicious counterteasing, and withdrawal.

SUGGESTED CONTENT FOR MODELING DISPLAYS

School or neighborhood: Main actor ignores classmate's comments when volunteering to help teacher after class.

Home: Main actor tells sibling to stop teasing about new haircut.

Peer group: Main actor deals with peer's teasing about a girlfriend or boyfriend by making a joke of it.

Skill 29: Avoiding Trouble with Others

STEPS	TRAINER NOTES
1. Decide if you are in a situation that might get you into trouble.	Examine immediate and long-range consequences.
2. Decide if you want to get out of the situation.	Consider risks versus gains.
3. Tell the other people what you decided and why.	
4. Suggest other things you might do.	Consider prosocial alternatives.
5. Do what you think is best for you.	

SUGGESTED CONTENT FOR MODELING DISPLAYS

School or neighborhood: Main actor tells classmates he/she will not cut class with them.

Home: Main actor refuses to take family car without permission.

Peer group: Main actor decides not to join peers in petty shoplifting.

COMMENTS

In Step 3, the reasons for decisions may vary according to the trainee's level of moral reasoning (e.g., fear of punishment, social conformity, concern for others).

Skill 30: Keeping Out of Fights

STEPS	TRAINER NOTES
1. Stop and think about why you want to fight.	
2. Decide what you want to happen in the long run.	What is the long-range outcome?
3. Think about other ways to handle the situation besides fighting.	You might negotiate, stand up for your rights, ask for help, or pacify the person.
4. Decide on the best way to handle the situation and do it.	

SUGGESTED CONTENT FOR MODELING DISPLAYS

School or neighborhood: Main actor tells classmate that he/she wants to talk out their differences instead of being pressured to fight.

Home: Main actor resolves potential fight with older sibling by asking parent to intervene.

Peer group: Main actor goes for help when he/she sees peers fighting on school steps.

COMMENTS

Prior to teaching this skill, it is often useful to review Skill 26 (Using Self-Control).

Skill 31: Making a Complaint

STEPS	TRAINER NOTES
1. Decide what your complaint is.	What is the problem?
2. Decide whom to complain to.	Who can resolve it?
3. Tell that person your complaint.	Consider alternative ways to complain (e.g., politely, assertively, privately).
4. Tell that person what you would like done about the problem.	Offer a helpful suggestion about resolving the problem.
5. Ask how he/she feels about what you've said.	

SUGGESTED CONTENT FOR MODELING DISPLAYS

School or neighborhood: Main actor complains to guidance counselor about being assigned to class that is too difficult.

Home: Main actor complains to sibling about unfair division of chores.

Peer group: Main actor complains to friend about spreading a rumor.

Skill 32: Answering a Complaint

STEPS	TRAINER NOTES
1. Listen to the complaint.	Listen openly.
2. Ask the person to explain anything you don't understand.	
3. Tell the person that you understand the complaint.	Rephrase; acknowledge the content and feeling.
4. State your ideas about the complaint, accepting the blame if appropriate.	
5. Suggest what each of you could do about the complaint.	You might compromise, defend your position, or apologize.

SUGGESTED CONTENT FOR MODELING DISPLAYS

School or neighborhood: Main actor responds to neighbor's complaint about noisy party.

Home: Main actor responds to parent's complaint about selection of friends.

Peer group: Main actor responds to friend's complaint about returning sporting equipment in poor condition.

Skill 33: Being a Good Sport

STEPS	TRAINER NOTES
1. Think about how you did and how the other person did in the game you played.	
2. Think of a true compliment you could give the other person about his/her game.	Say "Good try," "Congratulations," or "Getting better."
3. Think about his/her reactions to what you might say.	The reaction might be pleasure, anger, or embarrassment.
4. Choose the compliment you think is best and say it.	

SUGGESTED CONTENT FOR MODELING DISPLAYS

School or neighborhood: Main actor talks to classmate who has made starting team.

Home: Main actor wins Monopoly game with younger sibling.

Peer group: New acquaintance does well in pickup game.

Skill 34: Dealing with Embarrassment

STEPS	**TRAINER NOTES**
1. Decide if you are feeling embarrassed.	
2. Decide what happened to make you feel embarrassed.	
3. Decide on what will help you feel less embarrassed and do it.	Correct the cause; minimize it; ignore it; distract others; use humor; reassure yourself.

SUGGESTED CONTENT FOR MODELING DISPLAYS

School or neighborhood: Main actor deals with embarrassment the day after refusing pressure from peers to use drugs.

Home: Mother catches main actor necking with boyfriend or girlfriend.

Peer group: Main actor is embarrassed by being overheard when discussing private matter.

COMMENTS

Prior to teaching this skill, it is often useful to review Skill 15 (Knowing Your Feelings).

Skill 35: Dealing with Being Left Out

STEPS	TRAINER NOTES
1. Decide if you are being left out.	Are you being ignored or rejected?
2. Think about why the other people might be leaving you out of something.	
3. Decide how you could deal with the problem.	You might wait, leave, tell the other people how their behavior affects you, or ask to be included.
4. Choose the best way and do it.	

SUGGESTED CONTENT FOR MODELING DISPLAYS

School or neighborhood: Main actor tells teacher about disappointment after not being picked for committee.

Home: Main actor asks sibling to include him/her in planned activity with other friends.

Peer group: Main actor is left out of plans for party.

Skill 36: Standing Up for a Friend

STEPS	**TRAINER NOTES**
1. Decide if your friend has not been treated fairly by others.	Has your friend been criticized, teased, or taken advantage of?
2. Decide if your friend wants you to stand up for him/her.	
3. Decide how to stand up for your friend.	You might assert his/her rights, explain, or apologize.
4. Stand up for your friend.	

SUGGESTED CONTENT FOR MODELING DISPLAYS

School or neighborhood: Main actor explains to teacher that friend has been accused unjustly.

Home: Main actor defends friend's reputation when parent is critical.

Peer group: Main actor defends friend when peers are teasing.

Skill 37: Responding to Persuasion

STEPS	TRAINER NOTES
1. Listen to the other person's ideas on the topic.	Listen openly; try to see the topic from the other person's viewpoint.
2. Decide what you think about the topic.	Distinguish your own ideas from the ideas of others.
3. Compare what he/she said with what you think.	Agree; disagree; modify; postpone a decision.
4. Decide which idea you like better and tell the other person about it.	

SUGGESTED CONTENT FOR MODELING DISPLAYS

School or neighborhood: Main actor deals with high-pressure sales pitch.

Home: Main actor deals with parental pressure to dress in a particular way for a party or a job interview.

Peer group: Main actor deals with friend's persuasive argument to try drugs.

Skill 38: Responding to Failure

STEPS	TRAINER NOTES
1. Decide if you have failed at something.	The failure may be interpersonal, academic, or athletic.
2. Think about why you failed.	It could be due to skill, motivation, or luck. Include personal reasons and circumstances.
3. Think about what you could do to keep from failing another time.	Evaluate what is under your control to change: If a skill problem, practice; if motivation, increase effort; if circumstances, think of ways to change them.
4. Decide if you want to try again.	
5. Try again using your new idea.	

SUGGESTED CONTENT FOR MODELING DISPLAYS

School or neighborhood: Main actor deals with failing grade on exam.

Home: Main actor fails at attempt to help younger sibling with a project.

Peer group: Main actor deals with being turned down for date.

Skill 39: Dealing with Contradictory Messages

STEPS	TRAINER NOTES
1. Decide if someone is telling you two opposite things at the same time.	This could be in words, in nonverbal behavior, or in saying one thing and doing another.
2. Think of ways to tell the other person that you don't understand what he/she means.	Confront the person; ask.
3. Choose the best way to tell the person and do it.	

SUGGESTED CONTENT FOR MODELING DISPLAYS

School or neighborhood: Main actor deals with teacher who verbalizes approval but scowls at same time.

Home: Main actor confronts parent who verbalizes trust but refuses to grant privileges.

Peer group: Main actor deals with friend who makes general invitation but never really includes main actor in plans.

COMMENTS

In teaching this skill, it is important to encourage youngsters to observe closely the behaviors of others around them. See if they can think about a person who says yes but at the same time shakes his or her head to mean no. See if they can think about a person who says, "Take your time" but at the same time makes them hurry up. That is, be sure to include situations in which the person is told two conflicting things, as well as those involving a person saying one thing and doing the opposite. In Step 1, this deciphering of the message is essential; otherwise, the trainee will be unable to proceed to Steps 2 and 3.

Skill 40: Dealing with an Accusation

STEPS	**TRAINER NOTES**
1. Think about what the other person has accused you of.	Is the accusation accurate or inaccurate?
2. Think about why the person might have accused you.	Have you infringed on his/her rights or property? Has a rumor been started by someone else?
3. Think about ways to answer the person's accusation.	Deny it; explain your own behavior; correct the other person's perceptions; assert yourself; apologize; offer to make up for what happened.
4. Choose the best way and do it.	

SUGGESTED CONTENT FOR MODELING DISPLAYS

School or neighborhood: Main actor is accused of breaking neighbor's window.

Home: Parent accuses main actor of hurting sibling's feelings.

Peer group: Friend accuses main actor of lying.

Skill 41: Getting Ready for a Difficult Conversation

STEPS	TRAINER NOTES
1. Think about how you will feel during the conversation.	You might be tense, anxious, or impatient.
2. Think about how the other person will feel.	He/she may feel anxious, bored, or angry.
3. Think about different ways you could say what you want to say.	
4. Think about what the other person might say back to you.	
5. Think about any other things that might happen during the conversation.	Repeat Steps 1–5 at least twice, using different approaches to the situation.
6. Choose the best approach you can think of and try it.	

SUGGESTED CONTENT FOR MODELING DISPLAYS

School or neighborhood: Main actor prepares to talk with teacher about dropping subject.

Home: Main actor prepares to tell parent about school failure.

Peer group: Main actor prepares to ask for first date.

COMMENTS

In preparing for difficult or stressful conversations, it is useful for youngsters to see that the way they approach the situation can influence the final outcome. This skill involves rehearsing a variety of approaches and then reflecting upon which approach produces the best results. Feedback from group members on the effectiveness of each approach can be particularly useful in this regard.

Skill 42: Dealing with Group Pressure

STEPS	TRAINER NOTES
1. Think about what the group wants you to do and why.	Listen to other people; decide what the real meaning is; try to understand what is being said.
2. Decide what you want to do.	Yield; resist; delay; negotiate.
3. Decide how to tell the group what you want to do.	Give reasons; talk to one person only; delay; assert yourself.
4. Tell the group what you have decided.	

SUGGESTED CONTENT FOR MODELING DISPLAYS

School or neighborhood: Main actor deals with group pressure to vandalize neighborhood.

Home: Main actor deals with family pressure to break up friendship.

Peer group: Main actor deals with pressure to fight.

Skill 43: Deciding on Something to Do

STEPS

1. Decide whether you are feeling bored or dissatisfied with what you are doing.
2. Think of things you have enjoyed doing in the past.
3. Decide which one you might be able to do now.
4. Start the activity.

TRAINER NOTES

(Step 1) Are you not concentrating, getting fidgety, disrupting others who are involved in an activity?

(Step 3) Focus on prosocial alternatives; include others if appropriate.

SUGGESTED CONTENT FOR MODELING DISPLAYS

School or neighborhood: Main actor chooses after-school activity in which to participate.

Home: Main actor thinks up activity that will earn him/her money.

Peer group: Main actor suggests that friends play basketball instead of hanging around.

Skill 44: Deciding What Caused a Problem

STEPS	TRAINER NOTES
1. Define what the problem is.	
2. Think about possible causes of the problem.	Was it yourself, others, or events; intentional, accidental, or both?
3. Decide which are the most likely causes of the problem.	
4. Check out what really caused the problem.	Ask others; observe the situation again.

SUGGESTED CONTENT FOR MODELING DISPLAYS

School or neighborhood: Main actor evaluates reasons for teacher's abruptness.

Home: Main actor evaluates likely causes of parents having an argument.

Peer group: Main actor evaluates why he/she feels nervous with particular friend.

COMMENT

This skill is intended to help youngsters determine the degree to which they are responsible for a particular problem and the degree to which the causes of the problem are outside of their control.

Skill 45: Setting a Goal

STEPS	TRAINER NOTES
1. Figure out what goal you want to reach.	
2. Find out all the information you can about how to reach your goal.	Talk with friends; read; observe others; ask authorities.
3. Think about the steps you will need to take to reach your goal.	Consider your abilities, materials, help from others, and skills needed.
4. Take the first step toward your goal.	

SUGGESTED CONTENT FOR MODELING DISPLAYS

School or neighborhood: Main actor decides to find a job.

Home: Main actor decides to improve appearance.

Peer group: Main actor decides to have a party.

Skill 46: Deciding on Your Abilities

STEPS	**TRAINER NOTES**
1. Decide which abilities you might want to use.	Take the setting, circumstances, and goal into account.
2. Think about how you have done in the past when you have tried to use these abilities.	
3. Get other people's opinions about your abilities.	Ask others; take tests; check records.
4. Think about what you found out and decide how well you use these abilities.	Consider the evidence from both Steps 2 and 3.

SUGGESTED CONTENT FOR MODELING DISPLAYS

School or neighborhood: Main actor decides type of school curriculum.

Home: Main actor evaluates ability to repair broken bicycle.

Peer group: Main actor decides whether to try out for team (play).

COMMENTS

This skill is intended to help youngsters evaluate their capabilities realistically in view of available evidence. This skill is often tied to Skill 45 (Setting a Goal).

Skill 47: Gathering Information

STEPS	TRAINER NOTES
1. Decide what information you need.	
2. Decide how you can get the information.	You can get information from people, books, and so on.
3. Do things to get the information.	Ask questions; make telephone calls; look in books.

SUGGESTED CONTENT FOR MODELING DISPLAYS

School or neighborhood: Main actor gathers information on available jobs.

Home: Main actor gathers information on where to shop for particular item.

Peer group: Main actor finds out what kinds of things date likes to do.

COMMENTS

This skill often precedes Skill 49 (Making a Decision). Although each constitutes a separate skill, when taken together they often comprise an effective approach to problem solving.

Skill 48: Arranging Problems by Importance

STEPS	**TRAINER NOTES**
1. Think about the problems that are bothering you.	Make a list; be inclusive.
2. List these problems from most to least important.	
3. Do what you can to hold off on your less important problems.	Delegate them; postpone them; avoid them.
4. Go to work on your most important problems.	Plan first steps in dealing with the most important problem; rehearse these steps in your imagination.

SUGGESTED CONTENT FOR MODELING DISPLAYS

School or neighborhood: Main actor is worried about large number of school assignments.

Home: Parent tells main actor to take care of several chores before going out.

Peer group: Main actor has difficulty balancing school responsibilities, chores, and time with friends.

COMMENTS

This skill is intended to help the youngster who feels overwhelmed by a number of difficulties. The youngster is taught how to evaluate the relative urgency of the various problems and to deal with each according to the priority of its importance.

Skill 49: Making a Decision

STEPS	TRAINER NOTES
1. Think about the problem that requires you to make a decision.	
2. Think about possible decisions you could make.	Generate a number of possible alternatives; avoid premature closure.
3. Gather accurate information about these possible decisions.	Ask others; read; observe.
4. Reconsider your possible decisions using the information you have gathered.	
5. Make the best decision.	

SUGGESTED CONTENT FOR MODELING DISPLAYS

School or neighborhood: Main actor decides what job to apply for.

Home: Main actor decides how to spend money he/she has earned.

Peer group: Main actor decides whether to participate with friends in a weekend activity.

COMMENTS

This skill follows Skill 47 (Gathering Information) to constitute the general skill of problem solving.

Skill 50: Concentrating on a Task

STEPS	**TRAINER NOTES**
1. Decide what your task is.	
2. Decide on a time to work on this task.	Consider when and how long to work.
3. Gather the materials you need.	
4. Decide on a place to work.	Consider where: Minimize noise level, people present, possible interruptions.
5. Decide if you are ready to concentrate.	

SUGGESTED CONTENT FOR MODELING DISPLAYS

School or neighborhood: Main actor prepares to research and write a report.

Home: Main actor prepares to repair bicycle (appliance).

Peer group: Main actor gathers materials necessary for trip with friends.

COMMENTS

This skill helps youngsters overcome problems with distractions by focusing on relevant planning prior to undertaking a task. Planning, in this sense, involves scheduling and arranging materials and work environment.

CHAPTER 7
Skill Sequences and Combinations

The interpersonal challenges of adolescence are frequent and formidable. The need to deal with authority figures—parents, teachers, police, and others—comes early and often. Parents, for example (and the adolescents themselves!), frequently are not quite sure if these young people are children, young adults, a combination of the two, or a breed apart. Growing in part from the adolescent conflict between developing autonomy needs ("Leave me alone") and dependency needs ("Take care of me"), parents and adolescents not infrequently wage years-long interpersonal war against one another.

Peer influences loom especially large in the interpersonal lives of most young persons ages 12 to 18. Smoke pot? Drink beer? Have sex? Break a school window? Play ball? Hang out here? Hang out there? Steal that car? Raise a hand in class? Buy those pants? Walk like this? Talk like that? The answers to these questions, big and small, are often largely determined in youth interactions with adolescent peers. For most adolescents, the clique, the group, and the gang are powerful forces.

Thus, for many youngsters, relations with adults and peers present difficult interpersonal challenges—challenges that draw heavily upon their repertoire of interpersonal skills. Often, competence in single skills will prove insufficient. For example, Bob correctly tries to convince his mom of his views on a matter (Skill 14: Convincing Others), but Mom remains unconvinced. Teacher accuses Betty of cheating on a test. Betty responds with appropriate behavior (Skill 40: Dealing with an Accusation), but the teacher does not believe her. Fred is called a "fat slob" by three agemates in his neighborhood, and they refuse to stop badgering him. He responds to their teasing well (Skill 28: Responding to Teasing), but they continue making their nasty comments. One youth at school has drugs in his possession and asks a second to hold them for him until a school locker search is completed. The second youth refuses (Skill 37: Responding to Persuasion), but the pressure from the first continues and escalates.

These are all examples of the common experience that many youths have in response to difficult, demanding, and often complex interpersonal challenges. Single-skill responses, even when carried out correctly, prove inadequate. More potent skill combinations and sequences are necessary. Fortunately, after a Skillstreaming group has been meeting for several months, members have learned several skills. At this point, it is desirable for trainers to shift some of the group's time away from learning single new skills to practicing how to select, sequence, and enact combinations of previously learned skills adequate to meet these more demanding interpersonal challenges.

The transcript beginning on page 122 illustrates the modeling and role-playing portions of just such an advanced Skillstreaming session, one in which a combination of skills relevant to the challenge presented is demonstrated and rehearsed. This transcript is an edited excerpt from *The Refusal Skills Video* (Goldstein, 1990). The three skills—Dealing with Someone Else's Anger (Skill 18), Dealing with Fear (Skill 20), and Standing Up for Your Rights (Skill 27)—are first modeled by the trainers, then role-played by two of the group's trainees. The steps for these skills are presented in Table 4.

TABLE 4 A Sample Skill Sequence

Skill 18: Dealing with Someone Else's Anger

1. Listen to the person who is angry.
2. Try to understand what the angry person is saying and feeling.
3. Decide if you can say or do something to deal with the situation.
4. If you can, deal with the other person's anger.

Skill 20: Dealing with Fear

1. Decide if you are feeling afraid.
2. Think about what you might be afraid of.
3. Figure out if the fear is realistic.
4. Take steps to reduce your fear.

Skill 27: Standing Up for Your Rights

1. Pay attention to what is going on in your body that helps you know that you are dissatisfied and would like to stand up for yourself.
2. Decide what happened to make you feel dissatisfied.
3. Think about ways in which you might stand up for yourself and choose one.
4. Stand up for yourself in a direct and reasonable way.

Trainer: Okay, you guys, if I can get your attention, let's get started. Today is going to be a little different than what we did last week. Remember last week we just did one skill. It seemed to be enough in most refusal situations. Sometimes it's not enough. You try, but it doesn't seem to work. That's the kind of difficult situation we're going to practice today, how you handle, put together, a sequence or a group of skills. I'm going to do a modeling demonstration in a minute with Vernessa. She's going to offer me something that I don't want. I'm going to refuse. But this time, it's not going to work—in fact not only isn't it going to work, but she's going to get pissed off at me. She's really going to get angry at me, and I have to deal with her anger *(Skill 18).* So I try to do that. That turns out not to be enough. As a matter of fact, just about the time I'm through trying to deal with her anger unsuccessfully, along come two more friends. I've asked two more members of the group to get up there and join Vernessa. Now I got to deal with three people, and I'm getting a little frightened because the stakes have kind of gone up. So I think about how to deal with that fear *(Skill 20),* and I decide that the answer is to stand up for my rights *(Skill 27).* That's the sequence we're going to demonstrate, and that's what I'll get some of you to come up to actually try. Vernessa, let's do it. Hey, how you doing there?

Vernessa: Hi.

Trainer: What's that, gin?

Vernessa: Yeah, go ahead and take some. You know you've been here all of 3 hours and you haven't done nothing.

Trainer: What is it? I don't want that.

Vernessa:	Hey, this is the fifth time. Come on now, we're not going to invite you anymore. You're really pissing me off.
Trainer:	She is really angry. There's no doubt about this first step. *(Pointing to Step 1)* "Listen to the person who is angry." I've tried to just sort of listen and stay calm and not interrupt her, try to understand what she's feeling. *(Pointing to Step 2)* "Try to understand what the angry person is saying and feeling." I'm not sure I understand that. Could you tell me why you're so angry at me? Why are you so pissed off?
Vernessa:	You're giving me a bad reputation with my folks, okay? Everyone here is live except you, you know.
Trainer:	*(Pointing to Step 3)* "Decide if you can say or do something to deal with the situation." She's still angry. I could just keep listening to her. I could let her blow off steam. I could try to ignore her.
Vernessa:	Arnie, all the guys are going to come into the kitchen. They're going to see you standing there with a cup of water! You can't fool them with a cup of water. Arnie, take a sip. Okay, see. The home boys are coming. They are going to be looking at you, and you're going to be left out in the mud. You won't even take a sip.
Trainer:	Okay, now it's clear that this has not worked—she's still angry. I haven't been able to deal with it, and now there's three of them, and I'm getting a little more concerned. I got to move to this next skill *(Skill 20)*, Dealing with Fear. *(Pointing to Step 1)* "Decide if you are feeling afraid." I've got that feeling in the pit of my stomach, and it's bothering me. I got those butterflies. "Think about what you might be

afraid of" *(pointing to Step 2).* They might make fun of me; they'll probably tell me to get lost. "Figure out if the fear is realistic" *(pointing to Step 3).* Well, it's very realistic. Charlie got the business from them last week, Leroy the month before, and now it's my turn. "Take steps to reduce your fear" *(pointing to Step 4).* Okay, what can I do about this? I could leave, but I want to be at this party. That's why I came. I could make a joke out of it, I guess, but right now it doesn't feel very funny. They're looking at me like they're really angry. But I don't know—I'm not going to roll over on this, I'm going to deal with it head on. I got to move to this skill now *(Skill 27),* Standing Up for Your Rights. "Pay attention to what's going on in your body" *(pointing to Step 1).* That's easy. Tight stomach, butterflies, I'm still fearful. But I want to deal with this. "Decide what happened to make you feel dissatisfied" *(pointing to Step 2).* Well, they're sticking it to me. Just because I don't want to drink the gin, they're sticking it to me. I don't think that's fair. *(Pointing to Step 3)* "Think about ways in which you might stand up for yourself and choose one." I could walk away, or find other folks to hang with, or just tell them where I'm at. That's what I'll do, tell them straight out. *(Pointing to Step 4)* Listen, I hope we can still hang out together. I want to be here. I want to go to the scene that's happening next week, but I don't want to get hooked on that. I'm sorry, I'd like to stay at the party. I'm sorry I just don't want to drink that, and that's the way it is. So let's just hang out together. Be cool.

Vernessa: Well, Arnie . . . okay. I really like you, and if this is how you want to be, fine. I'm going to do my thing, you do yours.

Trainer: Okay, I want you guys to try this. Difficult refusal situations can be complicated. There certainly are other ways we could do this, with other sequences of two or three or four skills. What would be a situation that each of you have now that's pretty complicated, a refusal situation that's a pretty tough one, where just saying no hasn't worked terribly well? That's the kind of situation we want to role-play. Barbara, how about you?

Barbara: I was in school one day and they were having locker checks for drugs, and my friend had drugs in his locker and he wanted me to hold them for him until the check was over. So he wouldn't take the rap for it.

Trainer: And he got pretty angry.

Barbara: Yeah.

Trainer: Well, this might be a good situation. Let's try that one. Why don't you guys, Barbara and Ben, come up here. You can stand right over here. Ben, you ask her to hold this for you, and she's going to refuse. You're going to get angry. We want you to get good and angry. Don't hit her, but get good and angry. Barbara, you said your reaction was fear, and we want to see if you can sort of get into that way of feeling a little bit, and then we'll go through these skills, one, two, three. Let's go at it.

Ben: Barbara, you know about that locker check they're going to have today? Well, I kind of got some of this stuff, and they're going to check my locker, and I've already been in trouble once or twice before. So could you hold this for me until it's over?

Barbara: What is that?

Ben: It's some drugs that I have.

Barbara: No.

Ben: Can you please just hold this for me 'cause I've already been in trouble at least once or twice before. And if they catch up with me again . . . I don't know, I'll probably get expelled for it.

Barbara: I don't want you to get expelled.

Ben: I thought you were a friend, man. I'm going to get expelled from school for these.

Barbara: So will I.

Ben: No you won't. They won't get mad at you.

Trainer: He's starting to get angry at you, you're listening, you're doing a good job, you're staying cool, you're not interrupting, you're just listening. Try to understand why he's getting angry.

Barbara: Why are you getting so angry?

Ben: I'm not trying to make you *take* these pills or something. I just want you to hold on to them for me like for 2 hours or something.

Barbara: No.

Ben: Come on, Barbara!

Barbara: No.

Ben: Hold the pills. Here, I'll put them in your pocket. Just take them and keep them for me until after school, then give them back to me, that's all I'm asking.

Trainer: Okay, freeze the action. So his anger level seems to be creeping up and up. And from what you described earlier, with the real situation with the other boy, that started to make you fearful. How would you know if you're feeling fearful?

Barbara: Got butterflies.

Trainer: Okay. Think about what you might be afraid of, what could be happening here? What might he do, or what's going to be the thing to be fearful of here?

Barbara: I'm afraid that I'm going to give in or he's going to hit me or something.

Trainer: So the real other person might hit you.

Barbara: Yes.

Trainer: That sounds pretty realistic, doesn't it? What could you do to reduce your fear?

Barbara: I can leave. Take them. Or keep refusing.

Trainer: Okay, let's try the keep refusing in this form, standing up for your rights. You've told us what you're feeling, so we know what that's all about. What happened to make you feel that way is the pressure he's putting on you. How could you stand up for your rights here? What could you do?

Barbara: I could keep refusing, and then that would lead into leaving.

Trainer: If he didn't stop, you just split? Let's see what happens.

Ben: Just hold on to these until after school.

Barbara: No.

Ben: You will not be caught with these and if you do, just tell them somebody put them there, or tell them it's your mom's diet pills. I'm going to get expelled, if that's what you want.

Barbara: Ben, if you're that concerned, how come you can't just throw them away?

Ben: 'Cause they're too expensive to throw away. I don't want to lose these. Hold on to them until after school—you will not get in trouble. If you get in trouble, then I'll confess to it.

Barbara: No.

Ben: Come on, I'll just put them in your pocket until after school. *(Reaches out to her pocket.)*

Barbara: No, no. *(Walks out of room.)*

Trainer: Let's get some feedback.

Other illustrative skill sequences may be suggested. Earlier we indicated that Bob used the skill Convincing Others (Skill 14) in a dispute with his mother. He followed the skill steps correctly, but she remained unconvinced. For a successful outcome to be more likely, he may, in addition, need to employ Responding to Failure (Skill 38), Asking a Question (Skill 4), and Negotiating (Skill 25). Betty, in our earlier example, was accused of cheating by her teacher. Her use of Dealing with an Accusation (Skill 40) failed in its goal of resolving the confrontation. Perhaps Betty might have had a better result in her efforts with the teacher had she followed Skill 40 with, for example, Apologizing (Skill 13). As a final example, recall Fred, target of chronic teasing from his peers. His use of Responding to Teasing (Skill 28) proved insufficient. Perhaps more effective would have been the combination of Dealing with Fear (Skill 20), Standing Up for Your Rights (Skill 27), and Giving Instructions (Skill 11).

The real world of sometimes complex and challenging interpersonal tasks often will demand artfully chosen and sequenced skill combinations. As time and skill lessons already learned permit, we urge Skillstreaming trainers to apportion their training energies toward this valuable goal.

CHAPTER 8 Trainee Motivation and Resistance

Problems can and do occur in the Skillstreaming group. Trainees may not wish to attend, or their attendance may be sporadic. Once in the training room, they may be unmotivated to participate as requested. They may fail to see the relevance or utility of the skill curriculum to be taught to the demands of their everyday lives. In a variety of ways, they may actively resist meaningful group involvement. Their resistive behavior may interfere not only with their new skill acquisition, but also with the learning of others in the group. The present chapter speaks to such problems and offers suggestions for increasing trainee motivation and reducing trainee resistance.

INCREASING TRAINEE MOTIVATION

What means do we have at our disposal, or can we create, in order to increase the likelihood that trainees will actually (a) show up for planned Skillstreaming sessions (i.e., attendance motivation), (b) take part as requested in all group training procedures (i.e., participation motivation), and (c) use the skills they have learned on a continuing basis and in their own real-world contexts (i.e., generalization motivation)? The last concern, generalization, is the focus of chapter 9. Here we identify and describe means to motivate regular attendance and promote active, appropriate participation.

Motivation is not an easy task. A great many of the youths offered the opportunity to participate in Skillstreaming—a technique for training *prosocial* skills—are highly competent in the regular use of *antisocial* behavior. Further, this predilection is frequently encouraged, supported, and generously rewarded by many of the significant people in their lives—family, peers, and others. Motivating volitional attendance and meaningful participation in Skillstreaming is often a daunting task.

There are two types of motivation at our disposal for these purposes, extrinsic and intrinsic. *Extrinsic motivators* are tangible rewards provided contingent upon performance of desired behaviors. Such rewards have taken many forms, so many that they constitute a lengthy menu of reinforcers. In the early years of the behavior modification movement, the use of such extrinsic and tangible motivators was often denounced as "bribery." The youth, it was asserted, should *want* to engage in the desired behavior for its own sake and not for the external rewards it would bring. Some intervenors still offer similar protests (e.g., Kohn, 1986), but most agree that use of a combination of external and internal motivators is typically the most effective strategy.

Tangible motivators are, in fact, widely used in American schools and other institutions for adolescents. The points, checks, stars, and stickers of elementary school may have given way to pizza parties, movie privileges, club clothing, special activities, or other like events or objects, but the use of extrinsic rewards, in whatever form, is widespread. They seem especially useful in eliciting initial involvement, when the Skillstreaming activity is still unfamiliar.

It has been the consistent experience of many Skillstreaming trainers, however, that resting one's motivational effort strictly on a foundation of external rewards—whether in the form of tangible reinforcers, a token economy, a levels system, or other extrinsic incentives—is insufficient on a sustained basis. We and others believe substantial payoffs must be inherent in the activity itself. In Skillstreaming, such *intrinsic motivators* reside within the skills themselves, especially those trainees select and use successfully in their real-world settings. Our earlier discussion of a process we term negotiating the curriculum is central here. When youths are given the opportunity to select the skills *they* feel they need, a major step toward motivating positive attendance and participation has been taken. When such trainee-selected (or, to perhaps a somewhat lesser degree, trainer-selected) skills yield positive interpersonal outcomes for the trainee in interactions with family, peers, or significant others, motivation is further enhanced.

In addition to regular negotiation of the skill curriculum, we have used a second tactic to augment intrinsic motivation. It is to communicate to trainees, both during the initial structuring of the Skillstreaming process and periodically as the sessions unfold, that the goal of Skillstreaming is to teach alternatives, not substitutes. Many of the young men and women who are referred to a Skillstreaming program have been admonished, reprimanded, and punished perhaps hundreds of times for behaviors their parents, teachers, or others deemed inappropriate. In one or another way, they have been told, "Stop doing that, and do this *instead!*"

Although agreeing that it is certainly desirable to decrease the youth's antisocial or other inappropriate behavior, we believe that a more successful means toward this goal is to provide alternatives by expanding the youth's *behavioral repertoire*—the range of possible responses available. This is the goal of Skillstreaming. If, for example, someone falsely accuses the youth of stealing something and the only response the youth has learned, practiced, and been rewarded for before is to lash out, he or she will do so again. The youth has, in effect, no choice because there are no choices. If, however, Skillstreaming teaches that accusations may also be responded to by explanation, investigation, negotiation, walking away, and other means, at least some of the time the youth may use one of these means instead of counterattack. The fact that reprimands, punishments, and the like have had to be used hundreds of times in the past is stark testimony to their lack of enduring success. If the youth has skill response choices, some of the time, at least, he or she will use them.

The following excerpt is an example of an attempt to convey this provision-of-alternatives goal to a group of Skillstreaming trainees.

Trainee: This won't work.

Trainer: What do you mean, it won't work?

Trainee: Come on, get real, get out of that university, get out on the street more. We can negotiate up the wazoo in here, but you can't negotiate out on the street. Out on the street you got to hit the guy before he hits you.

Trainer: Now wait a second—what do you think we're doing in here? We're not teaching substitutes, we're teaching alternatives.

Trainee: I don't understand those words.

Trainer: All right, I'll give you a sports example. There's a team with a good quarterback, the only quarterback on the team, but for one reason or another, injury or whatever, one particular Sunday he can't throw long and he can't run. All he's got working for him is his short pass, and he's good at it. So on the first down, he goes out and he throws that short pass, and it's good. Same thing on the second down, another good short pass, but after that the defense in their huddle say, "Two short passes on two plays—maybe that's all the guy's got today. Let's look for it." Third down he throws it again, they knock it down. Fourth down, it's his only play, he throws it again and they intercept it. Son, you're like that quarterback. You have only one play—it's your fist. You've got a fist in every pocket. Someone looks at you, you hit them, they don't look at you, you hit them. They talk to you, you hit them, they don't talk to you, you hit them. That's why you've been in so much trouble. How about we try to help you become like a skilled quarterback, who has a variety of plays? Now you keep your fists, and if you need to hit someone, you hit them. I wish you wouldn't, but I can't follow you around to stop you, and I'm not going to teach you how to hit. You're already better at that than I am. But keep the fist in one pocket only, instead of every pocket. Back here, in the back pocket, another play. It's called negotiation. We'll not only teach you how to do it, but as a group we'll figure out where and when it fits. And back here, a miracle play. I think you're going to call it a miracle play—I actually wouldn't. I think you'll call it a miracle play because once I tell you what it is you're going to say to me it's a miracle if I can do that. But you know what, I've seen kids do it, and like any good

> football play, it fits some situations and it doesn't fit others. It's called walking away without losing face. There are times that adolescents like you can do it. Let's figure out together where and when. And in the fourth pocket yet another play. So like a good quarterback you have a variety of plays.

We have thus far suggested that trainee motivation to attend regularly and participate appropriately in Skillstreaming sessions will be enhanced by both extrinsic and intrinsic motivation, as well as by the trainers' communicating by word and deed that the goal of Skillstreaming is to provide trainees with behavioral options, alternative responses to be used or not used as the youngster chooses.

An additional motivational concern exists. Youngsters who frequently behave in their everyday lives in an angry, aggressive, intimidating, bullying, domineering, and threatening manner also often do so in the Skillstreaming group. If such negative behaviors are not dealt with—immediately, swiftly, and successfully—trainees will avoid the group. Their bodies may be present, but their participation will be guarded and minimal. The Skillstreaming trainer functions not only as a competent teacher, model, and role-play/feedback guide within the group, but also as a protector. In creating a safe learning environment, the trainer must be vigilant and immediately correct any participant efforts to bully, intimidate, dominate, or otherwise treat co-trainees in an inappropriate, aggressive manner. Such vigilance and responsiveness not only serve to protect the attacked but also provide additional skills training for the attacker. The following excerpt from a Skillstreaming trainer training workshop illustrates this dual benefit.

Trainer: You four pretend you are adolescents in a relatively new Skillstreaming group. Ellen and I have modeled a new skill, and Carolyn has just completed the group's first role-play of it. It is a skill that she needs badly in her personal life. Since I privately think she did a fine job in following the skill's steps during her role-play, I'm hoping she gets the kind of positive performance feedback from her peers in this group that will motivate her to really use the skill where and when it will be helpful for her. "Karen," I ask this first trainee, "Could you tell us what Carolyn did to carry out the first skill step, and how well you think she did it?" And Karen here says, "It was really nice what she said. When she turned to Barbara [the co-actor] and said 'I appreciate the invitation a lot, but I can't go,' it was right on target, firm but friendly." "Thanks, Karen," I say, as I think, "Good, this is just the kind of feedback I hoped she'd get." Then I turn to Bill and ask for his feedback to Carolyn on her handling of Step 2, and it, too, is clear and positive. Finally, I ask Pam for her appraisal of the enactment of Step 3, and she responds, "It was so bad I thought I would puke as she did it."

Pam's statement instantly initiates three problems for the group and for the trainers, and they all revolve around this issue of protection. The first concerns Pam. All Pam is doing is showing the very type of aggressive behavior that made her a part of the Skillstreaming group in the first place. Her behavior is threatening to another group member and must be dealt with, but dealt with in a manner that is instructive, constructive, and protective not only of Carolyn, but also of Pam. The second problem is Bill and Karen. They have not role-played yet, and they are thinking, "Oh, my god, when I get up to role-play, will Pam stick it to me the way she just stuck it to Carolyn?" The third problem is Carolyn. Carolyn is getting the kind of feedback that will discourage rather than encourage her to use the skill. So how does one serve as a protector for *all* of these group members?

Trainer: One way to do it would be to say to Pam, "Look, Pam, it's good that you could give Carolyn frank feedback, but the way you said it is not going to help her. Can you say it in a more constructive way?" If that's not in Pam's repertoire, if she doesn't know how to do that, I would stand Pam up, have her face Carolyn, and I would do what the psychodrama people do, the alter ego technique, where you stand behind her and whisper in her ear: "Pam, I'm going to say certain things to you—you say them to Carolyn." That teaches Pam a little bit about giving constructive feedback and lets her know that threatening comments are not acceptable. Carolyn gets the feedback, and this helps encourage real-world skill use. Bill and Karen get the message that if Pam sticks it to them the trainer will come to their aid. In an active manner, we have provided protection plus instruction to all four group members.

REDUCING TRAINEE RESISTANCE

Though not infinite (it just seems that way on occasion), the ways trainees may seek to thwart, circumvent, object to, or resist participation in the Skillstreaming group are numerous. Table 5 lists the more frequently observed types of trainee resistance. Each of these is discussed in the following pages.

Inactivity

Minimal participation involves trainees who seldom volunteer, provide only brief answers, and in general give the trainers a feeling that they are "pulling teeth" to keep the group at its various skills-training tasks.

A more extreme form of minimal participation is *apathy,* in which nearly everything the trainers do to direct, enliven, or activate the group is met with a lack of interest and spontaneity and little if any progress toward group goals.

While it is rare, *falling asleep* does occur from time to time. The sleepers need to be awakened, and the trainers might wisely inquire into the cause of the tiredness. Boredom in the group, lack of sleep, and physical illness are all possible reasons, each requiring a different trainer response.

Hyperactivity

Digression is a repetitive, determined, and strongly motivated movement away from the purposes and procedures of Skillstreaming. Here the trainees feel some emotion strongly, such as anger or anxiety or despair, and are determined to express it. Or the brief lecture given or the skill portrayed by the trainers or other trainees

Table 5 Types of Trainee Resistance

Inactivity

- Minimal participation
- Apathy
- Falling asleep

Hyperactivity

- Digression
- Monopolizing
- Interruption
- Excessive restlessness

Active Resistance

- Participation but not as instructed
- Passive-aggressive isolation
- Negativism, refusal
- Disruptiveness

Aggression

- Sarcasm, put-downs
- Bullying, intimidation
- Use of threats
- Assaultiveness

Cognitive Inadequacies and Emotional Disturbance

- Inability to pay attention
- Inability to understand
- Inability to remember
- Bizarre behavior

may set off associations with important recent experiences, which the trainees feel the need to present and discuss. Digression is also often characterized by "jumping out of role." Rather than merely wandering off track, in digression the trainees drive the train off its intended course.

Monopolizing involves subtle and not-so-subtle efforts by trainees to get more than a fair share of time during a Skillstreaming session. Long monologues, unnecessary requests to repeat role-plays, elaborate feedback, and other attention-seeking efforts to "remain on stage" are examples of such monopolizing behavior.

Similar to monopolizing but more intrusive and insistent, *interruption* is literally breaking into the ongoing flow of a trainer's modeling display, a role-play, or feedback period with comments, questions, suggestions, observations, or other statements. Interruption may be overly assertive or angry or may take the more pseudobenevolent guise of "help" to the trainer. In either event, such interruptions more often than not retard the group's progress toward its goals.

Excessive restlessness is a more extreme, more physical form of hyperactivity. The trainees may fidget while sitting; rock their chairs; get up and pace; or display other nonverbal, verbal, gestural, or postural signs of restlessness. Excessive restlessness will typically be accompanied by digression, monopolizing, or interrupting behavior.

Active Resistance

Trainees involved in *participation but not as instructed* are off target. They may be trying to role-play, serve as co-actor, give feedback, or engage in other tasks required in a given Skillstreaming session, but their own personal agendas or misperceptions interfere, and they wander off course to irrelevant or semirelevant topics. As such, this problem behavior is related to digression, although digression is perhaps a more intense manifestation of off-task behavior.

Passive-aggressive isolation is not merely apathy, in which the trainees are simply uninterested in participating. Nor is it participation but not as instructed, in which trainees actively go off task and raise personal agendas. Passive-aggressive isolation is the purposeful, intentional withholding of appropriate participation, an active shutting down of involvement. It can be thought of as a largely nonverbal "crossing of one's arms" in order to display deliberate nonparticipation.

When displaying *negativism,* trainees signal more overtly, by word and deed, the wish to avoid participation in the Skillstreaming group. Open *refusal* may take the form of unwillingness to role-play, listen to trainer instructions, or complete homework assignments. Or members may not come to sessions, come late to sessions, or walk out in the middle of a session.

Disruptiveness encompasses active resistance behaviors more extreme then negativism, such as openly and perhaps energetically ridiculing the trainers, other trainees, or aspects of the Skillstreaming procedures. Or disruptiveness may be shown by gestures, movements, noises, or other distracting nonverbal behaviors characteristically symbolizing overt criticism and hostility.

Aggression

Sarcasm and *put-downs* are denigrating trainee comments, made to ridicule the skill enactment or other behaviors of a fellow group member. The intent of such caustic evaluations is to criticize and diminish the appraised worth of such performance.

Bullying and *intimidation* are especially common problem behaviors, as they are characteristic of the youngsters selected for Skillstreaming participation. We distinguish it from the use of sarcasm and put-downs in that the behaviors in this category are often more severe in both their intent and consequences.

Further along on such a continuum, the overt use of explicit *threats* is the next category of Skillstreaming group management problems. One youth may warn another of impending embarrassment, revelation of confidences, or even bodily harm if compliance to one or another demand is not forthcoming.

Finally, on rare occasions, actual physical *assaultiveness* may occur in a Skillstreaming group. This very serious breach of group safety can have particularly harmful consequences for group functioning. The negative impact for skills training is not easy to dissipate.

Cognitive Inadequacies and Emotional Disturbance

Closely related at times to excessive restlessness, the *inability to pay attention* is often apparently the result of internal or external distractions, daydreaming, or other pressing agendas that command the trainees' attention. Inability to pay attention except for brief time spans may also be due to one or more forms of cognitive impairment.

Cognitive deficits due to developmental disability, intellectual inadequacy, impoverishment of experience, disease processes, or other sources may result in trainees' *inability to understand* aspects of the Skillstreaming curriculum. Failure to understand can, of course, also result from errors in the clarity and complexity of statements presented by trainers.

Material presented in the Skillstreaming group may be both attended to and understood by the trainees, but not remembered. *Inability to remember* may result not only in problems of skill transfer, but also in group management problems when what is forgotten includes rules and procedures for trainee participation, homework assignments, and so forth.

Bizarre behavior is uncommon, but when instances of it do occur they can be especially disruptive to group functioning. This type of group management problem may not only pull other trainees off task, it may also frighten them or make them highly anxious. The range of bizarre behaviors possible is quite broad, including talking to oneself or to inanimate objects, offering incoherent statements to the group, becoming angry for no apparent reason, hearing and responding to imaginary voices, and exhibiting peculiar mannerisms.

How shall such behaviors best be dealt with constructively, and their negative impact on skills training minimized? We wish to provide three sets of answers to this question. The first is based on the notion that the diagnosis of the resistive behavior suggests its cure. The second suggests techniques that have been employed successfully for these purposes in the context of the behavior modification movement. The third we term "capturing the teachable moment," a resistance reducing strategy in which problem behaviors occurring during the Skillstreaming session serve as stimuli for selecting and teaching the skills to resolve the problems displayed.

DIAGNOSIS DETERMINES CURE

As the Skillstreaming session unfolds, one or more trainees may display resistive behavior. One gets up and starts engaging in horseplay with a second. In another group, when asked to set the stage for her role-play, the trainee begins delivering a long monologue about largely irrelevant matters. In a third group, a trainee laughs at a group member's attempted role-play and shouts demeaning evaluations of the effort. In yet another group, a trainee sits, arms folded and silent, shaking his head "no" time and time again as he refuses the trainer's request to come up front for his turn at role-playing. Horseplay, digression, bullying, refusal. We urge as a first step in successfully managing such resistive behaviors that trainers ask themselves, Why? Why at this moment is this trainee engaging in that particular behavior? Trainers need to make a guess, a hypothesis, a diagnosis. The diagnosis will often suggest the cure. Perhaps one's hypothesis is that the trainee displayed a particular resistive behavior at a particular moment because what was being asked was too complicated (too many steps, too complex a challenge, too demanding a requirement). If this is the case, a good attempt at resistance reduction would be to simplify and decrease demands on the trainee's abilities. Table 6 lists steps trainers have taken to simplify what is being asked of trainees when it appears that a trainee experiences procedural requests as too complicated.

Alternatively, perhaps the trainer says inwardly, "No, it's not too complicated. Helen has handled even more difficult skills in here quite well. Perhaps she's feeling threatened. The feedback given by Charlie and Ed on the last role-play was really tough. Sarah had a hard time dealing with it. Maybe Helen fears she's about to become their next target." If threat and intimidation are central in the train-

TABLE 6
Simplification Methods for Reducing Trainee Resistance

1. Reward minimal trainee accomplishment.
2. Shorten the role-play.
3. Have trainer "feed" sentences to the trainee.
4. Have trainee read a prepared script portraying the behavioral steps.
5. Have trainee play co-actor role first.

er's diagnosis, threat-reduction steps should be taken immediately. Table 7 lists several possibilities of this type.

Our goal in seeking to reduce these problematic behaviors is straightforward: to maximize the level of youth involvement, on-task time, and, thus, potential learning, as well as to minimize time spent in distraction, aggression, or other off-task behaviors.

BEHAVIOR MODIFICATION TECHNIQUES

Both trainee behaviors promoting skill learning as well as behaviors inhibiting such progress can be managed via competent use of behavior modification techniques. The effectiveness of behavior modification technology rests upon a firm experimental foundation.

Beyond the repeated demonstration that "they work," behavior modification techniques are relatively easy to learn and use; may be teacher-, peer-, parent-, and/or self-administered; are generally cost-effective; yield typically unambiguous behavior-change results; have a long history of successful application (with aggressive youngsters in particular); and, for these reasons, can maximize time and

TABLE 7
Threat-Reduction Methods for Reducing Trainee Resistance

1. Employ additional live modeling by the trainers.
2. Postpone trainee's role-playing until last in sequence.
3. Provide reassurance to the trainee.
4. Provide empathic encouragement to the trainee.
5. Clarify aspects of the trainee's task that are experienced as threatening.
6. Restructure aspects of the trainee's task that are experienced as threatening.

student accessibility so trainers to do most what trainers do best: teach! The following discussion therefore briefly describes behavior modification procedures and the rules optimally governing their use, especially as regards interventions that may be readily employed in classroom settings to reduce aggression and enhance prosocial behavior.

Behavior modification is a set of techniques derived from formal learning theory, systematically applied in an effort to change observable behavior and rigorously evaluated by experimental research. Almost all of its techniques derive from the basic premise developed by Skinner and his followers (Ferster & Skinner, 1957; Skinner, 1938, 1953) that behavior is largely determined by its environmental consequences. In a broadly operational sense, this premise has found expression in techniques that, by one means or another, contingently present or withdraw rewards or punishments (i.e., environmental consequences) to alter the behavior preceding these consequences. It is this contingent quality that has led to the use of the term *contingency management* to describe most of the activities in which the behavior modifier engages. Specifically, if one's goal is to increase the likelihood that a given (e.g., prosocial) behavior will occur, one follows instances of its occurrence with positive consequences—that is, by presenting a reward or removing an aversive event. In a directly analogous management of contingencies, if one's goal is to decrease the likelihood that a given (e.g., antisocial) behavior will occur, one follows instances of its occurrence with negative consequences—that is, by presenting an aversive event or removing a rewarding one. To decrease a youngster's disruptiveness, aggression, or acting-out behavior and simultaneously to increase the chances that he or she will behave in a constructive, attentive, prosocial manner, the skilled behavior modifier will often use a combination of aversive or reward-withdrawing techniques (for the aggressive behaviors) and aversiveness-reducing or reward-providing techniques (for the constructive behaviors). A few definitions will help clarify further the substance of the contingency management process.

A *reinforcer* is an event that increases the subsequent frequency of any behavior it follows. When the presentation of an event following a behavior increases its frequency, the event is referred to as a *positive reinforcer*. Praise, special privileges, and tokens or points exchangeable for toys or snacks are a few examples of positive reinforcers. When the removal of an event following a behavior increases the subsequent frequency of the behavior, the event is referred to as a *negative reinforcer.* When a youngster ceases to behave in a disruptive manner following her teacher's yelling at her to do so, we may say that the youngster has negatively reinforced, and thus increased the future likelihood of, teacher yelling. When the presentation of an event following a behavior decreases its subsequent frequency, the event is referred to as a *punisher.* In the preceding example, the teacher's yelling, which was negatively reinforced by the student's decrease in disruptive behavior, functions as a punishment to the student to the extent that it decreases the likelihood of subsequent student disruptiveness. A second way of decreasing the probability of a given behavior is by removing positive reinforcers each time the behavior occurs. Ignoring the behavior or removing the reinforcer of attention (i.e., extinction), physically removing the person from important sources of reinforcement (i.e., time-out), and removing the reinforcers from the person (i.e., response cost) are three means of contingently managing behavior by *removing positive reinforcers.* To repeat, these four groups of techniques—positive reinforcement, negative reinforcement, punishment, and the removal of positive reinforcers—are the core methods of contingency management, from which stem all the specific contingency management techniques described later in this chapter.

It will aid in understanding the relationship among these four procedures, as well as their characteristic implementation in classroom settings, to point out that they are all means for either presenting or removing positive reinforcers or presenting or removing aversive stimuli. The various procedures for presenting or removing positive reinforcement are by far the more common uses of contingency management in school contexts. We will examine these two sets of procedures first and in some depth. Procedures for the presentation of aversive stimuli (i.e., punishment) or for their removal (i.e., negative reinforcement) are appropriately employed less frequently in school and agency settings, and we will examine them more briefly following our consideration of positive reinforcement.

Skillstreaming contingency management optimally begins by collaborating with the group to develop the *behavioral rules* to follow in order to create a safe and effective skill learning environment, then when necessary applying one or a combination of behavior-change procedures (the presentation or removal of positive reinforcement or the presentation or removal of aversive stimuli) in order to redirect current undesirable behaviors toward more desirable goals. Let us examine each step in this process in detail.

Communicating Behavioral Rules

A number of effective "rules for use of rules" have emerged in the contingency management literature (Greenwood, Hops, Delquadri, & Guild, 1974; Sarason, Glaser, & Fargo, 1972; Walker, 1979), including the following.

1. Define and communicate rules for trainee behavior in clear, specific, and, especially, behavioral terms. As Walker (1979) notes, it is better (more concrete and behavioral) to say, "Raise your hand before asking a question" than to say, "Be considerate of others." Similarly, "Listen carefully to trainer instructions" or "Pay attention to the feedback procedure" are rules more likely to find expression in student behavior than the more ambiguous "Behave in class" or "Do what you are told."
2. It is more effective to tell students what to do, rather than what not to do. This accentuation of the positive would, for example, find expression in rules about taking turns, talking over disagreements, or working quietly, rather than in rules directing students not to jump in, not to fight, or not to speak out.
3. Rules should be communicated in such a manner that trainees are aided in memorizing them. Depending on the age of trainees and the complexity and difficulty of following the rules, memorization aids may include keeping the rules short and few in number, presenting the rules several times, and posting the rules in written form where they can readily be seen.
4. Rule adherence is likely to be greater when trainees have had a substantial role in rule development, modification, and implementation. This sense of participation may be brought about by involving trainees in rule development, discussing rules with the entire group, selecting trainees to explain to the group the specific meaning of each rule, and having trainees role-play the behaviors identified by the rule.

5. In addition to the foregoing, further effective rules for rules are that they be developed at the start of the group; that they be fair, reasonable, and within the trainees' capacity to follow; that all members of the group understand the rules; and that they be applied equally and fairly to all trainees.

Skillstreaming group rules developed in this manner will enhance the likelihood that the group will be a safe and productive place for its members.

Applying Behavior-Change Procedures: Identifying Positive Reinforcers

Our overall purpose is to substitute appropriate for inappropriate behaviors by the skilled management of contingencies. As noted earlier, one major means for doing this is to present positive reinforcement to the trainee following and contingent upon the occurrence of an appropriate behavior. Before discussing optimal procedures for the actual presentation of positive reinforcers, however, we must first consider the process of identifying—both for a given youngster and for youngsters in general—just what events may in fact function as positive reinforcers.

Teachers and other school-based contingency managers have worked successfully with four types of positive reinforcers: material, social, activity, and token. *Material reinforcers* (sometimes called *tangible reinforcers*) are actual goods or objects presented to the individual contingent upon enactment of appropriate behaviors. One especially important subcategory of material reinforcement, *primary reinforcement,* occurs when the contingent event satisfies a basic biological need. Food is one such primary reinforcer.

Social reinforcers—most often expressed in the form of attention, praise, or approval—are particularly powerful and are frequently used in the Skillstreaming group. Both teacher lore and extensive experimental research testify to the potency of trainer-dispensed social reinforcement in influencing a broad array of personal, interpersonal, and academic student behaviors.

Activity reinforcers are those events the youngster freely chooses when an opportunity exists to engage in several different activities. Given freedom to choose, many youngsters will watch television rather than complete their homework. The parent wishing to use this activity reinforcer information will specify that the youngster may watch television for a given time period contingent upon the prior completion of the homework. Stated otherwise, the opportunity to perform a higher probability behavior (given free choice) can be used as a reinforcer for a lower probability behavior.

Token reinforcers, usually employed when more easily implemented social reinforcers prove insufficient, are symbolic items or currency (chips, stars, points, etc.) provided to the youngster contingent upon the performance of appropriate or desirable behaviors. Tokens thus obtained are exchangeable for a wide range of material or activity reinforcers. The system by which specific numbers of tokens are contingently gained or lost, and the procedures by which they may be exchanged for the backup material or activity reinforcers, is called a *token economy.*

In making decisions about which type of reinforcer to employ with a given youngster, the trainer should keep in mind that social reinforcement (e.g., trainer attention, praise, approval) is easiest to implement on a continuing basis and is most likely (for reasons discussed in chapter 9, dealing with transfer and maintenance) to lead to enduring behavior change. Thus, it is probably the type of reinforcement the trainer will wish to use most frequently. Unfortunately, in the initial stages of a behavior-change effort, aggressive, disruptive, and other inappropriate behaviors are probably being richly rewarded by the social reinforcement of trainer and peer attention, as well as by tangible reinforcers. As a result, the trainer will likely need to rely more heavily on material and activity reinforcers for desirable behaviors. Alternatively, a token reinforcement system may prove most effective as the initial reinforcement strategy. Youngsters' reinforcement preferences change over time, and trainer views of the appropriate reward value of desirable behaviors also change over time; both variable factors are easily reflected in token-level adjustments. For these and reasons related to ease of administration and effectiveness of outcome, the skilled contingency manager should be intimately acquainted with the full range of token economy procedures (Ayllon & Azrin, 1968; Kazdin, 1975; Morris, 1976). Again, however, it is crucial to remember that, with few exceptions, reliance on material, activity, or token reinforcement should eventually give way to reliance upon more "real-life" social reinforcement. Table 8 lists specific examples of commonly used material, social, activity, and token reinforcers.

Table 8 Commonly Used Reinforcers

Material
Favorite meal
Clothing
Books
Radio
Bicycle
Watch
Makeup
Stereo
Jewelry
Guitar
Tapes or CDs
Own room
Personal television
Private telephone

Social
Smiles
Hugs
Winks
Verbal praise
Head nods
Thumbs-up sign
Receiving attention when talking
Being asked for opinion

Activity
Having dating privileges
Getting driver's license
Reading
Having an extended curfew
Receiving car privileges
Staying up late
Staying overnight with friends
Having time off from chores
Dating during the week
Having the opportunity to earn money
Selecting television program
Using the family camera
Choosing own bedtime
Participating in activities with friends
Having a part-time job
Having friends over
Participating in dance or music lessons
Redecorating own room
Rollerblading/skate-boarding
Having additional time on the telephone
Listening to the stereo
Making a trip alone on a bus or plane

Token
Extra money
Own checking account
Allowance
Gift certificate

Note. From *Meeting the ADD Challenge: A Practical Guide for Teachers* (p. 101), by S.B. Gordon and M.J. Asher, 1994, Champaign, IL: Research Press. Copyright 1994 by the authors. Adapted by permission.

Given this wide, though nonexhaustive, array of potential reinforcers and the fact that almost any event may serve as a reinforcer for one individual but not another, how may the trainer decide which reinforcer(s) will be most effective with a particular youngster at a given point in time? Most simply, the youngster can be asked straightforwardly which items he or she would like to earn. Often, however, this approach will not prove sufficient because youngsters are not fully aware of the range of reinforcers available to them or, when aware, may discount in advance the possibility that the given reinforcer will actually be forthcoming. When this is the case, other identification procedures must be employed. Carr (1981) and others have reported three procedures typically used for this purpose.

First, the trainer can often determine whether a given event is functioning as a reinforcer by carefully *observing effects* on the youngster. The event probably is reinforcing if the youngster (a) asks that the event be repeated, (b) seems happy during the event's occurrence, (c) seems unhappy when the event ends, or (d) will work in order to earn the event. If one or more of these reactions are observed, the chances are good that the event is a positive reinforcer and that it can be contingently provided to strengthen appropriate, nonaggressive, or interactive behaviors.

Observing choices can also be helpful. As noted earlier in connection with activity reinforcers, when a youngster is free to choose from among several equally available activities, choice of activity and how long he or she engages in it are clues to whether an event is reinforcing.

A small number of *questionnaires* exist to identify positive reinforcers. Tharp and Wetzel's (1969) Mediation-Reinforcer Incomplete Blank is one often-used measure. It consists of a series of incomplete sentences that the youngster must complete by specifying particular reinforcers: for example, "The thing I like to do best with my mother/father is . . ." or "I will do almost anything to get. . . ." Most of the items help specify not only the nature of the events the youngster perceives as positive reinforcers, but also who the mediators of such reinforcers are. This is highly important information in carrying out a contingency management effort. Going to a ball game may be a powerful reinforcer if one is accompanied by peers, a weak one if accompanied by one's teacher or mother. Praise from a respected teacher may be a potent reinforcing event, whereas the same praise delivered by a peer considered by the youngster to be ignorant about the behavior involved may lack potency. This questionnaire also asks the youngster to indicate his or her sense of the potency of the reinforcer written in for each item. Thus, this measure provides a self-report of *which* events are reinforcing, when delivered or mediated by *whom,* and just *how* reinforcing each event is.

A rather different type of instrument for identifying positive reinforcers, especially appropriate for younger children and children with limited verbal abilities, is Homme, Csanyi, Gonzales, and Rechs's (1969) Reinforcing Event Menu. This measure is essentially a collection of pictures showing a variety of material reinforcers, activity reinforcers, and potential reinforcement mediators. It is the youngster's task to select from these pictures those reinforcers for which he or she would most like to work.

This process of identifying positive reinforcers for given youngsters completes the series of preparatory steps a trainer must undertake before presenting such events contingently upon the occurrence of appropriate behaviors.

Presenting Positive Reinforcers

The basic principle of contingency management is that the presentation of a reinforcing event contingent upon the occurrence of a given behavior functions to increase the likelihood of the reoccurrence of that behavior. Research has demonstrated a number of considerations that influence the success of this reinforcement effort and that should be reflected when presenting reinforcers.

Contingency

Although this rule may be obvious at this point, it is sometimes forgotten or inadequately implemented. The connection between the desirable behavior and the subsequent provision of reward should be made explicit to the youngster. As is true for all aspects of the contingency management effort, this description should be behaviorally specific—that is, the connection between particular behavioral acts and reinforcement should be emphasized over behaviorally ambiguous concepts like "good behavior," "being a good boy," "being well-behaved," or the like.

Immediacy

Related to the communication of the behavioral reinforcement contingency is the fact that the more immediately the reinforcer follows the desirable behavior, the more likely its effectiveness. Rapid reinforcement augments the message that the immediately preceding behavior is desirable, whereas delayed reinforcement increases the risk that the sequence will be A (desirable behavior), B (undesirable behavior), and C (reinforcement for A that actually reinforces B).

Consistency

The effects of positive reinforcement on behavior are usually gradual, not dramatic, working slowly to strengthen behavior over a period of time. Thus, it is important that positive reinforcement be presented consistently. Consistency refers not only to the trainer's efforts, it also means the trainer must attempt to match his or her reinforcement efforts with similar efforts from as many other important persons in the youngster's life as possible. This means, ideally, that when the youngster enacts the behavior to be reinforced—in school in the presence of other teachers, at home in the presence of parents or siblings, or at play in the presence of peers—such reinforcement will be forthcoming.

Frequency

When first trying to establish a new appropriate behavior, the trainer reinforces all or almost all instances of that behavior. This high frequency of reinforcement is necessary to establish the behavior in the individual's behavioral repertoire. Once it seems clear that the behavior has been acquired, the trainer thins the reinforcement schedule, decreasing the presentation of reinforcement so that only some of the youngster's desirable behaviors are followed by the reinforcement. This schedule, known as *partial reinforcement,* contributes to the continuation of the appropriate behavior because it closely parallels the sometimes reinforced/sometimes not reaction the youngster's appropriate behavior will elicit in other settings from other people. Partial reinforcement of the youngster's appropriate behaviors may be on a fixed-time schedule (e.g., at the end of each Skillstreaming session), on a fixed-number-of-response schedule (e.g., every fifth instance of the appropriate behavior), or on variable-time or number-of-response schedules. In any event, the basic strategy for reinforcement frequency remains a rich level for initial learning and partial reinforcement to sustain performance.

Amount

In our preceding discussion of frequency of reinforcement, we began to distinguish between learning (i.e., acquiring knowledge about how to perform new behaviors) and actual performance (i.e., overtly using these behaviors). The amount of reinforcement provided influences performance much more than learning. Youngsters will learn new appropriate behaviors just about as fast for a small reward as for a large reward, but they are more likely to perform the behaviors on a continuing basis when large rewards are involved. Yet rewards can be too large, causing a *satiation effect* in which youngsters lose interest in seeking the given reinforcement because it is "too much of a good thing." Or rewards can be too small: too little time on the playground, too few tokens, too thin a social reinforcement schedule. The optimal amount can be determined empirically. If a youngster has in the past worked energetically to obtain a particular reinforcer but gradually slacks off and seems to lose interest in obtaining it, a satiation effect has probably occurred, and the amount of reinforcement should be reduced. On the other hand, if a youngster seems unwilling to work for a reinforcer believed desirable, it can be given once or twice for free—that is, not contingent on a specific desirable behavior. If the youngster seems to enjoy the reinforcer and even wishes more of the same, the amount used may have been too little. The amount can be increased and made contingent; observations will then show whether it is yielding the desired behavior modification effect. If so, the amount of reinforcement offered is appropriate.

Variety

A type of satiation parallel to a reinforcement satiation effect due to an excessive amount of reinforcement occurs when the trainer uses the same approving phrase or other reward over and over again. Youngsters may perceive such reinforcement as mechanical, and they may thus lose interest in or decrease responsiveness to it. By varying the content of the reinforcer, the trainer can maintain its potency. Thus, instead of repeating "Nice job" four or five times, using a mix of comments ("I'm really proud of you," "You're certainly doing fine," or "Well done") is more likely to yield a sustained effect.

Pairing with praise

Earlier, we noted that social reinforcement is most germane to enduring behavior change, although there are circumstances under which material, activity, or token reinforcers are (at least initially) more appropriate. To aid in the desired movement toward social reinforcement, the trainer pairs all presentations of material, activity, or token rewards with some expression of social reinforcement: an approving comment, a pat on the back, a wink, a smile, and so forth. A major benefit of this tactic is noted by Walker (1979):

> By virtue of being consistently paired with reinforcement delivery, praise can take on the reinforcing properties of the actual reinforcer(s) used. This is especially important since teacher praise is not always initially effective with many deviant children. By systematically increasing the incentive value of praise through pairing, the teacher is in a position to gradually reduce the frequency of [material, activity, or token] reinforcement and to substitute praise. After systematic pairing, the teacher's praise may be much more effective in maintaining the child's appropriate behavior. (p. 108)

The preceding rules for maximizing the effectiveness of the presentation of positive reinforcement are all essentially remedial in nature. They are efforts to substitute appropriate prosocial behaviors for aggressive, disruptive, antisocial, withdrawal, or asocial behaviors that already exist. It is also worth noting, however, that positive reinforcement may also be used for preventive purposes. Sarason et al. (1972) urge teachers to present positive reinforcement openly to specific youngsters in such a manner that the entire class is aware of it. As they comment:

> Positive reinforcement for productive activity for the whole group is a powerful preventive technique. It can eliminate or reduce the great majority of behavior problems in classrooms. Try to praise the children who are paying attention. Attend to those who are sitting in their seats, doing their work in a nondisruptive manner. "That's right, John, you're doing a good job." "You watched the board all the time I was presenting the problem. That's paying attention." . . . These responses not only reinforce the child to whom they are directed, but they also help to provide the rest of the class with an explicit idea of what you mean by paying attention and working hard. Young children, especially . . . learn to model their actions after the positive examples established and noted by the teacher. (p. 18)

Such open use of attempts to "catch them being good" are strongly recommended for the Skillstreaming group.

Removing Positive Reinforcers

The teacher's behavior modification goal with youngsters displaying aggressive or other problematic behaviors is, in a general sense, twofold. Both sides of the behavioral coin—appropriate and inappropriate, prosocial and antisocial, desirable and undesirable—must be attended to. In a proper behavior-change effort, procedures are simultaneously or sequentially employed to reduce and eliminate the inappropriate, antisocial, or undesirable components of the youngster's behavioral repertoire and to increase the quality and frequency of appropriate, prosocial, or desirable components. This latter task is served primarily by the direct teaching of prosocial behaviors via Skillstreaming participation and by the contingent presentation of positive reinforcement following their occurrence. Conversely, the contingent removal of positive reinforcement in response to aggressive, disruptive, or other negative behaviors is the major behavior modification strategy for reducing or eliminating such behaviors. Therefore, in conjunction with the procedures discussed previously for presenting positive reinforcement, the trainer should also simultaneously or consecutively employ one or more of the following three techniques for removing positive reinforcement.

Extinction

Extinction is the withdrawal or removal of positive reinforcement for aggressive or other undesirable behaviors that have been either deliberately or inadvertently reinforced in the past. This technique can be thought of prescriptively as the procedure of choice with milder forms of aggression (e.g., sarcasm, put-downs, or other low-level forms of verbal aggression).

Knowing when to use extinction. Determining when extinction is appropriate is, of course, in part a function of each trainer's guiding group management philosophy and tolerance for deviance. Each trainer will have to decide individually the range of undesirable behaviors that can be safely ignored. Taking a rather conservative stance, Walker (1979) suggests that extinction "should be applied only to those inappropriate behaviors that are minimally disruptive to classroom atmosphere" (p. 40). Others are somewhat more liberal in its application (e.g., Carr, 1981). In any event, it is clear that the first step in applying extinction is knowing when to use it.

Providing positive reinforcement for appropriate behaviors. As noted earlier, attempts to reduce inappropriate behavior by withdrawing reinforcement should always be accompanied by efforts to increase appropriate behaviors by providing reinforcement. This combination of efforts will succeed especially well when the appropriate and inappropriate behaviors involved are opposite from, or at least incompatible with, each other (e.g., reward in-seat behavior, ignore out-of-seat behavior; reward talking at a conversational level, ignore yelling).

Identifying the positive reinforcers maintaining inappropriate behaviors. The reinforcers maintaining inappropriate behaviors are the ones to be withheld. The trainer should discern what the youngster is working for; what payoffs are involved; and what reinforcers are being sought or earned by aggression, disruptiveness, and similar behaviors. Very often, the answer will be attention. Laughing, looking, staring, yelling at, talking to, or turning toward are common teacher and peer reactions to a youngster's aggression. The withdrawal of such positive social reinforcement by ignoring the behaviors (by turning away and not yelling, talking, or laughing at the perpetrator) are the teacher and peer behaviors that will effect extinction. Ignoring someone who would normally receive one's attention is itself a talent, as the following extinction rules illustrate.

Knowing how to ignore aggressive behaviors. Carr (1981) has suggested three useful guidelines for ignoring low-level aggressive behaviors. These are summarized as follows:

1. Do not comment to the child that you are ignoring him or her. Long (or even short) explanations provided to youngsters about why trainers, peers, or others are going to avoid attending to given behaviors provide precisely the type of social reinforcement extinction is designed to withdraw. Such explanations are to be avoided. Ignoring behavior should simply occur with no forewarning, introduction, or prior explanation.
2. Do not look away suddenly when the child behaves aggressively or otherwise inappropriately. Jerking one's head away suddenly so as not to see the continuation of the aggressive behavior or other abrupt behaviors may communicate the message that "I really noticed and was impelled to action by your behavior," the exact opposite of an extinction message. As Carr recommends, "It is best to ignore the behavior by reacting to it in a matter of fact way by continuing natural ongoing activities" (p. 38).
3. Do protect the victims of aggression. If one youngster actually strikes another, the trainer must intervene. One may do so without subverting the extinction effort by providing the victim of aggression attention, concern, and interest and by ignoring the perpetrator.

Using extinction consistently. As is true for the provision of reinforcement, removal of reinforcement must be consistent for intended effects to be forthcoming. Within a given Skillstreaming group, this rule of consistency means both that the trainer and trainees must act in concert and that the trainer must be consistent across time. Within a given school, consistency means that, to the degree possible, all teachers having significant contact with a given youngster must strive to ignore the same inappropriate behaviors. In addition, to avoid the youngster's making a type of "I can't act up here, but I can out there" discrimination, parent conferences should be held to bring parents, siblings, and other significant real-world figures in the youngster's life into the extinction effort. As Karoly (1980) notes, when consistency of nonattending is not maintained, the aggressive behavior will be intermittently or partially reinforced, a circumstance that we noted earlier would lead to its becoming highly resistant to extinction.

Using extinction for a long enough period of time. Aggressive behaviors often have a long history of positive reinforcement. Especially if much of that history is one of intermittent reinforcement, efforts to undo aggressive behaviors must be sustained. Trainer persistence in this regard will usually succeed. There are, however, two types of events to keep in mind when judging the effectiveness of extinction efforts. The first is what is known as the *extinction burst.* When extinction is first introduced, it is not uncommon for the rate or intensity of the aggressive behavior to increase sharply before it begins gradually to decline toward a zero level. It is important for the trainer not to be discouraged during this short detour. In fact, the increase means extinction is beginning to work. In addition, inappropriate behaviors that have been successfully extinguished will reappear occasionally for reasons that are difficult to determine. Like the extinction burst, this *spontaneous recovery* is transitory and will disappear if the trainer persists in the extinction effort.

Time-out

In time-out, a youngster who engages in aggressive or other inappropriate behavior is physically removed from all sources of reinforcement for a specified time period. As with extinction, the purpose of time-out is to reduce the (undesirable) behavior that immediately precedes it and upon which its use is contingent. It differs from extinction in that extinction involves removing reinforcement from the person, whereas time-out usually involves removing the person from the reinforcing situation.

In school-based practice, time-out typically takes three forms. *Isolation time-out,* the most common form, requires that the youngster be physically removed from the classroom to a time-out room according to specific procedures described later in this section. *Exclusion time-out* is somewhat less restrictive but also involves physically removing the youngster from sources of reinforcement. Here the youngster is required to go to a corner of the classroom and perhaps to sit in a "quiet chair" (Firestone, 1976), which is sometimes behind a screen. The youngster is not removed from the classroom but is excluded from classroom activities for a specified time period. *Nonexclusion time-out* (also called *contingent observation*), the least restrictive time-out variant, requires the youngster to sit and watch on the periphery of classroom activities, to observe the appropriate behaviors of other youngsters. It is a variant that combines time-out with modeling opportunities and thus may be the preferred approach for Skillstreaming group use. All three of these variants of time-out may be effectively employed to deal with problematic behavior occurring in the Skillstreaming group. The implementation of time-out in any of its forms optimally employs the procedures next described.

Knowing when to use time-out. Extinction, it will be recalled, is the recommended procedure for aggressive or otherwise undesirable behaviors that can be safely ignored. Behaviors potentially injurious to other youngsters require a more active trainer response, possibly time-out. In the case of many youngsters at the upper middle school and senior high school levels, physical removal by the trainer is often not wise, appropriate, or even possible. For such youngsters, procedures other than extinction or time-out, discussed later in this chapter, must be employed. Time-out is recommended as a technique for youngsters ages 2 to 12 years who are displaying high rates of potentially dangerous, aggressive, or other disruptive behaviors. It is also the procedure to use for less severe forms of problematic behavior when the combination of extinction and positive reinforcement for other, more positive behaviors has been attempted and has failed.

Providing positive reinforcement for appropriate behaviors. As is the case for extinction, positive reinforcement for appropriate behaviors should accompany time-out. When possible, the behaviors positively reinforced should be opposite to, or at least incompatible with, those for which the time-out procedure is employed. Carr (1981) observes an additional basis for recommending the combined use of these two techniques:

> Although one important reason for using positive reinforcement is to strengthen nonaggressive behaviors to the point where they replace aggressive behaviors, there is a second reason for using reinforcement procedures. If extensive use of positive reinforcement is made, then time out will become all the more aversive since it would involve the temporary termination of a rich diversity of positive reinforcers. In this sense, then, the use of positive reinforcement helps to enhance the effectiveness of the time out procedure. (pp. 41–42)

Arranging an effective time-out setting. We will focus our description of an effective time-out setting on the isolation time-out arrangement because its general principles readily carry over to both exclusion and nonexclusion time-out environments. Essentially, two general principles are involved. The first concerns the youngster's health and safety. The time-out setting should be a small, well-lit, and well-ventilated room that provides a place for the youngster to sit. The second principle reflects the fact that the central quality of this procedure is time-out from positive reinforcement. Time-out must be a boring environment, with all reinforcers removed. There should be no attractive or distracting objects or opportunities; no toys, television, radio, books, posters, people, windows to look out, sounds to hear, or other obvious or not-so-obvious potential reinforcers. A barren isolation area is the optimal time-out environment.

Placing a youngster in time-out. A number of actions may be taken by the teacher when initiating time-out to increase the likelihood of its effectiveness. As with the immediate presentation of positive reinforcement contingent upon appropriate behaviors, time-out is optimally instituted immediately following the aggressive or other behaviors one is seeking to modify. Having earlier explained to the target youngster the nature of time-out, as well as when and why it will be used, the trainer should initiate the procedure in a more-or-less automatic manner following undesirable behavior—that is, in a manner that minimizes social reinforcement of the aggression. This means placing the youngster in time-out without a lengthy explanation but with a brief, matter-of-fact description of the precipitating behaviors. This process is best conducted without anger and, when possible, without physically moving the youngster from the setting in which Skillstreaming is being conducted to the time-out room. To minimize reinforcement of aggression during this process, it is also best if the distance between training room and time-out room is small: The shorter the distance and the briefer the transportation time, the less opportunity exists for inadvertent social reinforcement by the trainer. In addition to these considerations, the effectiveness of time-out is enhanced by its consistent application, when appropriate, by the same trainer on other occasions as well as by other trainers and teachers.

To summarize, immediacy, consistency, and various actions aimed at minimizing trainer presentation of reinforcement following inappropriate behavior thus function to augment the behavior-change effectiveness of time-out.

Maintaining a youngster in time-out. The skilled contingency manager must deal with two questions during a youngster's period in time-out: "What is the youngster doing?" and "How long should time-out last?" Monitoring makes certain that the time-out experience is not in fact functioning as a pleasant, positively reinforcing one for a given youngster. For example, rather than a removal from positive reinforcement, time-out may in reality be a removal from an aversive situation (negative reinforcement) if the trainer institutes it at a time when a youngster is in an unpleasant situation from which he or she would prefer to escape or if time-out helps the youngster avoid such a situation. Similarly, if monitoring reveals that the youngster is singing or playing enjoyable games, the effectiveness of time-out will be lessened. Unless the situation can be made essentially nonreinforcing, a different behavioral intervention may be necessary.

With regard to duration, most successful time-out implementations have been from 5 to 20 minutes long, with clear preference for the shorter levels of this range. When experimenting to find the optimal duration for any given youngster, it is best, as White, Nielson, and Johnson (1972) have shown, to begin with a short duration (e.g., 3 to 5 minutes) and to lengthen the time until an effective span is identified rather than to shorten successively an initially lengthier span. This latter approach would, again, risk the danger of introducing an event experienced as positive reinforcement by the youngster when the intention is quite the opposite.

Releasing a youngster from time-out. We noted earlier in connection with extinction that withdrawal of positive reinforcement not infrequently leads to an initial extinction burst, in which more intense or more frequent aggressiveness or other problem behaviors appear before they begin to subside. This same pattern is evident with withdrawal from positive reinforcement—that is, with time-out. The first few times a youngster is placed in time-out, what might be termed a *time-out burst* of heightened aggression or other problem behavior may occur. These outbursts will usually subside, especially if the trainer adds to the duration of the time-out span the same number of minutes that the outburst lasts.

Whether the release of the youngster from time-out is on schedule or is delayed for the reasons just specified, it should be conducted in a matter-of-fact manner, and the youngster should be quickly returned to regular Skillstreaming activities. Lengthy explanations or moralizing at this point are tactically erroneous provisions of positive reinforcement that communicate to the youngster that acting out in the classroom will bring a short period of removal from reinforcement and then a (probably lengthier) period of undivided trainer attention.

Response cost

Response cost involves the removal of previously acquired reinforcers contingent upon and in order to reduce future instances of inappropriate behavior. The reinforcers previously acquired and to be removed contingently may have been earned, as when the use of response-cost procedures is a component of a token economy, or they may have been simply provided, as is the case with a free-standing response-cost system. In either instance, reinforcers are removed (the cost) whenever previously targeted undesirable behaviors occur (the response). The two other means we have examined for the systematic removal of positive reinforcement, extinction and time-out, have sometimes proven insufficient for severely aggressive adolescents, even when combined with trainer praise or other reinforcement for appropriate behaviors. In a number of these instances, response-cost procedures have proven effective—especially when combined with the provision of positive reinforcement (via a token-economy system) for desirable prosocial behaviors.

We do not detail here the rules for the effective implementation of a token economy because they overlap considerably with rules delineated earlier in this chapter for the provision of nontoken positive reinforcers and are discussed at length elsewhere (e.g., Ayllon & Azrin, 1968; Kazdin, 1975; Walker, 1979). We do wish to specify, however, the rules for removing token or nontoken reinforcement that constitute the essence of the response-cost procedure.

Defining inappropriate behaviors in specific terms. As for the application of every other contingency management procedure, the trainer must think, plan, and act "behaviorally." When specifying the target behaviors that will cost tokens, points, privileges, or other commodities or events, the trainer must delineate specific overt acts, not broader behavioral or characterological categories. Thus, "is aggressive" (a characterological observation) or "acts withdrawn" (a broad behavioral observation) are too vague. "Swears," "makes threats," "raises voice," "raises hands," "pushes group mates," and "sits by self," are all useful specifications.

Determining the cost of specific inappropriate responses. As is the case for the amount, level, or rate of positive reinforcement to be provided contingent upon desirable behaviors, the specific cost of undesirable behaviors must be determined, whether such cost is a finite number of tokens or points, a finite amount of schoolyard time, or another outcome. Cost setting is a crucial determinant of the success or failure of this approach. For example, Carr (1981) notes that

> the magnitude of response costs must be carefully controlled. If fines are too large, bankruptcy will ensue and the child will be unable to purchase any back-up reinforcers. Further, if the child develops too large a deficit, he may adapt an attitude of "what do I have to lose?" and engage

> in considerable misbehavior. On the other hand, if the fines are too small, the child will be able to negate his loss easily by performing any of a variety of appropriate behaviors. (p. 52)

Yet other aspects of response-cost implementation will make demands on the trainer's skills as a creative economist. The relationship of points or other reinforcers available to earn to those that can be lost; the relationship of cost to the severity of the inappropriate behavior for which that cost is levied; and a host of similar marketing, pricing, and, ultimately, motivational considerations may come into play. A substantial level of contingency management expertise on the part of the trainer is required. This is especially true if the trainer is not only the implementer of the response-cost system, but also its originator, planner, and monitor.

Communicating contingencies. Once the trainer has decided upon the specific token, point, or privilege value of the appropriate and inappropriate behaviors relevant to the effective management of the Skillstreaming group, he or she communicates these values to the participating trainees.

Removing reinforcement. Group members not only must be able to know in advance what earnings and losses are contingent upon what desirable and undesirable behaviors, but must also have ongoing knowledge of their own earnings status. Walker (1979) has developed a simple, easily used delivery/feedback system that gives each youngster ongoing cumulative information indicating (a) when response cost or earnings have been applied; (b) to which specific behaviors response cost or earnings have been applied; and (c) how many points have been lost or earned as a result.

As is true for the other major procedures for the removal of positive reinforcement—extinction and time-out—optimal implementation of response-cost procedures requires that the trainer be (a) *consistent* in the application of procedures across students and across time for each student; (b) *immediate* in delivering contingent costs as soon as possible after the inappropriate behavior occurs; and (c) *impartial* and *inevitable* in ensuring that the instance of inappropriate behavior leads to an instance of response cost almost automatically, with an absolute minimum of exceptions.

Presenting and Removing Aversive Stimuli

The two contingency management approaches examined in this section—namely, the presentation of aversive stimuli (i.e., punishment) and the removal of aversive stimuli (i.e., negative reinforcement)—are in our view generally less recommendable than the positive reinforcement presentation and removal procedures discussed earlier. Our disinclination to recommend these procedures is explained in the following discussion.

Punishment

Punishment is the presentation of an aversive stimulus contingent upon the performance of a given behavior. It is usually intended to decrease the likelihood of future occurrences of that behavior. Two of the major forms that punishment has taken in United States classrooms are verbal punishment (i.e., reprimands) and physical punishment (i.e., paddling, spanking, slapping, or other forms of corporal punishment). The effectiveness of these and other forms of punishment in altering behaviors such as aggression has been shown to be a function of several factors:

1. Likelihood
2. Consistency
3. Immediacy
4. Duration
5. Severity
6. Possibility for escape or avoidance
7. Availability of alternative routes to goal
8. Level of instigation to aggression
9. Level of reward for aggression
10. Characteristics of the prohibiting agents

Punishment is more likely to lead to behavior-change consequences the more certain its application, the more consistently and rapidly it is applied, the longer and more intense its quality, the less the likelihood it can be avoided, the more available are alternative means to goal satisfaction, the lower the level of instigation to aggression or reward for aggression, and the more potent as a contingency manager the prohibiting agent. Thus, several factors determine the impact of an aversive stimulus on a youngster's behavior. Let us assume an instance in which these determinants combine to yield a substantial impact. What, ideally, may we hope the effect of punishment on aggression or other undesirable behavior will be? A reprimand or a paddling will not teach new behaviors. If the youngster is deficient in the ability to ask rather than take, request rather than command, and negotiate rather than strike out, all the scolding, scowling, and spanking possible will not teach the youngster desirable alternative behaviors. Thus, punishment, if used at all, must be combined with efforts to instruct the youngster in those behaviors in which he or she is deficient. When the youngster possesses high-quality appropriate behaviors but is not displaying them, punishment is optimally combined with any of the other procedures described earlier for the systematic presentation of positive reinforcement. In short, the application of punishment techniques should always be combined with a procedure to strengthen appropriate alternative behaviors, whether these behaviors are absent, weak, or merely unused.

This focus on teaching desirable alternative behaviors stems from the fact that most investigators report the main effect of punishment to be a temporary suppression of inappropriate behaviors. Although even a temporary suppression may be valuable to the harried trainer, it is not uncommon for the trainer to have to punish the same youngsters over and over again for the same inappropriate behaviors.

To recapitulate, if punishment is used, it must be combined with one or another means for simultaneously teaching desirable behaviors. This recommendation is underscored by the common finding that, when punishment does succeed in altering behavior, such effects are often temporary.

In part because of this temporary effect, but more so for some even more important reasons, a number of contingency management researchers have assumed an antipunishment stance, seeing little place for punishment, especially in the contemporary classroom. This view corresponds to punishment research demonstrating such undesirable side effects as withdrawal from social contact, counter-aggression toward the punisher, modeling of punishing behavior, disruption of social relationships, failure of effects to generalize, selective avoidance (refraining from inappropriate behaviors only when under surveillance), and stigmatizing labeling effects (Azrin & Holz, 1966; Bandura, 1973).

An alternative, propunishment view does exist. It is less widespread and more controversial, but it is based upon empirical evidence. These investigators hold that there are numerous favorable effects of punishment: rapid and dependable reduction of inappropriate behaviors; the opening up of new sources of positive reinforcement; the possibility of complete suppression of inappropriate behaviors; improved social and emotional behavior, imitation, and discrimination learning; and other potentially positive outcomes (Axelrod & Apsche, 1982; Newsom, Favell, & Rincover, 1982; Van Houten, 1982).

The evidence is clearly not all in. Data on which punishers should appropriately be used with which youngsters under which circumstances are incomplete. At present, decisions about using aversive stimuli in Skillstreaming to alter inappropriate behaviors must derive from partial data and from each trainer's carefully considered ethical beliefs regarding the relative costs and benefits of employing punishment procedures. Our own weighing of relevant data and ethical considerations leads to our favoring the selective use of verbal punishment techniques, such as reprimands. We reject under all circumstances the use of physical punishment techniques.

Negative reinforcement

As defined earlier, negative reinforcement is the removal of aversive stimuli contingent upon the occurrence of desirable behaviors. Negative reinforcement has seldom been used to modify behavior in a classroom context. The major exception to this rule is the contingent release of youngsters from time-out (an aversive environment), depending upon such desirable behaviors as quietness and calmness. Such release serves as negative reinforcement for these behaviors. Unfortunately, negative reinforcement often proves important in a classroom context in a less constructive way. Consider a teacher-student interaction in which the student behaves disruptively (shouts, swears, fights), the teacher responds with anger and physical punishment, and the punishment brings about a temporary suppression of the youngster's disruptiveness. The decrease in student disruptiveness may also be viewed as a decrease in aversive stimulation experienced by the teacher, which functions to negatively reinforce the immediately preceding teacher behavior (in this case, corporal punishment). The net effect of this sequence is to increase the likelihood that the teacher will use corporal punishment in the future. Analogous sequences may occur and function to increase the likelihood of other ineffective, inappropriate, or intemperate teacher behaviors.

Other Behavior Modification Procedures

In addition to procedures for the presentation or removal of positive reinforcement and the use of aversive stimuli, two other behavior modification procedures are useful in Skillstreaming. These procedures do not rely upon the management of contingencies for their effectiveness.

Overcorrection

Overcorrection is a behavior modification approach developed by Foxx and Azrin (1973) for circumstances in which extinction, time-out, and response cost have either failed or are impractical and when few alternative appropriate behaviors are available to reinforce. Overcorrection is a two-part procedure, having both restitutional and positive practice components. The restitutional aspect requires that the target individual return the behavioral setting (e.g., the classroom) to its status prior to disruption or better. Thus, objects broken by an angry youngster must be repaired, classmates struck in anger apologized to, papers scattered across the room picked up. The positive practice component of overcorrection requires that the disruptive youngster then, in the specific examples just cited, be made to repair objects broken by others, apologize to classmates who witnessed the classmate being struck, or clean up the rest of the classroom (including areas not disturbed by the target youngster). It is clear that the restitution and positive practice requirements serve both punitive and instructional functions.

Contingency contracting

A contingency contract is a written agreement between a trainer and trainee. It is a document each signs that specifies desirable trainee behaviors and their contingent positive consequences, as well as undesirable trainee behaviors and their contingent undesirable consequences (See Figure 7 for an example). As Homme et al. (1969) specify in their initial description of this procedure, such contracts will more reliably lead to desirable trainee behaviors when the contract payoff is immediate; approximations to the desirable behavior are rewarded; the contract rewards accomplishment rather than obedience; accomplishment precedes reward; and the contract is fair, clear, honest, positive, and systematically implemented.

CAPTURING TEACHABLE MOMENTS

Thus far, discussion has focused on two strategies for successfully managing trainee resistance in Skillstreaming groups. The first emphasized letting your diagnosis determine your intervention—for example, problems due to complexity are managed with simplification, threat with threat-reduction steps, and so forth. The second centered on modifying problematic behaviors by providing and withdrawing reinforcement contingent upon the presence or absence of appropriate or inappropriate behaviors. A third strategy may be offered. In effect, it employs Skillstreaming itself to better manage the Skillstreaming group.

The problematic behaviors of concern in this chapter—minimal participation, disruptiveness, digression, bullying, bizarreness, and so forth—may each be viewed as a behavioral *excess* to be reduced by one or more of the means already examined. Each such behavior, however, may equally well be construed as a behavioral *deficiency* (e.g., too much monopolizing is too little listening to others, too much bullying is too little empathy directed to others). Thus, an additional means for reducing problem behaviors is to replace them with desirable behaviors. The Skillstreaming curriculum includes just such alternatives; the skills may be taught as previously scheduled, as part of the regular sessions, or at opportune times (teachable moments) that serve to reduce resistance and open up opportunity to learn yet other skills.

For example, imagine that two trainers are conducting the session-opening homework report segment of a Skillstreaming meeting. The skill role-played the previous session was Expressing Affection. In role-playing this skill, one group member, Jane, had rehearsed with another member skill steps involving approaching a male student to invite him to an upcoming party.

Trainer: Jane, how did your homework work out? Did you go to Lee and ask him to go to that Saturday party with you?

Jane: No, I didn't. I didn't say anything to Lee, and I want you to know that I'm really pissed off today.

Trainer: Oh, what's going on?

Jane: You said this group was a confidential group, that one of our rules was whatever happens in the group stays in the group. Somebody told Lee that I think he's cute. It really makes me mad as hell, and embarrassed as hell. I don't know who told him, but right after the meeting last week I saw Jennifer go over to Lee and say something. I think she told him, and I'm going to smack her in the face right now.

Jane stands up and begins moving toward Jennifer. At this point it is the trainer's responsibility to do two things. The first is to make clear that the first trainee will not be permitted to physically harm the second and to take immediate, proper steps to make sure such containment occurs. Elsewhere, we have described our program to train teachers and other school personnel in skills for the safe and rapid management of such confrontations (Goldstein, Palumbo, Striepling, & Voutsinas, 1995). Once safety is assured, the trainer captures the teachable moment presented by the confrontation and turns it into an opportunity for learning. The trainee, Jane, seeks to resolve her anger by attacking the peer she believes is its source. The chance here is to teach Jane an alternative, more prosocially skilled way of handling the same situation. As a bonus, the situation described presents the opportunity to accomplish the same prosocial skill training goal for the second youngster, too, the one Jane was seeking to attack.

Trainer: *(To Jane)* Jane, we are not going to permit you to hit Jennifer, but I know you're really angry. I think there are better ways to express how you feel. Do you remember about three sessions back we learned the skill Standing Up for Your Rights? As I recall, you did a pretty good job role-playing it, but your homework on it with your father was a bit of a problem. Remember? Here's the Skill Card for it. I'd like you to practice it right now with Jennifer. Rather than hit her, let her know what you think and feel by acting out these steps. *(To Jennifer)* Jennifer, you can see that Jane is really angry with you. She's going to say something to you about her suspicion that you spoke to Lee about what happened in here. You may get angry back at her—I don't know—but I want you to try to respond to her with a skill we haven't learned yet. It's called Dealing with an Accusation. Here is the Skill Card for it. Got it?

Youngsters will master the Skillstreaming curriculum to the degree that their motivation for attendance and participation is high and their resistance to such involvement is low. In this chapter we have examined a number of procedures for enhancing the former and reducing the latter. Which particular means of increasing motivation and reducing resistance are best for any given Skillstreaming group will vary according to trainer, trainee, and setting characteristics. We urge trainers to experiment. We believe the methods described here are the best available in group management technology. Trial use of various combinations and sequences will enable each trainer to determine which means, used in which sequence, are most effective for any particular Skillstreaming group and setting.

CHAPTER 9
Enhancing Generalization of Skill Performance

As the social skills training movement in general and Skillstreaming in particular have matured, and relevant evidence regarding effectiveness has accumulated, it has become clear that skill acquisition is a reliable finding across both training methods and populations. However, generalization is quite another matter. Both generalization to new settings (transfer) and over time (maintenance) have been reported to occur in only a minority of training outcomes. This chapter examines the alternative approaches that have been taken toward enhancing generalization. In it, we propose that the embedding and delivery of social skills training within a comprehensive psychoeducational curriculum, including both social skills and other supportive psychological competencies, has substantial potential for maximizing both transfer and maintenance of acquired social skills.

INTERVENTIONS AS INOCULATION

Many traditional interventions have reflected a core belief in personality change as both the target and the outcome in effective treatment, as well as a strong tendency to downplay environmental influences on behavior. In brief, these approaches have viewed successful intervention as a sort of "psychological inoculation." It has been assumed that the positive changes purported to take place within the individual's personality structure would enable the client to deal effectively with problematic events wherever and whenever they might occur. That is, transfer and maintenance would occur automatically. With reference to the prevailing psychoanalytic view on this matter, Ford and Urban (1963) note:

> If the patient's behavior toward the therapist is modified, the changes are expected to transfer automatically to other situations. The conflicts involved in the neurosis all become directed toward the therapist during the "transference neurosis." They are not situation-specific. They are responses looking for an object to happen to. Thus, if they are changed, while they are occurring in relation to the therapist, they will be permanently changed, and can no longer attach themselves to any object in their old form. No special procedures are necessary to facilitate the transfer from the therapist to other situations if the therapist has successfully resolved the transference pattern of behavior. (p. 173)

Such purported automatic maintenance and transfer, variously explained, also characterize the therapeutic positions of Adler (1924), Horney (1939), Rank (1945), Rogers (1951), and Sullivan (1953). In each instance, the view put forth is that, when the given therapy process results in positive intrapsychic changes in the patient, the patient is able to "take these changes with him" and apply them where and when needed in the real-life environment. As Ford and Urban (1963) comment, Rogers, like Freud,

> assumes that changes in behaviors outside of the therapy interview will follow automatically upon changes in the self-evaluative thoughts and associated emotions during the therapy hour. Changes in the self-evaluative thoughts and their emotional concomitants result in reduced anxiety, improved discrimination among situational events and responses, more accurate symbolization of them, and greater confidence in one's own decisions. These provide the conditions from which more appropriate instrumental and interpersonal responses will naturally grow. (p. 435)

This intervention-as-inoculation perspective was widespread during the 1950s. Because transfer and maintenance were held to occur inexorably as a consequence of within-treatment gains, no call emerged for the development of purposeful means for their enhancement.

TRAIN AND HOPE

Psychotherapy research as a viable enterprise was initiated in the 1950s and grew in both quantity and scope during the 1960s and 1970s. Much of the outcome research conducted at the time included systematic follow-up probes, which sought to ascertain whether gains evident at the termination of formal intervention had generalized across settings and/or time. Stokes and Baer (1977) described this phase as one in which transfer and maintenance were hoped for and noted but not pursued:

> Studies that are examples of Train and Hope across time are those in which there was a change from the intervention procedures, either to a less intensive but procedurally different program, or to no program or no specifically defined program. Data or anecdotal observations were reported concerning the maintenance of the original behavior change over the specified time intervening between the termination of the formal program and the postchecks. (p. 351)

The overwhelming result of these many investigations was that, much more often than not, transfer and maintenance of intervention gains did not occur. Treatment and training did not often serve as an inoculation; gains did not persist automatically; transfer and maintenance did not necessarily follow (Goldstein & Kanfer, 1979; Keeley, Shemberg, & Carbonell, 1976). The failure of the inoculation model, as revealed by the evidence accumulated during the train-and-hope phase, led to a third phase of concern with generalization—the energetic development, evaluation, and use of a number of procedures explicitly designed to enhance transfer and maintenance of intervention gains.

DEVELOPMENT OF TRANSFER AND MAINTENANCE ENHANCERS

The early call by us and by others for the development of transfer and maintenance enhancers made explicit the belief that any enhancement that might result would have its roots in the empirical literature on learning and its transfer:

> A different assumption regarding response maintenance and transfer of therapeutic gains has in recent years begun to emerge in the psychotherapy research literature, especially that devoted to the outcome of behavior modification interventions. This assumption also rests on the belief that maintenance and transfer of therapeutic gain are not common events but, instead of positing that they should occur via an automatic process whose instigation lies within the procedures of the therapy itself, the position taken is that new maintenance-enhancing and transfer-enhancing techniques must be developed and purposefully and systematically incorporated into the ongoing treatment process. Thus, not satisfied that "behaviors usually extinguish when a program is withdrawn" (Kazdin, 1975, p. 213), or that "removal of the contingencies usually results in a decline of performance to or near baseline levels" (Kazdin, 1975, p. 215), a number of therapy practitioners and researchers are actively seeking to identify, evaluate, and incorporate into ongoing treatment a series of procedures explicitly designed to enhance the level of transfer which ensues. As we have stated elsewhere, the starting point in this search for effective gain maintenance and transfer-enhancers is clear: We need specific knowledge of the conditions under which learning or other changes that take place in therapy will be carried over into extra-therapy situations. . . . We cannot assume that a behavior acquired in the therapy situation, however well learned, will carry over into other situations. Unquestionably the phenomena of therapy are orderly and lawful; they follow definite rules. We must, then, understand the rules that determine what responses will be generalized, or transferred, to other situations and what responses will not. As a first approximation to the rules obtaining in psychotherapy, we suggest the knowledge gained from study of transfer of other habits. (Goldstein, Heller, & Sechrest, 1966, p. 244)

The effort to develop effective and reliable means for maximizing transfer and maintenance, though clearly still in progress, has shown considerable success. A variety of useful techniques, which collectively constitute the current technology of transfer and maintenance enhancement, are listed in Table 9 and are discussed further in the following pages.

TABLE 9 Transfer- and Maintenance-Enhancing Procedures

Transfer

1. Provision of general principles (general case programming)
2. Overlearning (maximizing response availability)
3. Stimulus variability (training sufficient exemplars, training loosely)
4. Identical elements (programming common stimuli)
5. Mediated generalization (self-recording, self-reinforcement, self-punishment, self-instruction)

Maintenance

1. Thin reinforcement (increase intermittency, unpredictability)
2. Delay reinforcement
3. Fade prompts
4. Provide booster sessions
5. Prepare for real-life nonreinforcement
    - Teach self-reinforcement
    - Teach relapse and failure management skills
    - Use graduated homework assignments
6. Program for reinforcement in the natural environment
7. Use natural reinforcers
    - Observe real-life settings
    - Identify easily reinforced behaviors
    - Teach reinforcement recruitment
    - Teach reinforcement recognition

Provision of General Principles

Transfer of training may be facilitated by providing the trainee with the general mediating principles that govern satisfactory performance of both the original and the transfer task. The trainee can be given the rules, strategies, or organizing principles that lead to successful performance. The general finding that understanding the principles that underlie successful performance can enhance transfer to new tasks and contexts has been reported in a number of domains of psychological research, including studies of labeling, rules, advance organizers, learning sets, and deutero-learning. It is a robust finding, with empirical support in both laboratory and psychoeducational settings.

No matter how competently the Skillstreaming trainer seeks to create in the role-play setting the "feel" of the real-life setting in which the trainee will need to use the skill, and no matter how well the coactor in a given role-play matches the actual qualities of appearance and response of the real target figure, there will always be differences that matter between role-play and real world. Even when the trainee has role-played the skill a number of times, the demands of the actual situation will depart at least in some respects from the demands portrayed in the role-play. And the real parent, real peer, real teacher is likely to respond to even correct skill use at least somewhat differently than did the trainee's role-play partner. When the trainee has a good grasp of the principles underlying the situations, whether role-play or real (why *these* steps, in *this* order, toward *which* ends) a successful training to real-life transfer of skilled performance becomes more likely. Correctly discerning the general principles associated with diverse skill-relevant settings can be enhanced by trainee participation in a process we have termed Situational Perception Training, described later in this chapter.

Overlearning

Transfer of training has been shown to be enhanced by procedures that maximize overlearning or response availability: The likelihood that a response will be available is very clearly a function of its prior use. We repeat and repeat foreign language phrases we are trying to learn, we insist that our child spend an hour per day in piano practice, and we devote considerable time practicing to make a golf swing smooth and "automatic." These are simply expressions of the response-availability notion—that is, the more we have practiced responses (especially correct ones), the easier it will be to use them in other contexts or at later times. We need not rely solely on everyday experience to find support for this conclusion. It has been well established empirically that, other things being equal, the response emitted most frequently in the past is more likely to be emitted on subsequent occasions. However, it is not sheer practice of attempts at effective behaviors that is of most benefit to transfer, but practice of successful attempts. Overlearning involves extending learning over more trials than would be necessary merely to produce initial changes in the individual's behavior. In all too many instances of near-successful training, one or two successes at a given task are taken as evidence to move on to the next task or the next level of the original task. This is a training technique error if one wishes to maximize transfer. To maximize transfer through overlearning, the guiding rule should not be "practice makes perfect" (implying that one simply practices until one gets it right and then moves on), but "practice of perfect" (implying numerous overlearning trials of correct responses after initial success).

Youths who have just received feedback from co-trainees and trainers to the effect that their just-completed role-play was a good one (i.e., all steps followed and well portrayed) may object to the request that they role-play the skill a second or third time. Although valid concerns exist about the consequences of repetition and boredom when conducting training with a group of restless adolescents, the likely value of skill overlearning cannot be overstressed. To assuage trainee objections, we point to the value for professional athletic performance of grossly repetitive pregame practice (warm-ups, shoot-arounds, batting practice). Such practice makes core skills nearly automatic and frees the player to concentrate on strategic efforts.

The need to be responsive to the value of overlearning means it is common and appropriate for a Skillstreaming group to spend two, three, or even more sessions role-playing a single skill. Given that in many real-life contexts, people and events often work *against* the use of prosocial behaviors by Skillstreaming trainees, the need for overlearning becomes all the more apparent.

Stimulus Variability

The previous section concerned enhancement of transfer by means of practice and repetition—that is, by the sheer number of correct skill responses the trainee makes to a given situation. Transfer is also enhanced by the variability or range of situations to which the individual responds. Training even on two situations is better than training on one. As we noted several years ago in response to research on stimulus variability, "The implication is clear that in order to maximize positive transfer, training should provide for some sampling of the population of stimuli to which the response must ultimately be given" (Goldstein et al., 1966, p. 220). As Kazdin (1975) comments:

> One way to program response maintenance and transfer of training is to develop the target behavior in a variety of situations and in the presence of several individuals. If the response is associated with a range of settings, individuals, and other cues, it is less likely to be lost when the situations change. (p. 21)

Epps, Thompson, and Lane (1985) discuss stimulus variability for transfer enhancement as it might operate in school contexts under the rubrics "train sufficient examples" and "train loosely." They observe that generalization of new skills or behaviors can also be facilitated by training students under a wide variety of conditions. Manipulating the numbers of trainers, settings, and response classes involved in the intervention promotes generalization by exposing students to a variety of situations. Thus, if for purposes of overlearning trainees are asked to role-play a given skill correctly perhaps three times, each attempt should involve a different co-actor, a different constructed setting, and, especially, a different need for the same skill.

Identical Elements

In perhaps the earliest experimental work dealing with transfer enhancement, Thorndike and Woodworth (1901) concluded that, when there was a facilitative effect of one habit on another, it was to the extent that and because the habits shared identical elements. Ellis (1965) and Osgood (1953) have more recently emphasized the importance for transfer of similarity between characteristics of the training and application tasks. As Osgood (1953) notes, "The greater the similarity between practice and test stimuli, the greater the amount of positive transfer" (p. 213). This conclusion rests on particularly solid experimental support.

In Skillstreaming, the principle of identical elements is implemented by procedures that increase the "real-lifeness" of the stimuli (places, people, events, etc.) to which the trainer is helping the trainee learn to respond with effective, satisfying behaviors. Two broad strategies exist for attaining such high levels of correspondence between in-group and extra-group stimuli. The first concerns the location in which Skillstreaming takes place. Typically, we remain in the school or institution and by use of props and imagination try to re-create the physical feel of the real-world context in which the trainee plans to use the skill. Whenever possible, however, the Skillstreaming group leaves the formal training setting and meets in the actual physical locations in which the problem behaviors have occurred: "Fight in the schoolyard? Let's have our session there." "Argument with the principal's secretary? Let's move the group to her office." "Stare-downs in the hallway? Today's group will meet out there."

In addition to implementing identical elements via in-vivo locations, Skillstreaming employs the principle of transfer enhancement by having co-trainees in the group be the same people the youngster interacts with on a regular basis outside the group. It is especially valuable to employ such a strategy when the others involved are persons the trainee is not getting along with well and with whom more prosocially skilled interactions are desired. Suppose, for example, you are starting two Skillstreaming groups of six adolescents each. Two of the 12 youngster fight a lot. For most interventions, for behavior management purposes and for purposes of being better able to carry out the goals of the interventions, one youth would be placed in one group, the second in the other. Not so in Skillstreaming. Fight outside? Put the youths in the same group and even hope that they fight during a group session. These two youths are real-world figures for one another. They employ poor quality prosocial (and "high quality" antisocial) behaviors in their chronic inability to get along outside the group. What a fine opportunity their participation in the same group presents to teach them positive alternatives for dealing with their real-life difficulties.

Thus, if given the choice in starting a single Skillstreaming group, we would select all members from one class or unit, rather than one or a few from more than one class or unit. Live together, play together, go to class together, fight together—you get trained together. For the same reason, when implementing Skillstreaming in residential, agency, or institutional settings, our training groups are most often constructed to parallel the facility's unit, crew, cottage, or ward structure.

Mediated Generalization

The one certain commonality, which by definition is present in both training and application settings, is the individual target trainee. Mediated generalization—mediated by the trainee, not by others—is an approach to transfer enhancement that relies on instructing the trainee in a series of context-bridging self-regulation competencies (Kanfer & Karoly, 1972; Neilans & Israel, 1981). Operationally, it consists of instructing the trainee in self-recording, self-reinforcement, self-punishment, and self-instruction. Epps et al. (1985), working in a special education setting, have structured these generalization-mediating steps as follows:

Self-recording

1. The teacher sets up the data collection system—that is, selects a target behavior, defines it in measurable terms, and decides on an appropriate recording technique.
2. The teacher tries out the data collection system.
3. The teacher teaches the trainee how to use the data collection system.
4. The teacher reinforces the trainee for taking accurate data.

Self-reinforcement

1. The teacher determines how many points a trainee has earned, and the trainee simply records these.
2. The teacher tells the trainee to decide how many points should be awarded for appropriate behavior.
3. The trainee practices self-reinforcement under teacher supervision.

4. The trainee employs self-reinforcement without teacher supervision.

Self-punishment

Self-punishment, operationalized in this example by response cost (taking away points), is taught in a manner directly parallel to that just described for self-reinforcement, in which the teacher employs the technique of fading.

Self-instruction

1. The teacher models the appropriate behavior while talking through the task aloud so the trainee can hear.
2. The trainee performs the task with overt instructions from the teacher.
3. The trainee performs the task with overt self-instructions.
4. The trainee performs the task with covert self-instructions.

In recent years, as cognitive behavior modification therapies (especially those relying heavily on self-instructional processes) have grown in popularity, the use of self-mediated approaches to generalization has grown correspondingly.

MAINTENANCE-ENHANCING PROCEDURES

The persistence, durability, or maintenance of behaviors developed by diverse skills training approaches is primarily a function of the manipulation of reinforcement both during the original training and in the youngster's natural environment. There are several specific means for such maintenance-enhancing manipulation of reinforcement. We will examine first the use of rewards during the Skillstreaming session. Then we will turn to the role of the youth's family and peer system, beyond the Skillstreaming group.

During the Skillstreaming Session

Thinning of reinforcement

A rich, continuous reinforcement schedule is optimal for the establishment of new behaviors. Maintenance of such behaviors will be enhanced if the reinforcement is gradually thinned. Thinning of reinforcement will proceed best by moving from a continuous (every trial) schedule, to some form of intermittent schedule, to the level of sparse and infrequent reinforcement characteristic of the natural environment. In fact, the maintenance-enhancing goal of such a thinning process is to make the trainer-offered reinforcement schedule indistinguishable from that typically found in real-world contexts.

Delay of reinforcement

Resistance to extinction is also enhanced by delay of reinforcement. As Epps et al. (1985) note:

> During the early stages of an intervention, reinforcement should be immediate and continuously presented contingent on the desired response. . . . After the behavior becomes firmly established in the student's repertoire, it is important to introduce a delay in presenting the reinforcement. Delayed reinforcement is a closer approximation to reinforcement conditions in the natural environment. (p. 21)

Delay of reinforcement may be implemented, according to Sulzer-Azaroff and Mayer (1977), by (a) increasing the size or complexity of the response required before reinforcement is provided; (b) adding a time delay between the response and the delivery of reinforcement; and (c) in token systems, increasing the time interval between the receipt of tokens and the opportunity to spend them and/or requiring more tokens in exchange for a given reinforcer.

Fading prompts

Maintenance may be enhanced by the gradual removal of suggestions, reminders, prompts, or similar coaching or instruction. Fading of prompts is a means of moving away from artificial trainer control to more natural self-control of desirable behaviors. As with all the enhancement techniques examined here, fading of prompts should be carefully planned and systematically implemented.

Booster sessions

Notwithstanding the importance of fading of prompts, it may be necessary periodically to reinstate instruction in the specifics of given appropriate behaviors in order for those behaviors to continue in the natural environment. Booster sessions between trainer and trainee, either on a preplanned schedule or as needed, have often proven valuable in this regard (Feindler & Ecton, 1986; Karoly & Steffen, 1980).

Preparation for real-life nonreinforcement

Both trainer and trainee may take several energetic steps to maximize the likelihood that reinforcement for appropriate behaviors will occur in the natural environment. Nevertheless, on a number of occasions, reinforcement will not be forthcoming. Thus, it is important for maintenance purposes that the trainee be prepared for this eventuality. As described in our earlier examination of mediated generalization, self-reinforcement is one means of promoting maintenance when the desirable behaviors are performed correctly but are unrewarded by external sources.

Another way in which the Skillstreaming trainee may bc prepared for nonreinforcement in the natural environment is the use of graduated homework assignments. In Skillstreaming, it becomes clear at times as the homework is discussed that the real-life figure is too difficult a target, too harsh, too unresponsive, or simply too unlikely to provide reinforcement for competent skill use. When faced with this circumstance, with the newly learned skill still fragile and a potentially unrewarding homework environment, we have recast the homework assignment toward two or three more benevolent and more responsive target figures. When the trainee finally does use the skill correctly with the original target figure and receives no contingent reinforcement, his or her previously reinforced trials help minimize the likelihood that the behavior will be extinguished.

Beyond the Skillstreaming Session

Programming for reinforcement in the natural environment

The maintenance-enhancing techniques examined thus far are targeted toward the individual trainee and his or her own reinforcement schedule, instruction, booster sessions, and preparation for nonreinforcing consequences. But maintenance of appropriate behaviors also may be enhanced by efforts directed toward others, especially those in the natural environment who function as the main providers of the trainee's reinforcement.

This larger interpersonal world consists of a variety of persons—parents, siblings, peers, teachers, neighbors, classmates, and others. By their responsiveness or unresponsiveness to the trainee's newly learned skill behaviors, to a large extent they hold the destiny of these behaviors in their hands. In contrast to the earlier "inoculation" view, our view is that we all, including Skillstreaming trainees, react to what the important people in our lives think or feel about our behavior. What they reward, we are more likely to continue doing. What they are indifferent or even hostile to will fall into disuse.

During the past several years, we and others have suggested a number of ways to increase the likelihood that school, agency, and institutional staff, as well as parents and peers, will respond to trainees' newly learned skills with active approval, encouragement, or other social reward. Our discussion in chapter 3 has focused on training staff as transfer coaches to facilitate the generalization of skills developed in the Skillstreaming group to school and other real-life settings.

Parents have been our second target for procedures designed to enhance the likelihood that prosocial skills, once learned, will be maintained. Figure 11, the Skillstreaming School-Home Note, has helped increase the chance that parents will reward trainee skill performances. Each time a new skill is introduced in the group, the trainees' parents are sent this note, informing them about the purpose and value of the skill, its constituent steps, and the homework assigned (often involving the parents themselves as the homework targets). The note enumerates a series of requests to the parents to reward competent skill use, reciprocate (another type of reward) if the skill (like Negotiating) requires reciprocation, and pass on to the trainers any suggestions to make the training and homework aspects of Skillstreaming more effective and more of a collaborative effort. The Parent/Staff Skill Rating Form in Figure 12 has been used to build a skill-maintaining collaboration between the group's trainers and parents, teachers, and other significant adults.

In a major elaboration of Skillstreaming, also designed primarily to increase the likelihood of skill maintenance, Skillstreaming sessions were also provided to parents (Goldstein et al., 1989). These

FIGURE 11 School-Home Note

Student: ______________________________ Date: ________

DESCRIPTION OF LESSON

Skill name: ______________________________

Skill steps:

Skill purpose, use, value: ______________________________

____

DESCRIPTION OF SKILL HOMEWORK

____

____

REQUEST TO PARENTS

1. Provide skill homework recognition and reward.
2. Provide skill homework reciprocation.
3. Return this School-Home Note with your comments (on the back) about:
   - Quality of homework done
   - Rewards that work/don't work at home
   - Suggestions or questions regarding this skill, other skills, additional homework assignments, other ways to promote school-home collaboration, and so on
4. Please sign and return this form to ______________________________

   by ______________________________

Signature: ______________________________ Date: ________

FIGURE 12 Parent/Staff Skill Rating Form

Date: ______________________

____

(student's name)

is learning the skill of ______________________________

The steps involved in this skill are:

1. Did he or she demonstrate this skill in your presence?

   ☐ yes ☐ no

2. How would you rate his or her skill demonstration? *(check one)*

   ☐ poor ☐ below average ☐ average
   ☐ above average ☐ excellent

3. How sincere was he or she in performing the skill? *(check one)*

   ☐ not sincere ☐ somewhat sincere ☐ very sincere

Comments: ______________________________________

____

____

Please sign and return this form to ______________________

by ______________________________

Signature: ______________________________ Date: __________

parent training groups met independently from the adolescent group three out of every four sessions, the fourth being a joint meeting. In the same spirit, we have also conducted major Skillstreaming training programs for the peers of trainees. In one instance, the peers involved were fellow members of the trainees' juvenile gangs (Goldstein et al., 1994). In the second, the peers trained were fellow residents in a state facility for juvenile delinquents (Gibbs, Potter, & Goldstein, 1995). Research evaluations of these programs demonstrated, as was true for the parent training effort, that enhancing the skills of significant people in trainees' lives enhances trainees' skill maintenance. These research outcomes reflect a belief long-held by many who work with troubled and troubling youth—namely, that serious attempts to alter such behaviors for the better *must* be directed simultaneously to the youths and to the people constituting the youth's system, those persons who possess the ability to reward, punish, or ignore given trainee behaviors.

Using natural reinforcers

A final and especially valuable approach to maintenance enhancement is the use of reinforcers that occur naturally in the trainee's real-world environment. Stokes and Baer (1977) observe that

> perhaps the most dependable of all generalization programming mechanisms is the one that hardly deserves the name; the transfer of behavioral control from the teacher-experimenter to stable, natural contingencies that can be trusted to operate in the environment to which the subject will return, or already occupies. To a considerable extent, this goal is accomplished by choosing behaviors to teach that normally will meet maintaining reinforcement after the teaching. (p. 353)

Galassi and Galassi (1984) offer the following similar comment:

> We need to target those behaviors for changes that are most likely to be seen as acceptable, desirable, and positive by others. Ayllon and Azrin (1968) refer to this as the "Relevance of Behavior Rule." "Teach only those behaviors that will continue to be reinforced after training." (p. 10)

Alberto and Troutman (1982) suggest a four-step process that facilitates effective use of natural reinforcers:

1. Observe which specific behaviors are regularly reinforced and how they are reinforced in the major settings that constitute the trainee's natural environment.
2. Instruct the trainee in a selected number of such naturally reinforced behaviors (e.g., certain social skills, grooming behaviors).
3. Teach the trainee how to recruit or request reinforcement (e.g., by tactfully asking peers or others for approval or recognition).
4. Teach the trainee how to recognize reinforcement when it is offered because its presence in certain gestures or facial expressions may be quite subtle for many trainees.

To summarize, the call in the 1960s for a technology of transfer and maintenance enhancement has been vigorously answered. The technology examined in this section is substantial and still growing. Its full employment in the context of Skillstreaming is strongly recommended.

EMBEDDING SKILLSTREAMING IN A BROADER CURRICULUM

We contend that generalization of acquired skills will be further promoted if the trainee is concurrently taught an array of companion, supportive psychological competencies. As we have noted elsewhere:

> Growing evidence suggests that generalization of gain will be more likely when the psychological treatment offered is both broad and multichannel. Bandwidth in this context refers to the breadth or number of client qualities targeted by the treatment; multichannelness refers to the range of different modes of client response targeted, respectively, by the different components of the treatment. Our approach to chronically aggressive adolescents, Aggression Replacement Training, consisting of separate but integrated weekly sessions of prosocial skills training (the behavior-targeted

> component), anger control training (the affect-targeted component), and moral reasoning (the values-targeted component), is an example of such a broad band, multi-channel treatment. Demonstrations of reductions in recidivism associated with this intervention are initial evidence of its generalization promoting efficacy. (Goldstein et al., 1994, p. 103)

In 1988, we expanded Aggression Replacement Training (which itself was an earlier expansion of Skillstreaming) into a 10-course prosocial competency training program called the Prepare Curriculum (Goldstein, 1988). Although each course teaches competencies that are of value in their own right (empathy, cooperation, etc.), a major benefit of each course is its generalization-promoting relationship to the curriculum's focus, Skillstreaming. The remainder of this chapter describes the Prepare Curriculum courses, specifically in terms of each one's potential to promote skill generalization. Because the potential of Prepare Curriculum courses other than Skillstreaming has only recently begun to be investigated, assertions about them are stated in the form of hypotheses.

Prepare Curriculum Course 1: Skillstreaming

Since the early 1970s, we have sought to teach an array of interpersonal, prosocial competencies to aggressive, withdrawn, immature, developmentally delayed, and other skill-deficient children and youth. Skillstreaming's history, procedures, and curriculum have been described in earlier chapters.

Hypothesis I

Skill generalization will be promoted to the degree that the probability of competing responses is reduced.

Prepare Curriculum Course 2: Anger Control Training

Anger Control Training was developed by Feindler and her research group at Adelphi University (Feindler, 1979; Feindler & Ecton, 1986) and modified in separate programs involving incarcerated juvenile delinquents (Goldstein, Glick, Carthan, & Blancero, 1994; Goldstein,

Glick, Irwin, Pask-McCartney, & Rubama, 1989; Goldstein, Glick, Reiner, Zimmerman, & Coultry, 1986). In contrast to the direct facilitation of prosocial behavior in Skillstreaming, Anger Control Training facilitates such skill behavior indirectly, by teaching means for inhibiting anger and loss of self-control. Participating youngsters are taught, over an 8-week span, how to respond to provocations to anger by (a) identifying their external and internal anger triggers; (b) identifying their own physiological/kinesthetic anger cues; (c) using anger reducers to lower arousal via deep breathing, counting backwards, imagining a peaceful scene, or contemplating the long-term consequences of one's anger-associated behavior; (d) using reminders, or self-statements that function opposite to triggers (i.e., to lower one's anger arousal level); and (e) self-evaluating, in which one judges how adequately anger control worked and rewards oneself when it has worked well.

Prepare Curriculum Course 3: Stress Management

It has been demonstrated by Arkowitz (1977) and by Curran (1977) that individuals may possess an array of prosocial skills in their repertoires but may not employ them in particularly challenging or difficult situations because of anxiety. A youth may have learned well the Skillstreaming skill Responding to Failure, but his embarrassment at receiving a failing grade in front of his teacher or at missing a foul shot in front of his friends may engender a level of anxiety that inhibits proper skill use. A young woman may possess the problem-solving competency to plan well for a job interview but may perform poorly in the interview itself as anxiety "takes over." Anxiety and resulting inhibition may be particularly strong sources of prosocially incompetent and unsatisfying behavior in the highly peer-conscious adolescent years.

A series of self-managed procedures can substantially reduce stress-induced anxiety: the Prepare Curriculum Stress Management Training course. Participating youngsters are taught systematic deep muscular relaxation (Benson, 1975; Jacobson, 1938), meditation techniques (Assagioli, 1973; Naranjo & Ornstein, 1971), environmental restructuring (Anderson, 1978), exercise (Walker, 1979), and related means for the management, control, and reduction of stress-induced anxiety.

Hypothesis II

Skill generalization will be promoted to the degree that the trainee's level of motivation for skill utilization is increased.

Prepare Curriculum Course 4: Moral Reasoning Training

In a long and pioneering series of investigations, Kohlberg (1969, 1973) demonstrated that exposing youngsters to a series of moral dilemmas, in a discussion group that includes youngsters reasoning at differing levels of moral thinking, arouses an experience of cognitive conflict whose resolution will frequently advance a youngster's moral reasoning to that of the higher level peers in the group. Although such stage advancement is a reliable finding, as with other single interventions, efforts to use this method by itself to change overt moral behavior have yielded only mixed success (Arbuthnot & Gordon, 1983; Zimmerman, 1983). We would speculate that this is the case because such youngsters did not have in their behavioral repertoires either the skills to act prosocially or those to inhibit the antisocial. We have been able to show that Kohlbergian Moral Education has the potential to enhance prosocial behavior and reduce antisocial behavior in youngsters who have received both Skillstreaming and Anger Control Training (Goldstein et al., 1986).

Prepare Curriculum Course 5: Cooperation Training

Chronically aggressive and other skill-deficient youth have been shown to display a personality high in egocentricity and competitiveness and low in concern for others and cooperativeness (Slavin, 1980). Cooperation is a valuable social goal in itself; in addition, cooperation heightens motivation to employ prosocial skills. One major set of approaches to cooperation training, namely *cooperative learning,* has yielded outcomes of enhanced self-esteem, group cohesiveness, altruism, and cooperation itself, as well as reduced egocentricity. As long ago as 1929, Maller commented:

> The frequent staging of contests, the constant emphasis upon the making and breaking of records, and the glorification of the heroic individual achievement . . . in our present

> educational system lead toward the acquisition of competitiveness. The child is trained to look at the members of his group as constant competitors and urged to put forth a maximum effort to excel them. The lack of practice in group activities and community projects in which the child works with his fellows for a common goal precludes the formation of habits of cooperativeness. (p. 163)

It was many years before the educational establishment responded concretely to this Deweyan challenge, but when it did, it created a number of innovative, cooperation-enhancing methodologies, each of which deserves careful application and scrutiny both in general educational contexts as well as with particularly noncooperative youth. Specifically, these include Student Teams–Achievement Divisions (Slavin, 1980), Teams-Games-Tournaments (Slavin, 1980), Jigsaw Classrooms I (Aronson, Blaney, Stephan, Sikes, & Snapp, 1978), Jigsaw Classrooms II (Slavin, 1980), Group Investigation (Sharon & Sharon, 1976), and Co-op Co-op (Kagan, 1985). Using shared materials, interdependent tasks, group rewards, and similar features, these methods (applied to any content area—mathematics, social studies, etc.) have consistently yielded the interpersonal, cooperation-enhancing group and individual benefits noted previously.

In our Prepare Curriculum course, we make use of the many valuable features of cooperative learning. In addition, we respond to the physical orientation typical of many skill-deficient youth by relying heavily on cooperative sports and games. Cooperative athletics are more popular outside the United States (Fluegelman, 1981; Orlick, 1978). Collective score basketball, no-hitting football, cross-team rotational hockey, track meets based on collective fastest times, and other sports restructured to be what creators term "all touch," "all play," "all positions," "all shoot," and cooperative in other playing and scoring ways may seem strange to typical American youth, weaned on competition, but they appear to be valuable for enhancing both cooperation and skill generalization.

Hypothesis III

Skill generalization will be promoted to the degree that the trainee concurrently acquires strategies for determining which skills to employ and where, when, and with whom to use them.

Prepare Curriculum Course 6: Problem-Solving Training

Adolescents and younger children may, as Ladd and Mize (1983) point out, be deficient in such problem-solving competencies as "(a) knowledge of appropriate goals for social interaction, (b) knowledge of appropriate strategies for reaching a social goal, and (c) knowledge of the contexts in which specific strategies may be appropriately applied" (p. 130). An analogous conclusion flows from the research program on interpersonal problem solving conducted by Spivack, Platt, and Shure (1976). During early and middle childhood, as well as in adolescence, chronically aggressive youngsters are less able than their nonaggressive peers to function effectively in most problem-solving subskills, such as identifying alternatives, considering consequences, determining causality, and engaging in means-ends thinking and perspective taking.

Several programs have been developed to remediate such youngsters' problem-solving deficiencies (DeLange, Lanham, & Barton, 1981; Giebink, Stover, & Fahl, 1968; Sarason et al., 1972). Such programs represent a fine beginning, but these youths' problem-solving deficiency is substantial (Chandler, Greenspan, & Barenboim, 1974; Selman, 1980; Spivack et al., 1976), and substantial deficiencies require long-term, more comprehensive interventions. The Prepare Curriculum course is a long-term sequence of graduated problem-solving skills such as reflection, problem identification, information gathering, perspective taking, identification of alternatives, consideration of consequences, and decision making. Our initial evaluation of this sequence with an aggressive adolescent population has yielded significant gains in problem-solving skills thus defined, encouraging further development of this course (Grant, 1987). These results give substance to our assertion that

> individuals can be provided systematic training in problem solving skill both for purposes of building general competence in meeting life's challenges and as a specific means of supplying one more reliable, prosocial alternative to aggression. (Goldstein, 1981)

The potential value of problem-solving training for the enhancement of skill generalization seems high but remains untested.

Prepare Curriculum Course 7: Situational Perception Training

Once armed with the interpersonal skills necessary to respond prosocially to others (Course 1) and the problem-solving strategies underlying skill selection and use (Course 6), the chronically skill-deficient youngster may still fail to behave prosocially because he or she misreads the context in which the behavior is to occur. A major thrust in psychology during the past 15 years concerns the role of the situation or setting, as perceived by the individual, in determining overt behavior. As Morrison and Bellack (1981) comment:

> Adequate social performance not only requires a repertoire of response skills, but knowledge about when and how these responses should be applied. Application of this knowledge, in turn, depends upon the ability to accurately "read" the social environment: determine the particular norms and conventions operating at the moment, and to understand the messages being sent . . . and intentions guiding the behavior of the interpersonal partner. (p. 70)

Dil (1972), Emery (1975), and Rothenberg (1970) have each shown that emotionally disturbed youngsters, as well as those "socially maladjusted" in other ways, are characteristically deficient in such social perceptiveness. Argyle (1981) observes:

> It has been found that people who are socially inadequate are unable to read everyday situations and respond appropriately. They are unable to perform or interpret nonverbal signals, unaware of the rules of social behavior, mystified by ritualized routines and conventions of self-presentation and self-disclosure, and are hence like foreigners in their own land. (p. 37)

Argyle (1981) and Backman (1979) have emphasized this same social-perceptual deficit in their work with aggressive individuals.

We believe that the ability to "read" social situations accurately can be learned; this course attempts to teach this set of skills. Its content reflects three salient dimensions of accurate social perceptiveness, as identified by Brown and Fraser (1979):

1. The setting of the interaction and its associated rules and norms
2. The purpose of the interaction and its goals, tasks, and topics
3. The relationship of the participants—their roles, responsibilities, expectations, and group memberships

Prepare Curriculum Course 8: Understanding and Using Groups

The acute responsiveness to peer influences of adolescents and preadolescents is a truism frequently cited in both lay and professional literature on child development. It is a conclusion resting on solid research (e.g., Baumrind, 1975; Field, 1981; Guralnick, 1981; Manaster, 1977; Moriarty & Toussieng, 1976; Rosenberg, 1975). Therefore, it is especially important that the Prepare Curriculum include a segment giving special emphasis to group—especially peer—processes. The course title includes both *understanding* and *using* because both are clearly part of the instructional goal. Participating youth will be helped to understand such group forces and phenomena as peer pressure, clique formation and dissolution, leaders and leadership, cohesiveness, imitation, reciprocity, in-group versus out-group relations, developmental phases, competition, within group communication and its failure, and similar processes, with special emphasis on the role of Skillstreaming skills and skill sequences in dealing with these processes.

This course's instructional format relies heavily on group activities in which, experientially, participants can learn means for resisting group pressure, for seeking and enacting a group leadership role, for helping to build and enjoy the fruits of group cohesiveness, and so forth. Examples of specific activities for such group-experiential learning include group simulations, structured experiences, and gaming (Pfeiffer & Jones, 1974; Thayer & Beeler, 1975).

Hypothesis IV

Skill generalization will be promoted to the degree that the trainee concurrently acquires enhanced competence in assuming the perspective of the skill-use target person(s).

Prepare Curriculum Course 9: Empathy Training

Expression of empathic understanding can simultaneously serve as both an inhibitor of negative interactions and a facilitator of positive ones. Evidence clearly demonstrates that

> responding to another individual in an empathic manner and assuming temporarily their perspective decreases or inhibits one's potential for acting aggressively toward the other.... Stated otherwise, empathy and aggression are incompatible interpersonal responses, hence learning to be more skilled in the former serves as an aid to diminishing the latter. (Goldstein et al., 1986, p. 309)

The notion of empathy as a facilitator of positive interpersonal relations has an even broader base of research evidence. Our recent review of the hundreds of investigations inquiring into the interpersonal consequences of empathic responding reveal empathy to be a consistently potent facilitator of interpersonal attraction, dyadic openness, conflict resolution, and individual growth (Goldstein & Michaels, 1985).

This same review led us to define empathy as a multistage process of perception of emotional cues, affective reverberation of the emotions perceived, cognitive labeling, and communication. This Prepare Curriculum course is a multistage training program by which these four constituent components can be taught.

Hypothesis V

Skill generalization will be promoted to the degree that the trainee learns to construct, employs, and is rewarded for employing in his or her real-life environment skill sequences and combinations.

Prepare Curriculum Course 10: Recruiting Supportive Models

Aggressive youth typically are exposed regularly to highly aggressive models in their interpersonal worlds. Parents, siblings, and peers are frequently chronically aggressive individuals themselves (Knight & West, 1975; Loeber & Dishion, 1983; Robins, West, & Herjanic, 1975). Simultaneously, relatively few countervailing prosocial models are available to be observed and imitated. When prosocial models are available, however, they can make a tremendous difference in the daily lives and development of such youth. In support of this assertion are community models such as Big Brothers, Big Sisters, the Police Athletic League, Scouts, and the like. Laboratory research also consistently shows that rewarded prosocial behaviors (e.g., sharing, altruism, cooperation) are often imitated (Bryan & Test, 1967; Canale, 1977; Evers & Schwartz, 1973). Even more direct evidence suggests the value of supportive models. For example, Werner and Smith (1982), in their impressive longitudinal study of aggressive and nonaggressive youth *Vulnerable but Invincible,* clearly demonstrated that many youngsters growing up in a community characterized by high crime, high unemployment, high secondary school dropout rates, and high levels of aggressive models were indeed able to develop into effective, satisfied, prosocially oriented individuals if they had experienced sustained exposure to at least one significant prosocial model—parent, relative, teacher, coach, neighbor, or peer.

Because such models are often scarce in the real world environments of the youths the Prepare Curriculum is intended to serve, efforts must be put forth to help them identify, attract, and at times perhaps even create sources and attachments to others who function prosocially themselves and who also can serve as sustained sources of direct support for the youths' own prosocially oriented efforts. Prepare course content for cultivating supportive models relies on the Skillstreaming teaching procedures as well as on sequences of particular Skillstreaming skills.

In summary, over the past 65 years the perspective of the helping professions on generalization of gain has progressed from the assumption that treatment would have an "inoculation effect," to a train-and-hope stance, to the proactive development and use of an array of transfer- and maintenance-enhancing techniques. Longer term outcomes have improved, but positive effects limited to the place and time of intervention still frequently occur. This mixed outcome appears to characterize many helping interventions, including social skills training. We have in this chapter urged consideration, implementation, and evaluation of an additional strategy, designed to be used in conjunction with, not as a replacement for, the generalization-enhancing strategies described previously. This approach is the teaching of an array of companion psychological competencies, coordinated with social skills instruction. The Prepare Curriculum exemplifies this approach. Partial tests of simultaneous training in social skills, anger control, and moral reasoning do in fact yield evidence of relatively long-term skill use (Goldstein et al., 1989; Goldstein et al., 1994; Gibbs et al., 1995). We urge further implementation and, especially, evaluation of the generalization strategy proposed here.

CHAPTER 10
The Skillstreaming Setting: Safe and Unsafe Schools

Skillstreaming sessions take place not only in a training room, but in a place that itself is part of a larger outcome-influencing context. Very often that context is a school. The school's social and administrative climate, as well as its physical characteristics, may have profound effects not only on initial skill acquisition (Do trainees learn the skills?), but also on skill transfer and maintenance (Do they perform them?). In terms of both its social and physical ecology, is the school a safe or a dangerous environment; a skill-use promoting or a skill-use inhibiting context; a place in which teachers, administrators, and staff (and the building and grounds themselves) discourage aggression or enable it? These are the issues addressed in this chapter.

THE SOCIAL ECOLOGY OF THE SCHOOL

Administrator Qualities in Low-Aggression Schools

An extensive examination of the relevant educational literature and our personal experience over the course of three decades in hundreds of schools within and outside of the United States consistently suggest that a number of characteristics of principals, assistant principals, and other administrative personnel are associated with low levels of student aggression.

Administrator visibility and availability to students and teachers

A number of factors associated with student aggression appear connected to large institutional size. These include greater marginalization of low-performing students, higher levels of vandalism, and the impersonality that occur when students are more "numbers" than names. In smaller schools and in house-plan arrangements (a few largely autonomous smaller schools all within a single building or campus, each with its own administrators), the principal can greet students by name, make welcoming and friendly small talk at the front door at the start of each day, and, more generally, help create a feeling among students that this school is their school. It is no wonder that this administrator quality is associated with lower levels of student aggression.

Effective intelligence network

In low-aggression schools, the administrators not only know a great many students (and all staff!) by name, they are also aware of Larry's need for a math tutor, Harris's ankle injury and his readiness to return to the football team, and the state of Mary's mother's health. Because high levels of mutual trust have been developed and nurtured, such administrators also more readily learn about potentially dangerous situations, often before they take place. In the 1993–1995 school years, 47 bombs were planted in American schools. Six were fakes, 12 were found and removed before they exploded, and 29 actually went off. Several of the bombs found were discovered because students, staff, and administrators in the schools involved had earlier developed free and open lines of communication.

"Effective intelligence network" does not mean a spy system. It describes an administrative climate in which principal and assistant principal know what is likely to happen, whether these events are as serious as bombs, weapons, or gang fights—or less serious, such as bullying or harassment. All concerned (students, staff, administration) feel the school is *their* school and communicate because they care about its climate and quality.

Fair and consistent rule enforcement

Safe environments are predictable environments. A well-thought-out, widely disseminated, and fairly and consistently enforced set of school rules helps establish such predictability. "Fair" rule enforcement means rules apply to all—no teacher's pets, no whipping boys, no bias in application. "Consistent" enforcement means all administrators (and staff) are aware of and evenhandedly enforce agreed-upon rules and that, over time, each administrator does so in a manner consistent with herself or himself. The demands of fairness and consistency may be contradictory at times (e.g., consistency requires rule enforcement on all applicable occasions; fairness may require taking special circumstances into account and *not* enforcing a given rule in some instances). Both are important, but if and when a choice must be made, we believe that in the safe school fairness will be chosen.

Fair and consistent response to grievances

When students or staff believe rules have been applied unfairly or protest other decisions or actions, administrators respond by openly considering each complaint made on its issues. Although the school is not a democracy, "input from below" is listened to respectfully, considered on its merits, and acted upon if it is constructive for the parties involved as well as the school.

Support of teachers

In addition to carrying out consequences for aggression in a manner consistent with that of teachers, administrators in low-aggression schools support staff in numerous other ways. They back up teachers in angry or other confrontations with parents, citizens, or even the school board. Administrator-teacher disagreements are resolved fairly and in private. The best administrators consistently empower teachers—for example, by asking the teacher, in front of her or his class, how the teacher wants the administrator to handle a student's infraction or aggression.

Openness to intervention

We live in a global village. Via near-instantaneous mass media, the violence in one part of the world is known rapidly in other parts—even thousands of miles away. The "how to" of aggression spreads swiftly. For decades, school has been viewed as neutral turf—the fights and weapons within the community largely stayed outside of the classroom and schoolyard. When that changed, beginning mostly in the 1970s, some were surprised. We are surprised that the violence took so long to get to the schools! Schools are, after all, part of the community in which they are located. The United States is increasingly an armed camp. Why wouldn't schools also become, as they most unfortunately have, firing ranges for a portion of these arms? Yet a number of administrators fail to appreciate this national perspective. Somehow, they conclude, weapons or violence in *their* schools reflects badly on them. They fear the school board, the taxpayers, and others will view their failure to protect their schools as incompetence. So they minimize or deny the problem, fail to take precautions, and pay the price later. Competent administrators, in contrast, recognize the problem of growing aggression early in its development and take decisive steps to retard its growth.

Culturally appropriate and appreciative interventions

Many American classrooms are looking more and more like miniature United Nations. Different cultures, languages, customs, and learning styles increasingly characterize our students. To reach students academically, administrators and teachers will employ, to the degree possible, materials that are consistent with diverse backgrounds and learning styles (i.e., "appropriate") and that are selected in collaboration with persons representing the cultural groups to be taught (i.e., "appreciative"). Such appropriate and appreciative programming also characterizes the way administrators and teachers design interventions to reduce student aggression in low-violence, high-safety schools.

Ongoing assessment of interventions

Currently, over 200 different approaches to the management of student aggression are claimed to exist in America's schools. This estimate is likely accurate. Yet the effectiveness of these approaches in actually reducing violent and vandalistic incidents (or in increasing positive, alternative student behaviors) is largely unmeasured and unknown. Most such programs are initiated because they "sound good" and persist based on mere anecdote or impression. Effective administrators do more. Before the intervention begins, they carefully track the frequency of the target behaviors they hope to change (e.g., referrals to the office, fights, detentions, suspensions, calls to parents, and so forth). Systematic tracking of effectiveness continues during the intervention. If frequency of occurrence comparisons reveal that the intervention is in fact changing student behavior for the better, the intervention is continued or even expanded. If not, it is dropped and a new approach tried.

Safety-oriented policies and procedures

Schools and school systems have a number of means available to formalize safe school policies and procedures. These include, but are not limited to, controlling campus access; establishing visitor screening procedures; developing a school mission statement, codes of rights and responsibilities, dress codes, and school procedure manuals; disseminating a summary of laws pertaining to school disorder; and organizing school safety and discipline committees. Wise administrators carefully choose among these options, selecting those that best fit their own schools and particular circumstances. Rather than overrely on punitive techniques or elaborate technology, these administrators create a governance structure that works smoothly, is clearly understood by the staff who must carry it out, and is subject to change as changing circumstances warrant.

Learning from administration in high-aggression schools

Finally, it may help identify administrator qualities in low-aggression schools to enumerate governance characteristics of high-aggression schools. Research has shown that both vandalism (aggression toward property) and violence (aggression toward persons) are more frequent in schools whose administration is (a) either autocratic (too strict) or laissez-faire (too lax), rather than "firm but fair"; (b) impersonal, unresponsive, nonparticipatory, overregulated, oppressive, arbitrary, or inconsistent; (c) characterized by overuse of punitive control methods; or (d) weak or inconsistent in its support of faculty. Each of these negative qualities implies its opposite as a further administrative means to promote low-aggression schools and classrooms.

Teacher Qualities in Low-Aggression Schools

For most youngsters, classroom teachers typically assume an even more prominent role than the school's administrators in shaping the environment's social ecology. A number of teacher qualities and teaching characteristics have been shown to be associated with low levels of student aggression.

Planning for success

Before the school term starts, the teacher takes a number of steps to facilitate the transition into a well-organized and smoothly running school day. She or he gets to know the school and its formal and informal rules, the general nature of its student population, and, in at least a general way, the students in the new class. In the course of acquiring such knowledge, the teacher avoids the types of aggression-eliciting self-fulfilling prophecies that often follow when one learns that students who have been in trouble in the past are included on one's class list. Because the opening days and weeks of the term can be particularly stressful, with numerous agendas to be served, the teacher does a good bit of academic planning before school opens. Such anticipatory efforts include a long-range general outline of materials to be covered, specific 2-week lesson plans, consideration of optimal instructional methods given the particular students, and concrete preparations for the use of effective classroom behavior management procedures.

Community building

It is common in low-aggression schools for teachers to spend a considerable amount of time at the beginning of the school term creating a sense of community, of "we-ness," among students. Teacher effort is devoted to instilling a climate of cooperation and collaboration, rather than indifference to one another or competition. The curriculum is not ignored during this effort to enhance group identity; however, it is treated more as a vehicle for community building than as an academic target in its own right. Students learn one another's names and discuss likes, strengths, and similarities. Activities carried out involve the whole class, and games and simulations may be employed to enhance cooperation.

Relevant curricula

For too many youngsters, school days are "school daze." Much of what is being taught seems quite aside from both their daily lives and their future aspirations. When asked, they complain that school is boring, boring, boring. The importance of such perceived irrelevance to aggression has been suggested by a number of researchers. Csikszentmihalyi and Larsen (1978), for example, in proposing their enjoyment theory of vandalism, note that a large percentage of students find their school experiences to be especially boring and irrelevant to their planned life goals and often respond to such boredom and irrelevance with vandalistic acts directed toward the institution they perceive as its source. In this context, we note that expanded availability of vocational education opportunities, an option offered to fewer and fewer students, might serve to diminish this sense of irrelevance and boredom.

Managing the classroom

What do teachers actually *do* in low-aggression classrooms? Kounin's (1970) observations, as well as our own (Goldstein et al., 1995) suggest a clear set of important teacher behaviors. First, the teacher knows what is going on. Such *with-it-ness* is communicated to the class in a number of ways, including swift and consistent recognition and, when necessary, consequating of low-level behaviors likely to grow into disruptiveness or more serious aggression. Closely connected to such attentiveness is *overlapping,* the ability to more-or-less simultaneously manage two or more classroom events, be they instructional or disciplinary. *Smoothness,* the ability to transition from one activity to another without downtime, is a third facilitative teacher behavior. Downtime is a good time for boredom-engendered acting out; avoiding or minimizing it significantly deters such behaviors. Another way to minimize boredom is by instructing with *momentum,* maintaining a steady sense of progress or movement throughout a particular lesson, class, or school day. A *group focus,* the ability to keep the entire class involved in a given instructional activity, also diminishes the likelihood of student aggression. Finally, and, to us, an especially significant contributor to a low-aggression classroom, is the teacher's communication of consistently *optimistic expectations.* Students live up to (and, unfortunately, also down to) what important people in their lives—such as teachers—expect of them. The teacher who expects an eighth grader to read at fifth-grade level because of his or her past record, or a sibling's past poor performance in the same school, or the neighborhood the student came from will likely be rewarded with fifth-grade performance. By contrast, the teacher who, in the wide variety of ways available to teachers, lets the student know he or she can achieve and will have the teacher's help along the way is likely to motivate the student to be more academically successful and less behaviorally disruptive. The message is, Expect the best of your students—you may well get it.

Rules and procedures

Teachers with low-aggression classrooms teach rules and procedures as explicitly as they teach academic content. Rules are guidelines governing appropriate and inappropriate student behaviors. Procedures are what students need to know and follow in order to meet their own personal needs and to perform routine instructional and classroom housekeeping activities. Effective teachers integrate their rules and procedures—as well as consequences for not following them appropriately—into their classroom routine. In chapter 8 we presented a series of useful "rules for use of rules" as they might profitably be applied within the Skillstreaming group: few in number, negotiated with students, stated behaviorally, stated positively, sent home to parents, and posted in the classroom. All of these recommendations apply to the use of rules for the class as a whole. As with rules, classroom procedures need to be explicitly taught; one cannot assume that students know them. Unlike rules, which ought to be taught "up front," procedures usually can be explained as the need arises—for obtaining help, leaving the room, using bathroom passes, disposing of trash, and so forth. As with rules, however, procedures need to be clearly stated, closely monitored, consistently followed, and consequated when not followed.

Consistent application of rules and procedures provides clear expectations for student behavior and establishes that the teacher is in charge of the classroom. Yet such consistency is difficult to maintain over time. Teachers get tired, harried, overworked, distracted. It sometimes seems easier to "let it go just this once." When this occurs, students are quick to get the message that perhaps "just this once" can become more than once, and that maybe the boundary between what is and is not acceptable is no longer firm. They begin to push a bit, to test limits in order to reestablish the boundary line between "yes" and "no." As a result, the foundation for a safe, low-aggression classroom begins to erode. "Every time with every student" may be a difficult rule of consistency to follow without exception, but it should be every teacher's goal.

Home-school collaboration

Schools have always sought home-school contact, but many times contact has meant the school (the experts) telling the parents (the nonexperts) what to do. Traditionally, contact has taken the form of PTA meetings, parent-teacher conferences, or, as far too often is the case with youngsters who behave aggressively, the "bad news call" in which the school phones home to, in effect, tell the parents what a lousy kid they have. Teachers able to create and maintain low levels of aggression in their classrooms often view and deal with parents quite differently. They recognize and appreciate parents as the youth's first (and continuing) teachers and actively seek contact early and frequently, seeing this contact as an opportunity to collaborate in a supportive, mutually reinforcing way. Such an attitude helps create the opportunity for the parents, the teacher, and, it is hoped, the student to become a problem-solving team. The opportunity for the student to be successful in school is enhanced, and, because those experiencing success are less likely to be disruptive, aggression in the classroom is diminished.

In middle and high schools, parents may not always be welcomed by their own adolescent children due to peer pressure and anticipated embarrassment. When this is the case, parent participation programs can be designed to avoid or minimize this potential problem. For example, parents might assist students in classes other than their own child's or work outside of the classroom tutoring or mentoring students in need of extra assistance. In both of these instances, parent connection to the academic enterprise in general and the school in particular is heightened, thus increasing the chances of parents' attentiveness to their youngsters' academic progress and receptivity to teacher initiatives.

Learning from teachers in high-aggression schools

Just as it is useful to consider administrative qualities in schools with high levels of aggression, much may be gained by examining the behavior of teachers in such settings. Remboldt's (1994) exploration of the several ways in which teachers may actually promote, encourage, or enable student aggression is most helpful for this purpose. Stated simply, student aggression will be reduced and a safe, skill-use-promoting environment enhanced to the degree that teachers avoid the following aggression-enabling behaviors:

1. Ignoring student complaints of being threatened
2. Avoiding high-violence school locations
3. Ignoring low-level violence: put-downs, bullying, harassment
4. Ignoring student threats of planned violence
5. Ignoring rumors about students who may have weapons
6. Failing to intervene or report witnessed student violence
7. Excusing violent behavior of "good kids" as necessary for self-defense

Aggression is an unpleasant act to confront. Nonetheless, it is the duty of the responsible adults in the school to do so.

THE PHYSICAL ECOLOGY OF THE SCHOOL

Physical qualities of the school as a whole, including classrooms and other locations, may operate for better or for worse with regard to student aggression, student safety, and the presence or absence of skill-use-promoting environmental features.

School size has been shown a number of times to be an important correlate of school violence. The larger the school, the more likely the per capita occurrence. The lower size-to-violence relationship in smaller schools may grow from the easier identification of students and by students with the school. In larger schools, such consequences as nonparticipation in governance, impersonality, and crowding may come into play. As Garbarino (1973) observes:

> As schools increase in size, student objections to strict controls, the lack of choice . . . and uniformity rather than individual attention are very likely to increase as well. As an adaptation to an unresponsive environment, many students (and staff) will become passive and uncommitted to school; others will react with anger or frustration. The marginal or unsuccessful student is particularly likely to experience the negative effects of the large school and,

> as increasing numbers of such students are compelled to remain in school, the likelihood of their "finding" one another and forming educationally and socially deviant peer groups is enhanced. As school size increases, administration becomes more centralized, bureaucratic, and inflexible. Large educational bureaucracies and the accompanying proliferation of rules also decreases innovation, responsiveness, and adaptation, a fact which has important implications for school crime. Controlling crime in the school requires not only a personalized social climate, but considerable flexibility and responsiveness to the need for change. (p. 28)

Precise optimal numbers are difficult to establish. Stefanko (1989) asserts that a school with over 2,000 students is too large. Turner and Thrasher (1970) suggest 700 to 1,000 as appropriate; Rosenberg (1975) proposes 400 to 500 as an optimal range. Whatever the specific number, a consensus favoring smaller schools for aggression reduction is apparent. Concern for this feature of the physical ecology of our schools is certainly justifiable.

An ecological concern closely related to school size (i.e., number of registered students) is the amount of space available to these students (i.e., crowding). Crowding is a second significant correlate of in-school aggression, with such behavior occurring more frequently in more crowded school locations—stairways, hallways, and cafeterias—and less frequently in classrooms. Other chronic "causality zones" include lavatories, entrance and exit areas, and locker rooms. These locations tend to be prime venues for "bad looks," bumps, or other common provocations that set off student fights.

In addition to size of the student body and the density of interaction, the school's general physical appearance and state of repair also operate for better or worse vis à vis student aggression. High-aggression schools tend to be poorly maintained, poorly lit, and run down. Of concern is not the age of the school per se, but the school's overall appearance. Vandalism-prone schools are, for example, "rigid, uninspired buildings with cheerless square rooms and bleak hallways, surrounded by asphalt and chain link fences [which] foster perceptions of a rigid, harsh authoritarian environment" (Stefanko, 1989, p. 16).

One interesting study of the physical ecology of the school sought to identify school qualities associated with low violence and vandalism levels. Pablant and Baxter (1975) constituted 16 pairs of schools—one having a high violence and vandalism rate, the other low—and matched them within each pair for size, ethnic composition, grade level, and location. As the authors had predicted, the schools with lower rates (a) were characterized by better aesthetic quality and maintenance of school property; (b) were located in more densely populated areas with higher activity levels; (c) permitted a more unobstructed view of school property by surrounding residents; and (d) were located in better illuminated neighborhood areas.

Let us move from the school building as a whole to the classroom. What does a low-aggression classroom look like? Each child has his or her own desk or space. The aisles are wide enough to be "traffic-friendly," making bumps and congestion less likely. The teacher's desk is placed so the teacher can see the entire room. The room has personal touches here and there to convey the message that "this is our room" to the students. The classroom's door is lockable, made of solid wood, with a small window of unbreakable glass.

If the school has had a history of high levels of student violence, physical changes may have been made to enhance its real and perceived safety. Grillwork may cover the windows, or polycarbon windows may have been put in place. Desks and tables may be bolted to the floor, and a graffiti board may be affixed to one wall. Other features and arrangements may serve to decrease the opportunity to initiate violence or vandalism. Ideally, such measures are put in place only after careful consideration of their possible negative impact on the school's primary educational mission.

When a youngster in a school or other setting behaves aggressively, most typically the adults in his or her environment behave as if the source of the aggression exists entirely within the youth. In their punitive, administrative, counseling or other interventions, they (teacher, administrator, security officer, etc.) assume that aggression is in the perpetrator, by the perpetrator, and from (and only from) the perpetrator. Although perpetrator qualities do largely determine where, when, how, and even if an aggressive act will occur, the social and physical ecology in which the youth functions also plays a crucial part. The environmental features examined in this chapter all influence whether or not youths will be likely to learn, perform, and generalize the positive, nonaggressive, prosocial behaviors they learn via Skillstreaming. Skillstreaming group trainers, master trainers, and program and school administrators must be competent teachers, program planners, and performance monitors. They must also be effective social and physical ecologists.

CHAPTER 11
Future Directions and Opportunities

This book has been a recounting and updating of the Skillstreaming method. Drawing upon our own 20 years of experience in its use, and that of its many practitioners, we have examined its background, arrangements, and procedures. We have considered obstacles to its success, generalization of its outcomes, nature of its contexts, and more. We have, as best we are able, brought Skillstreaming up to date.

It is clear from this review, however, that since its inception Skillstreaming has been—as it should be—an intervention in transition, open to change as practitioner insights and researcher findings warrant. We hope that it will always be an intervention in transition, and in the present chapter we offer some future directions for program revision and growth. This is our brainstorming chapter, our place to suggest possible leads and opportunities for enhancing Skillstreaming's impact and effectiveness. Based on past and current trends, or seeds perhaps barely planted, or fantasies about what we would like to see happen though we currently have little idea how to get there, we offer in this chapter our hopes for the development of Skillstreaming over the next 20 years.

District and Schoolwide Application

For any given youngster, the potential for success in a Skillstreaming program (skill acquisition and generalization) is greatly enhanced the more his or her environment is involved in the program. The environment can provide motivation, skill awareness, reward for correct skill use, prompting and coaching following incorrect skill use, and so on. (It is in large part for such benefits that in the next section we advocate the increased future use of family and peer-group Skillstreaming.) Most current Skillstreaming groups in most secondary and elementary schools in the United States involve one or a small number of teachers who, usually on their own initiative, institute this approach. In some places, the program infuses an entire school and, in a few places, an entire school district.

We hope these district and schoolwide applications will increase in the years ahead. The advantages are several. The most obvious benefit is that the number of students whose interpersonal skill repertoires may be expanded is larger. When this is the case, trainees' prosocial interactions work toward their reciprocal and mutual benefit. When entire schools or districts are involved, including especially the lower grade levels, Skillstreaming is more likely to operate at a preventive level, before youngsters get into difficulty in school, at home, or with the law. Such an approach, with *all* students in the system becoming Skillstreaming trainees, also avoids the labeling or stigmatizing that may occur when youngsters are pulled out of class for special programming. Further, large-scale program involvement means many more teachers or other staff are involved as trainers, thus providing greater opportunity for such persons to receive mutual benefit from peer supervision.

Finally, as noted earlier, many different interventions are now in place in America's schools, each designed to reduce school violence. Most commonly these well-intentioned efforts rest on a base of anecdote and impression and only rarely on sound, objective evaluation. Involving greater numbers of trainees, schoolwide or districtwide, greatly enhances the possibility of such evaluation.

It is thus our hope and expectation that, in Skillstreaming's next 20 years, those initiating Skillstreaming programs will knock first not on the classroom door but instead at the door of the school principal or district superintendent.

Alternative Schools

School administrators are in a quandary. Their primary responsibility is the education of the children in their charge, yet at times a disruptive minority of students severely diminishes the quality of education for the majority. When such disruptiveness is chronic, out-of-school suspension has been the most frequent solution. While suspension perhaps frees up the school environment to better serve its intended purpose, the possibilities for redirecting the suspended youths are diminished. Far too often, out-of-school suspension at best yields idle days in front of the television set or hanging out on the street or at worst transfer of the disruptiveness and even major antisocial behavior from school to community.

One encouraging response to this educational dilemma that has emerged in recent years is the alternative school. While taking diverse physical, administrative, and curricular forms, alternative schools are those to which seriously disruptive students are assigned for their educational programming. Typically, they are locations apart from the schools in which students are causing difficulties. Alternative schools that work well share a number of common features. Small classes are led by a motivated, empathic, and culturally diverse teaching staff. High behavioral and academic performance standards and expectations are set and are clearly communicated to students. Full days of study and rigorous work loads characterize the school day, as do continual monitoring and evaluation, reflected in daily attendance records and progress reports. Staff make a major effort to be responsive to individual student learning styles.

High-quality alternative schools are remedial in their guiding orientation, not just "soft jails." A substantial role therefore exists in this alternative context for Skillstreaming. A number of alternative schools in the United States already devote a significant portion of their efforts to skill-enhancement programming, and we hope more will do so. The exclusionary practice of suspension provides no opportunity to teach youths alternative, prosocial means for dealing with events that led to the behaviors of concern. Some refer to the use of Skillstreaming in the alternative school as "instructional discipline." Whatever it is called, it is a method particularly relevant to the difficult youths now so frequently dealt with by removal from school altogether.

Family Skillstreaming

Aggression is a difficult behavior to change. It is primarily a learned behavior, and many youths learn it well. From their early years, aggressive youths live with family and peers who repeatedly model, reward, and overtly encourage actions hurtful to others. In a real sense, aggression is for many adolescents a behavior that "works"—both for them and for the significant people in their lives.

In school, agency, and institutional settings, many chronically aggressive youths participate in interventions such as Skillstreaming, designed to teach prosocial alternatives to such antisocial behaviors. The youngster learns to negotiate, maintain self-control, or walk away from a confrontation, rather than incite, attack, or fight. He or she then uses one of these prosocial alternatives in the presence of one of his familial or peer "trainers" of aggression. Rather than reward the constructive attempt, family member or peer responds critically, disparagingly, even with hostility: "No son of mine is going to be a punk. You hit him before he hits you!" says the parent.

In chapter 9, we emphasized the significance for enduring skill effectiveness of the responses of important people in the lives of trainees. As suggested, such responses may be for better or for worse. To increase the likelihood that they will be for better (i.e., rewarding, supportive, and even reciprocal to newly learned skills), we have carried out programs in which these significant others also participate in Skillstreaming training programs. Guzzetta's (1974) early effort of this type yielded higher levels of empathy by adolescent trainees when *both* they and their parents (either separately or together) underwent Skillstreaming training focused on this skill.

In later evaluations, we showed not only greater skills learning and reduced aggression, but also reduced recidivism—defined in terms of rearrest—when both delinquent youths and their families (parents and siblings) participated in our skills training sequence (Goldstein et al., 1989). Further, both we (Goldstein, Glick et al., 1994) and Gibbs et al. (1995) have found similarly positive prosocial consequences for both immediate behaviors (more skilled, less aggressive) and recidivism when the "family" being trained along with the delinquent youths was not their biological family, but their adolescent peer group. In Goldstein, Glick et al. (1994) the peers were fellow members of 10 highly aggressive youth gangs. Our skills training in this program was always directed to the gang as a unit. For Gibbs et al. (1995), trainees—again taught together as a group—were all of the residents on a particular unit in a state facility for delinquent youth. The success of these programs strongly encourages interventions in which skills training is directed to both the aggressive or otherwise skill-deficient youths and the significant people in their lives, who hold within their grasp the rewards and punishments influential in determining the sustained outcome of such training.

As Dryfoos (1994) accurately notes in her book *Full-Service Schools,* the American school has increasingly provided not only traditional educational services but also a wide variety of other services for children and adolescents. For students and their families, school is increasingly a community resource, offering all manner of health-related and social service programming. Such growing expansion of the purposes of schools in the United States is likely to continue. We strongly urge that family Skillstreaming become a regular offering in this context.

New Intervention Combinations

Skillstreaming teaches skills, no more, no less. A great deal of research convincingly demonstrates that youngsters who participate in a series of Skillstreaming sessions do indeed acquire new interpersonal competencies. That, as they say, is the good news. It is also true, unfortunately, that a substantial number of the skills learned are not performed by trainees where and when needed. In chapter 9, we examined at length the bases for such failures of generalization, as well as potential means for their remediation. In an extended and fruitful research program, we identified yet one further approach to increasing skill transfer and maintenance—namely, the construction and implementation of new intervention combinations.

We reasoned that some youngsters failed to display newly learned (prosocial) skill behaviors because earlier learned (antisocial) behaviors, such as aggression, were prepotent (i.e., well practiced and thus more readily available and frequently used). For this purpose, we incorporated Feindler's Anger Control Training into our developing new intervention package. Yet, one could know what to do (from Skillstreaming) and what not to do (from Anger Control Training) and still decide that an aggressive response in a given situation was optimal. We therefore added a third component, one targeted to trainee values, to increase their motivation to choose the prosocial skill alternative. This component was Kohlberg's (1969, 1973) Moral Education. This three-part intervention combination we labeled Aggression Replacement Training (ART; Goldstein et al., 1986). An extended series of efficacy evaluations conducted by ourselves as well as others makes clear that ART is a potent means both for initial skills acquisition and for extended skill use over time and settings.

We have shared this brief history of Aggression Replacement Training as an example of both an intervention package and the line of reasoning that led to its construction. The Prepare Curriculum (see chapter 9) is a second new intervention combination; Gibbs et al.'s (1995) EQUIP program is a third. In each instance, skill acquisition, performance, and generalization were substantially enhanced by going beyond Skillstreaming to larger rationally composed intervention combinations. The success of these initial efforts speaks well for their continued integration in schools and agencies to serve youngsters yet to come.

Virtual Reality

Reel-to-reel tape recorders and filmstrips are largely gone from the educational scene. Computer-assisted instruction in several forms is here and growing. Over the technological horizon, as a potentially outstanding means of teaching interpersonal skills, lies one of technology's most promising expressions—*virtual reality.* Throughout this book, we have time and again returned to concerns for what is clearly the single most significant and challenging dimension of *all* intervention efforts, including Skillstreaming—namely, generalization. In several ways, we have made the point that new interpersonal skills are readily acquired but often fail to transfer or be maintained. To the technology of generalization enhancement techniques discussed in chapter 9, we hope and expect to add virtual reality. We would first expect Skillstreaming to be offered in an interactive computer program via CD-ROM. This effort would eventually evolve into a virtual reality program.

Broadly, virtual reality is an interactive, three-dimensional multisensory experience that the user experiences as real. Pioneered by the military for training purposes (e.g., simulated midair refueling, air traffic control, mechanized vehicle operation), virtual reality has also been employed in medicine (e.g., simulated surgeries), architecture (e.g., to "walk through" buildings planned but yet to be built), and entertainment (e.g., simulations and games). Its use for prosocial skills training in educational settings has been proposed (Muscott & Gifford, 1994) but not yet undertaken.

Virtual reality systems can mimic the real world with computer generated images, sounds, and sensations in such a way that the user gets the feeling of, as Aukstakalnis and Blatner (1992) put it, "being actually inside and surrounded by the environment" (p. 4). Possible simulated environments would easily include an active classroom, crowded hallway, busy schoolyard, moving school bus, and other school-related sites that are frequent locations for mischief, mayhem, or worse.

The hardware needed to create a virtual reality environment is still quite expensive. It includes a computational engine (the single or multiple computers that create and drive the virtual experience); a head-mounted display (which contains the visual display system, tracker, earphones, and microphone); data gloves (which enable the user to detect the position and orientation of his or her hands and thus to interact with objects in the virtual environment); and a flying mouse (which is similar to a conventional computer mouse but with the added ability to move up and down in the air.

Muscott and Gifford (1994) observe:

> One possible structure begins with a student entering a virtual world depicting an environment familiar to them, for example, a school. This school is populated with computer controlled agents that play the parts of other students and teachers. The student enters a preset situation . . . an agent or group of agents whose preprogrammed goal is to instigate a situation. This turn of events forces the user to react to stimuli from the antagonist agent. The user is given three or four choices of actions that (s)he can take. These actions are natural and implicit to the situation. They could include both motor and social behaviors such as moving away, starting to fight, or making any number of verbal comments. Each choice leads to a different branch of the program which in turn plays out the consequences of the student's choice. Branches can lead to more decision points which lead to more branches. In this way we can lead a child through an example situation and show intuitively the outcome of many different courses of action. (p. 429)

Doing our illustrative work for us, Muscott and Gifford continue:

> Let's take a look at one specific example. Take the social skill, responding to peer pressure, which is part of the *Skillstreaming the Elementary School Child* program

> (McGinnis & Goldstein, 1984). In one VR role play scenario we could create a cafeteria in a local elementary school. Paul, the child who is entering the virtual world, is the user. Students could be eating and conversing with each other. One student, a fifth grader named Bruiser, who is streetwise and savvy, could lean over to Paul, who is socially immature and withdrawn, and tell him to take the lunch money left on the table by a classmate. . . . Scaling could be used to increase the physical size of Bruiser as he makes the request and shrivel the size of Paul if he chooses to give in to the threat. Should Paul choose to use his previously learned sequence of social skills as outlined in the Skillstreaming program, his character could be enlarged to be equal to or larger in stature than his adversary. Each choice that the students make in this computer generated scenario could be observed by classmates and the teacher. Additional conditions such as the teacher walking over could be included to increase the complexity of the experience. . . . Simulations could be set up to reinforce prosocial behaviors so that repeated antisocial behaviors terminate the game, much like a tilt in a pinball game. Once the scenario has been completed, the entire episode can be replayed on a screen and analyzed by the class. Copies of the interaction could be taken home on videotape for review by the students and their families. The advantages over real role playing include the novel nature of the experience, the potential for convincing the participants that they are immersed in an experience that has real outcomes, the ability to heighten various aspects of the situation, and the ability to play out a variety of consequences that could not be played out in a real situation (e.g., a fight breaking out). (pp. 429–430)

Muscott and Gifford have creatively detailed the manner in which the technology of virtual reality might be applied to the interpersonal skills training domain, emphasizing not only skill acquisition but also generalization. Their observations chart a valued course along which to begin our virtual exploration.

Training for the Work World

Both public and private schools in the United States typically do poorly at training youths in the wide variety of job-related interpersonal skills that foster success in the employment market. Finding a job for which to apply, applying for it, being hired, keeping the job over time, performing in it effectively, and progressing along a career ladder all demand the skilled performance of a number of interpersonal behaviors. In chapter 7, we described what might be viewed as "advanced Skillstreaming," in which youths are taught skill sequences and combinations adequate to deal with the complex interpersonal challenges life frequently brings. The area of employment is full of such challenges. The school of the future, we would hope, would incorporate into its curricula and regularly offer employment-oriented advanced Skillstreaming.

In 1976, Goldstein, Sprafkin, and Gershaw implemented a program of just such skill sequence training for employment purposes. We used a somewhat different terminology then. Skillstreaming in its first incarnation was called Structured Learning Therapy. And the skill combinations taught were termed "application skills." Our trainee population also differed from that of concern here. Back then we focused on the hundreds of adult psychiatric patients who, after lengthy mental hospital stays, were about to be "deinstitutionalized" into community living, for which they typically were ill-prepared. Among their longstanding and major skill problems were the very types of employment-relevant skills in which contemporary adolescents are also deficient. Therefore, we urge the school of the future to devote major attention to such illustrative skill combinations as the following.

Job seeking

Skill 46: Deciding on Your Abilities

Skill 47: Gathering Information

Skill 49: Making a Decision

Skill 41: Getting Ready for a Difficult Conversation

Skill 14: Convincing Others

Job keeping

Skill 50: Concentrating on a Task
Skill 9: Asking for Help
Skill 12: Following Instructions
Skill 38: Responding to Failure
Skill 47: Gathering Information
Skill 21: Rewarding Yourself

Organizing time

Skill 45: Setting a Goal
Skill 50: Concentrating on a Task
Skill 46: Deciding on Your Abilities

Dealing with crises

Skill 15: Knowing Your Feelings
Skill 26: Using Self-Control
Skill 48: Arranging Problems by Importance
Skill 46: Deciding on Your Abilities
Skill 45: Setting a Goal

Receiving telephone calls

Skill 1: Listening
Skill 17: Understanding the Feelings of Others
Skill 32: Answering a Complaint
Skill 11: Giving Instructions
Skill 18: Dealing with Someone Else's Anger

These few examples illustrate a much broader need. Using the 50 Skillstreaming skills, trainers and trainees can construct a great number of individualized, employment-relevant skill sequences. These can then be modeled, role-played, and practiced to the criterion of effective use in the real world of work.

Mass Media Skillstreaming

Ninety-nine percent of American homes have a television set, and two-thirds have two or more. The average adolescent in the United States watches television approximately 35 hours per week. Many of these same youngsters learn their lessons in how and why to behave aggressively not only from family and peers, but also during these 5 hours per day of television viewing. In fact, there are an average of 6 violent acts per hour on prime time evening programming and 25 such acts per hour on Saturday morning cartoons. By age 16, youngsters have seen 200,000 violent acts, about 30,000 of them murders or attempted murders.

Four distinctly negative consequences have been reliably demonstrated to occur as a result of this remarkably high diet of televised violence. The first has been called an *aggressor effect* or a *copy-cat effect.* A substantial minority of viewers will actually do what they have seen portrayed on the screen. Males copy more than females, younger children more than older. There is more copying the more violence the youngster has seen, when the violence depicted is justified by the show's script ("He deserved it"), when it is shown in "how-to" detail, and when it has that odd quality of painlessness so often portrayed—no suffering, injury, or bodily consequences. The second demonstrated effect has been called the *victim effect.* Increased fearfulness, mistrust, and self-protectiveness are its main features. Viewers come to see the world as more threatening, less safe. A third and perhaps most serious consequence is the *desensitization effect.* As the violence shown increases in intensity and explicitness, we adapt, we adjust, we get used to it. Higher and higher levels become tolerable—spurting arteries, chainsaw dismemberment, violent rape. Finally, there is the *appetite effect.* Its main feature is increased self-initiated behavior to further expose oneself to violent behavior. The more seen, the more efforts there are to view yet additional violence, which in turn feeds back on and facilitates the first three effects.

Our nation's adolescents and younger children go to two schools every day. One is a building with teachers, classrooms, books, chalk, and erasers. The other is a box at home with a large picture tube, dials, cables, and the demonstrated ability to exert a tremendous influence. Thus far, most of that influence has been for the worse.

Television can also function for the better. A small amount of research has demonstrated the prosocial effects television viewing may have. Helpfulness, charity, intervention in crisis situations, empathy, and other positive and antiviolent consequences have been demonstrated as a result of viewing prosocial programming. As part of this prosocial effort, it is our hope that the modeling methodology central to Skillstreaming, as well as its interpersonal skills curriculum, will find a place in future mass media programming.

Appreciative Programming

Adolescent Skillstreaming trainees are male and female; of lower, middle, and sometimes upper socioeconomic status; Caucasian, African American, Hispanic American, Asian American, and other; from families with roots in any of several dozen nations; and in numerous other ways from truly diverse cultures. We have earnestly sought to be responsive to such cultural diversity in our implementations of Skillstreaming to date, and we urge that programming appreciative of cultural diversity continue to be a prime feature of its future implementation.

What skills are to be taught? Constructed of which particular behavioral steps? What is the optimal size and membership of the trainee group? Who might serve as the most effective models—their age, gender, behavior? How might training procedures ideally be altered to better fit trainee learning styles or channels of accessibility? And, perhaps most important, what appear to be productive means for enhancing the likelihood that, once learned, skill use will generalize to the youths' real-world environments? Each of these important questions may be at least in part answerable by assuming an appreciative perspective on intervention.

Appreciative programming is an attempt to plan and carry out interventions in a manner involving major and sustained consultation with members of the group represented by Skillstreaming trainees, whether in terms of gender, age, ethnicity, or otherwise. An accurate and sensitive understanding of culture-associated issues, beliefs, motivations, perceptions, and aspirations cannot adequately be obtained from the outside looking in. Such understanding, and its implications for alterations to the Skillstreaming process, depends on input from members of the cultural group involved.

The following life concerns, and many, many more, are shaped by cultural traditions and standards: The meaning and value of aggression. The degree to which such skills as negotiation, compromise, or ignoring may be seen as weakness rather than strength. One's perception of family and its significance in one's life. Means for acquiring status and perceived success. One's place in the community. It is vital to the success of future Skillstreaming efforts that trainers be adequately appreciative of and responsive to such cultural definitions, as well as to the role their own cultural values and biases may play in facilitating or inhibiting responsiveness.

District and schoolwide use in alternative schools, family Skillstreaming, new intervention combinations, virtual reality, training for the world of work, mass media Skillstreaming, and appreciative programming are but some of our hopes for the future development and application of Skillstreaming. In addition, distance learning, instructional means already well out of the starting gate, ought to be commonplace. Perhaps Skillstreaming lessons interactively telecast in city W will be received and learned in cities X, Y, and Z.

This book has introduced a number of procedural, curricular, and group management refinements of the Skillstreaming approach, based on the successful outcomes of most Skillstreaming evaluation studies and in the spirit of "If it ain't broke, don't fix it." Nonetheless, the original (1980) and present (1997) incarnations of Skillstreaming for adolescents contain the same 50 skills, delivered by essentially the same demonstration-rehearsal-feedback-generalization procedures. Perhaps such constancy will not be appropriate in the years ahead, as the adolescent population in the United States expands from its current 25 million to an expected 32 million by 2015, as new and perhaps yet even more multicultural trainee populations are served, as new and higher levels of prosocial skill deficiency become manifested in an ever-more aggressive society. As yet unforeseeable social and cultural changes may lead to the desirability of both additional Skillstreaming skills and more individualized training techniques. However, present applications of Skillstreaming are diverse and substantial. Its future promise seems bright.

APPENDIX A
Skillstreaming Research: An Annotated Bibliography

Training and treatment approaches that aspire to help people lead more effective and satisfying lives must not be permitted to endure simply on the basis of the faith and enthusiasm of their proponents. Whether psychoeducational or of another type, such interventions must be subjected to careful, objective, and continuing evaluation. Only those approaches that research demonstrates to be effective deserve continued use and development. Those that fail such evaluations justly must not survive.

The present appendix references and briefly describes studies examining the effectiveness of Skillstreaming. Generally, these investigations combine to support the effectiveness of Skillstreaming with diverse trainee groups and diverse skill-training targets. Continuing tests of Skillstreaming's efficacy are necessary. But on the basis of this evidence, we confidently recommend its continued and expanded use with adolescents.

Beeker, M., & Brands, A. (1986). Social skills training in retardates. *Bedragstherapie, 19,* 3–14.

A series of studies employing Skillstreaming with mentally retarded individuals. Authors report substantial levels of enhanced skill competency and interpersonal interaction.

Berlin, R.J. (1979). *Teaching acting-out adolescents prosocial conflict resolution with Structured Learning Therapy.* Unpublished doctoral dissertation, Syracuse University.

Trainees: Adolescent boys with history of acting-out behaviors (N=42)

Skill(s): Empathy

Experimental design: (1) Skillstreaming for empathy in conflict situations, (2) Skillstreaming for empathy in nonconflict situations, versus (3) No-treatment control by (a) High Interpersonal Maturity Level versus (b) Low Interpersonal Maturity Level

Results: Skillstreaming for empathy (conflict) significantly > Skillstreaming for empathy (non-conflict) or controls on acquisition. High I level significantly > Low I level. No significant generalization effects.

Bleeker, D.J. (1980). *Structured Learning Therapy with skill-deficient adolescents.* Unpublished master's thesis, Syracuse University.

Trainees: Adolescent boys identified as disruptive in regular junior high school (N=55)

Skill(s): Responding to a complaint

Experimental design: A 2×2 plus control factorial design reflecting high versus low perceived (by the trainee) similarity between Skillstreaming trainer and generalization test figure by high versus low objective similarity, plus brief instructions control

Results: Significant effects for both Skillstreaming and similarity

Bryant, S.E., & Fox, S.K. (1995). Behavior modeling training and generalization: Interaction of learning point type and number of modeling scenarios. *Psychological Record, 45,* 495–503.

Trainees: Undergraduate volunteers (N=80)

Skill(s): Cooperative problem solving

Experimental design: One versus three modeling exposures by rule code versus summary label skill step presentation

Results: Significant interaction effect on skill generalization attributable to the superiority of the multiple model plus rule code condition

Cobb, F.M. (1973). *Acquisition and retention of cooperative behavior in young boys through instructions, modeling, and structured learning.* Unpublished doctoral dissertation, Syracuse University.

Trainees: First-grade boys (N=80)

Skill(s): Cooperation

Experimental design: (1) Skillstreaming for cooperation, (2) instructions plus modeling of cooperation, (3) instructions for cooperation, (4) attention control, (5) no-treatment control

Results: Skillstreaming significantly > all other conditions on both immediate and delayed tests of cooperative behavior

Coleman, M., Pfeiffer, S., & Oakland, T. (1991). *Aggression Replacement Training with behavior disordered adolescents.* Unpublished manuscript, Department of Special Education, University of Texas.

An evaluation of the effectiveness of a 10-week Aggression Replacement Training program used with behavior-disordered adolescents in a residential treatment center. Results indicated significant increases in skill knowledge but not actual overt skill behaviors.

Cross, W. (1977). *An investigation of the effects of therapist motivational predispositions in Structured Learning Therapy under task versus relationship stress conditions.* Unpublished doctoral dissertation, Syracuse University.

Trainees: College undergraduates (N=120)

Skill(s): Skillstreaming group leadership skills

Experimental design: Task-motivated versus relationship-motivated trainers by task-relevant versus relationship-relevant trainee-originated trainer stress plus no-treatment control

Results: Relationship-motivated trainers significantly > task-motivated trainers on Skillstreaming effectiveness under task threat conditions

Curulla, V.L. (1990). *Aggression Replacement Training in the community for adult learning disabled offenders.* Unpublished manuscript, Department of Special Education, University of Washington, Seattle.

Trainees: Young adult offenders in a community treatment center (N=67)

Skill(s): "Tendency toward recidivism" skills

Experimental design: Compared (1) Aggression Replacement Training, (2) Aggression Replacement Training absent its Moral Education component, (3) no-training control

Results: Significant reduction in tendency toward recidivism in (1), but not (2) or (3)

Cutierrez, M.C., & Hurtado, S. (1984). Effects of transfer enhancers on generalization of social skills in handicapped adolescents. *Revista de Analisis del Comportamiento, 21,* 81–88.

Trainees: Physically handicapped adolescents (N=15)

Skill(s): Social competency subset

Experimental design: Three training conditions: (1) Skillstreaming plus transfer enhancers, (2) Skillstreaming, (3) wait-list control

Results: For skill acquisition, both (1) and (2) > (3). For skill maintenance at 4-week follow-up probe, (1) > (2) and (3).

Davis, C. (1974). *Training police in crisis intervention skills.* Unpublished manuscript, Syracuse University.

Description of a training program utilizing Skillstreaming to develop skills among a 225-person urban police force for the competent handling of family fights, rapes, accidents, suicides, and variety of other crises common in everyday police work. Skills taught included (1) preparing to deal with threats to your safety, (2) calming the emotional aspects of the crisis, (3) gathering relevant information, and (4) taking appropriate action.

Dominquez, Y.A., & Garrison, J. (1977). Towards adequate psychiatric classification and treatment of Mexican American patients. *Psychiatric Annals, 7,* 86–96.

Responding to the several ways in which the core procedures of the Skillstreaming approach were selected for use in response to characteristic learning styles of low-income populations, this article recommends Skillstreaming as one of four intervention methods for bridging the gap between primarily Anglo middle class therapists and primarily lower class Chicano patients.

Edelman, E. (1977). *Behavior of high versus low hostility-guilt Structured Learning trainers under standardized client conditions of expressed hostility.* Unpublished master's thesis, Syracuse University.

Trainees: Nurses and attendants at state mental hospital (N=60)

Skill(s): Structured Learning trainer group leadership behaviors

Experimental design: Skillstreaming trainers high versus low in hostility-guilt by (1) high, (2) low, or (3) no expressed client hostility

Results: High hostility-guilt trainers responded to trainee hostility with significantly less counterhostility than did low hostility-guilt trainers. Low hostility-guilt trainers significantly > counterhostility to hostile than neutral trainees; no similar effect for high hostility-guilt trainers.

Epstein, M., & Cullinan, D. (1987). Effective social skills curricula for behavior-disordered students. *Pointer, 31,* 21–24.

A comparative description of six social skills curricula for secondary and elementary behavior-disordered students.

Figueroa-Torres, J. (1979). Structured Learning Therapy: Its effects upon self-control of aggressive fathers from Puerto Rican low socioeconomic families. *Hispanic Journal of Behavioral Sciences, 14,* 345–354.

Trainees: Family-abusing fathers (N=60)

Skill(s): Self-control

Experimental design: Skillstreaming for self-control versus no treatment

Results: Skillstreaming-trained fathers significantly > controls on self-control on acquisition and minimal generalization criteria

Fleming, D. (1977). *Teaching negotiation skills to preadolescents.* Unpublished doctoral dissertation, Syracuse University.

Trainees: Adolescents (N=96)

Skill(s): Negotiation

Experimental design: High self-esteem versus low self-esteem adolescents by adult Skillstreaming trainer versus peer Skillstreaming trainer by presence versus absence of pre-Skillstreaming enhancement of expectancy for success

Results: All Skillstreaming groups showed significant increase in negotiation skill acquisition but not transfer. No significant effects observed between trainer type or between esteem level effects.

Fleming, L.R. (1977). *Training aggressive and unassertive educable mentally retarded children for assertive behaviors, using three types of Structured Learning Therapy.* Unpublished doctoral dissertation, Syracuse University.

Trainees: Mentally retarded children (N=96)

Skill(s): Assertiveness

Experimental design: (1) Skillstreaming for assertiveness plus fear-coping training, (2) Skillstreaming for assertiveness plus anger-coping training, (3) Skillstreaming for assertiveness, (4) attention control by aggressive versus unassertive children

Results: All three Skillstreaming groups significantly > controls on increase in assertiveness. No significant in vivo transfer effects.

Friedenberg, W.P. (1971). *Verbal and nonverbal attraction modeling in an initial therapy interview analogue.* Unpublished master's thesis, Syracuse University.

Trainees: Psychiatric inpatients (all male, mostly schizophrenic; N=60)

Skill(s): Attraction

Experimental design: High versus low attraction to interviewer displayed via nonverbal cues by high versus low attraction to interviewer displayed via verbal cues

Results: Significant modeling effect for attraction for the high-high group (high modeled attraction using both the verbal and nonverbal cues) as compared to the other three conditions

Gibbs, J.C., Potter, G.B., & Goldstein, A.P. (1995). *The EQUIP program: Teaching youth to think and act responsibly through a peer-helping approach.* Champaign, IL: Research Press.

EQUIP is a multimethod intervention for delinquent youth consisting of a positive peer culture, Aggression Replacement Training, and means to correct disordered, criminal thinking. This book describes these procedures in "how-to" detail and presents an extensive and successful evaluation of their efficacy when used with a sample of incarcerated delinquents.

Contents: (1) Introduction and Description; (2) Developing a Positive Youth Culture; (3) Equipping with Mature Moral Judgment; (4) Equipping with Skills to Manage Anger and Correct Thinking Errors; (5) Equipping with Social Skills; (6) Program Implementation; (7) Developing a Positive Staff Culture; (8) Program Adaptations and Expansions

Gibbs, J.C., Potter, G.B., Goldstein, A.P., & Brendtro, L.K. (1996). Frontiers in psychoeducation: The EQUIP model with antisocial youth. *Reclaiming Children and Youth, 4,* 22–29.

A discussion of the intervention challenges presented by antisocial youth, the development of earlier psychoeducational methods, and the rationale that led to the construction of the EQUIP approach, which combines skills-oriented and peer-oriented components.

Gilstad, R. (1977). *Acquisition and transfer of empathic responses by teachers through self-administered and leader-directed Structured Learning Training and the interaction between training method and conceptual level.* Unpublished doctoral dissertation, Syracuse University.

Trainees: Elementary school teachers (N=60)

Skill(s): Empathy

Experimental design: Skillstreaming for empathy training conducted by a trainer in "standard" Skillstreaming groups versus Skillstreaming for empathy self-instructional training format by high versus low conceptual level trainees, plus attention control

Results: Both Skillstreaming groups significantly > control on empathy acquisition and transfer criteria. No significant effects between Skillstreaming conditions or between conceptual levels.

Glick, B., & Goldstein, A.P. (1987). Aggression Replacement Training. *Journal of Counseling and Development, 65,* 356–362.

A description of the Skillstreaming, anger control training, and moral reasoning training components of Aggression Replacement Training, including the institutional evaluation studies on juvenile delinquent populations conducted to ascertain its effectiveness.

Golden, R. (1975). *Teaching resistance-reducing behavior to high school students.* Unpublished doctoral dissertation, Syracuse University.

Trainees: High school students (N=43)

Skill(s): Resistance-reducing behavior (reflection of the other's feeling plus appropriate assertiveness regarding one's own view in an interpersonal conflict situation with authority figures)

Experimental design: (1) Discrimination training ("good" modeled skill behavior versus "bad" modeled skill behavior) for resistance-reducing behavior, (2) Skillstreaming for resistance-reducing behavior, (3) no-treatment control by internal versus external locus of control

Results: Both discrimination training and Skillstreaming significantly > controls on resistance-reducing behavior on both acquisition and generalization criteria. No significant locus of control effects.

Goldstein, A.P. (1973). A prescriptive psychotherapy for the alcoholic patient based on social class. In *Proceedings of the Second Annual Alcoholism Conference of NIAAA.* Washington, DC: U. S. Department of Health, Education and Welfare.

An overview of the development of Skillstreaming and relevant evaluative research, with special emphasis upon its implications for alcoholic patients.

Goldstein, A.P. (1973). *Structured Learning Therapy: Toward a psychotherapy for the poor.* New York: Academic.

A comprehensive statement of the origin and rationale for Structured Learning Therapy and a full presentation of relevant evaluative research. Modeling scripts from both inpatient and outpatient studies are presented.

Contents: (1) Psychotherapy: Income and Outcome; (2) Personality Development and Preparation for Patienthood; (3) Language and Malcommunication; (4) Psychopathology and Sociopathology; (5) Structured Learning and the Middle-Class Patient; (6) Structured Learning and the Lower-Class Inpatient; (7) Structured Learning and the Lower-Class Outpatient; (8) Structured Learning and the Working-Class Paraprofessional; (9) Future Directions; (10) Appendix: Modeling Scripts

Goldstein, A.P. (1981). *Psychological skill training: The Structured Learning technique.* New York: Pergamon.

A comprehensive description of Skillstreaming research and application with diverse trainee populations. Trainer manuals for implementing this approach are also provided.

Contents: (1) Introduction; (2) Origins of Structured Learning; (3) Mental Hospital Patient Trainees; (4) Adolescent Trainees; (5) Child Trainees; (6) Change Agent Trainees; (7) Other Trainees; (8) Issues in Skill Training: Resolved and Unresolved

Goldstein, A.P. (1985). Prosocial education: Aggression replacement via psychological skills training. *International Journal of Group Tensions, 15,* 6–26.

Prosocial education is the intentional teaching of a curriculum of effective interpersonal, conflict management, and anger control skills. This paper describes the rationale underlying this strategy and means for its implementation.

Goldstein, A.P. (1985). Structured Learning Therapy. In D. Larsen (Ed.), *Giving psychology away.* San Francisco, Brooks/Cole.

A review of prescriptive need for new interventions to serve underserved populations. Describes how and why Skillstreaming was developed to meet the psychoeducational needs of low-income trainee populations.

Goldstein, A.P. (1986). Teaching prosocial skills to antisocial youth. In C.M. Nelson, R.B. Rutherford, & B.T. Wolford (Eds.), *Special education and the criminal justice system.* Columbus, OH: Charles E. Merrill.

A review of the educational and correctional philosophy underlying a psychoeducational intervention orientation toward changing antisocial behavior. Described are the Skillstreaming and Aggression Replacement Training implementations of this philosophy.

Goldstein, A.P. (1988). *The Prepare Curriculum: Teaching prosocial competencies.* Champaign, IL: Research Press.

A major expansion of the Skillstreaming approach, this 10-course curriculum collectively proposes that a diverse array of prosocial competencies can be taught, learned, and effectively employed in various settings by diverse trainees.

Contents: (1) Introduction; (2) Problem-Solving Training; (3) Interpersonal Skills Training; (4) Situational Perception Training; (5) Anger Control Training; (6) Moral Reasoning Training; (7) Stress Management Training; (8) Empathy Training; (9) Recruiting Supportive Models; (10) Cooperation Training; (11) Understanding and Using Groups; (12) Transfer and Maintenance; (13) Classroom Management; (14) Future Directions

Goldstein, A.P. (1989). Refusal skills: Learning to be positively negative. *Journal of Drug Education, 19,* 271–277.

A description of the application of the Skillstreaming method and curriculum to the problem of alcohol or drug refusal by adolescents. In effect, responding to the failure of a "just say no" philosophy, the goal is to teach youth how to say no in challenging situations.

Goldstein, A.P. (1989). Teaching alternatives to aggression. In D. Biklen, D.L. Ferguson, & A. Ford (Eds.), *Schooling and disability.* Chicago: The National Society for the Study of Education.

A review of psychoeducational philosophy and procedures for use in expanding the behavioral repertoires of chronically aggressive youngsters, thus making alternatives to aggression more available and more likely.

Goldstein, A.P. (1991). El curriculum de preparation. *Revista de Analisis del Comportemiento, 4,* 108–129.

A description in Spanish of the background, methods, constituent courses, and range of applicability of the Prepare Curriculum.

Goldstein, A.P. (1992). Teaching prosocial behavior to low-income youth. In P. Pedersen & J. Carey (Eds.), *Multicultural counseling in schools.* Fairfield, CT: Greenwood.

An examination of the developmental life path typical for low-income youth and the manner in which this path leads to particular channels of accessibility for learning. The Skillstreaming, Aggression Replacement Training, and Prepare Curriculum methods are each described, as is their compatibility with a low-income learning style.

Goldstein, A.P. (1993). Interpersonal skills training interventions. In A.P. Goldstein & C.R. Huff (Eds.), *The gang intervention handbook.* Champaign, IL: Research Press.

A review of the Skillstreaming approach—its rationale, procedures, and curriculum—and the main expansions of this intervention (Aggression Replacement Training, Prepare Curriculum) as they have been and might be employed with gang youth.

Goldstein, A.P. (1995). Coordinated multitargeted skills training: The promotion of generalization enhancement. In W. O'Donohue & L. Krasner (Eds.), *Handbook of psychological skills training: Clinical techniques and applications.* Boston: Allyn & Bacon.

An examination of the problem of generalization failure, which has plagued interventions of all kinds, including those oriented toward teaching prosocial skills. Reviewed are the content and research base of procedures for the enhancement of both setting generalization (transfer) and temporal generalization (maintenance) of newly learned skills.

Goldstein, A.P., Amann, L., & Reagles, K.W. (1990). *Refusal skills: Preventing drug use in adolescents.* Champaign, IL: Research Press.

A presentation of procedures and materials needed to focus Skillstreaming efforts on refusal skills needed by adolescents being pressured to use drugs or alcohol. Designates 20 of the 50 Skillstreaming skills for adolescents as core refusal skills.

Contents: (1) Introduction; (2) Issues in Drug Use; (3) The Refusal Skill Curriculum; (4) Refusal Skill Training Procedures; (5) Transfer and Maintenance; (6) Skillstreaming Curriculum for Adolescents; (7) Commonly Abused Drugs

Goldstein, A.P., Blake, G., Cohen, R., & Walsh, W. (1971). The effects of modeling and social class structuring in paraprofessional psychotherapist training. *Journal of Nervous and Mental Disease, 153,* 47–56.

Trainees: Nurses and attendants (N=135)

Skill(s): Attraction, empathy, warmth

Experimental design: High, low, and no attraction modeling by middle, low, and no social class structuring

Results: Significant modeling by social-class structuring interaction effects for attraction, empathy, and warmth.

Goldstein, A.P., Blancero, D.A., Carthen, W., & Glick, B. (1994). *The prosocial gang: Implementing Aggression Replacement Training.* Thousand Oaks, CA: Sage.

A description of the use of Aggression Replacement Training, an expansion of Skillstreaming, with 10 criminally oriented youth gangs. Comparison of treated versus untreated gang youth reveals significant benefits from participation, including reduced recidivism.

Contents: (1) Gangs in the United States; (2) Gang Aggression; (3) A Historical Review; (4) Aggression Replacement Training: Background and Procedures; (5) Aggression Replacement Training: Evaluations of Effectiveness; (6) Gangs in the Hood; (7) The Program: Management and Evaluation; (8) Future Perspectives: Enhancing Generalization of Gain

Goldstein, A.P., Coultry, T., Glick B., Gold, D., Reiner, S., & Zimmerman, D. (1985). Entrenaminto en sustitucion de agresion: Un modelo de intervencion integral endelincuencia. *Revista de Analisis del Comportamiento, 2,* 325–335.

Aggression Replacement Training—both methods and evaluation research—is described as it has been and might be profitably used with delinquent youth.

Goldstein, A.P., Coultry, T., Glick B., Gold, D., Reiner, S., & Zimmerman, D. (1986). Aggression Replacement Training: A comprehensive intervention for the acting-out delinquent. *Journal of Correctional Education, 37,* 120–126.

Aggression Replacement Training—both methods and evaluation research—is described as it has been and might be profitably used with delinquent youth.

Goldstein, A.P., Erne, D., & Keller, H. (1985). *Changing the abusive parent.* Champaign, IL: Research Press.

Child abuse is a major and growing social problem. This book describes the development and application of a Skillstreaming approach to teaching parenting skills to chronically abusive parents.

Contents: (1) Child Abuse: The Problem; (2) Child Abuse: Intervention Approaches; (3) An Introduction to Structured Learning; (4) Preparing for Structured Learning; (5) Conducting the Structured Learning Group; (6) Structured Learning

Skills for Abusive Parents; (7) A Typical Structured Learning Session; (8) Managing Problem Behaviors; (9) Structured Learning in the Agency Context; (10) Structured Learning Research

Goldstein, A.P., Gershaw, N.J., Glick, B., Sherman, M., & Sprafkin, R.P. (1978). Training aggressive adolescents in prosocial behavior. *Journal of Youth and Adolescence, 7,* 73–92.

A comprehensive review of research employing Skillstreaming with aggressive adolescent trainees. Study designs and findings are presented and examined. The value of prescriptively designed practice and research is emphasized. Special emphasis is placed upon transfer of training, particularly reasons for its infrequency and possible means for its enhancement.

Goldstein, A.P., Gershaw, N.J., Klein, P., & Sprafkin, R.P. (1980). *Skillstreaming the adolescent: A structured learning approach to teaching prosocial skills.* Champaign, IL: Research Press.

A practitioner-oriented trainer's manual presenting the background, procedures, materials, and measures necessary to organize and manage Skillstreaming groups for adolescents.

Contents: (1) A Prescriptive Introduction; (2) Structured Learning: Background and Development; (3) Structured Learning Procedures for Adolescents; (4) Selection and Grouping of Trainees; (5) Structured Learning Skills for Adolescents; (6) Structured Learning in Use; (7) Management of Problem Behavior in a Structured Learning Group; (8) Structured Learning Research: An Annotated Bibliography

Goldstein, A.P., Gershaw, N.J., Klein, P., & Sprafkin, R.P. (1983). Structured Learning: A psychoeducational approach to teaching social competencies. *Behavior Disorders, 8,* 161–170.

A presentation of the Skillstreaming method—its history, development, procedures, and curriculum—as it might optimally be employed with troubled and troubling youth.

Goldstein, A.P., Gershaw, N.J., & Sprafkin, R.P. (1975). Structured Learning Therapy: Skill training for schizophrenics. *Schizophrenia Bulletin, 14,* 83–88.

A description of the procedures that constitute Skill-streaming and their evaluation. Relevant modeling tapes and related materials are also described. This article places special emphasis on the community-relevant needs of a variety of types of schizophrenic patients and the manner in which daily living skill deficits may be systematically reduced by the use of this approach.

Goldstein, A.P., Gershaw, N.J., & Sprafkin, R.P. (1976). *Skill training for community living: Applying Structured Learning Therapy.* New York: Pergamon.

A detailed, applied presentation regarding the use of Skillstreaming with adult psychiatric patients and similar trainees.

Contents: (1) Introduction; (2) Trainer Preparation and Training Procedures; (3) Inpatient and Outpatient Trainees; (4) Modeling Tapes; (5) Skillstreaming Research; (6) Supplement A: Trainer's Manual; (7) Supplement B: Trainee's Notebook; (8) Supplement C: An Advanced Skillstreaming Session; (9) Supplement D: Resistance and Resistance Reduction; (10) Supplement E: Skill Surveys

Goldstein, A.P., Gershaw, N.J., & Sprafkin, R.P. (1979). *I know what's wrong, but I don't know what to do about it.* Englewood Cliffs, NJ: Prentice Hall.

A self-administered version of Skillstreaming, presented in stepwise, concrete detail. Oriented in content and procedures toward the general adult population.

Contents: (1) How to Use This Book; (2) Knowing What's Wrong: Diagnosing the Problem; (3) Getting Ready: Preparing to Change Your Behavior; (4) What to Do about It: Changing Your Behavior; (5) Personal Skills in Action: Guidelines, Steps and Examples; (6) Making Changes Stick; (7) More Personal Skills

Goldstein, A.P., Gershaw, N.J., & Sprafkin, R.P. (1979). Structured Learning Therapy: Training for community living. *Psychotherapy: Theory, Research and Practice, 16,* 199–203.

An examination of existing approaches to the resocialization of mental hospital patients, which, while often yielding positive changes at the termination of treatment, typically do not result in enduring transfer of such changes into community functioning. Skillstreaming is described as an intervention deliverable in association with transfer-enhancing features, thus overcoming this typical weakness in generalization.

Goldstein, A.P., Gershaw, N.J., & Sprafkin, R.P. (1985). Structured Learning: Research and practice in psychological skills training. In L. L'Abate & M.A. Milan (Eds.), *Handbook of social skills training and research.* New York: Wiley.

Explores the history and development of psychological skills training in general and the Skillstreaming approach in particular, including its constituent methods, curriculum, and research evaluations.

Goldstein, A.P., Gershaw, N.J., & Sprafkin, R.P. (1995). Teaching the adolescent: Social skills training through Skillstreaming. In G. Cartledge & J.F. Milburn (Eds.), *Teaching social skills to children and youth.* Boston: Allyn & Bacon.

A description of the Skillstreaming method as utilized with adolescent populations. Examined are the developmental relevance of this approach, methods and application, curriculum, means for enhancing trainee motivation, and the Aggression Replacement Training and Prepare Curriculum expansions of the approach.

Goldstein, A.P., & Glick, B. (1987). *Aggression Replacement Training: A comprehensive intervention for aggressive youth.* Champaign, IL: Research Press.

A description of a major expansion of the Skillstreaming approach. Skillstreaming teaches youths skill alternatives to aggression. Anger control training inhibits use of the alternative antisocial behaviors. Moral Education provides the concern with the rights of others that encourages use of the skills taught. This book describes this three-part approach and provides evaluation results for two investigations of its effectiveness with incarcerated delinquents. *Contents:* (1) Juvenile Delinquency: Incidence and Interventions; (2) The Behavioral Component of ART: Structured Learning; (3) Trainer's Manual for Structured Learning; (4) The Affective Component of ART: Anger Control Training; (5) Trainer's Manual for Anger Control Training; (6) The Cognitive Component of ART: Moral Education; (7) Trainer's Manual for Moral Education; (8) Program Description and Evaluation; (9) Future Directions; (10) Administrator's Manual for ART

Goldstein, A.P., & Glick, B. (1987). Angry youth—reducing aggression. *Corrections Today, 49,* 38–42.

A description of the purposes, methods, curricula, and evaluations of Aggression Replacement Training as used with juvenile delinquent populations.

Goldstein, A.P., & Glick, B. (1994). Aggression Replacement Training: Curriculum and evaluation. *Simulation and Gaming, 25,* 9–26.

A description of the history, development, and evaluation of Aggression Replacement Training (i.e., Skillstreaming, anger control training, and Moral Education). Its curriculum, methods, and outcomes in institutional, community, and school settings are presented.

Goldstein, A.P., & Glick, B. (1995). Aggression Replacement Training for delinquents. In R.R. Ross, D.H. Antonowicz, & G.A. Dhlival (Eds.), *Going straight: Effective delinquency prevention and offender rehabilitation.* Ottawa, Canada: AIR Training and Publications.

A review of research examining the effectiveness of Aggression Replacement Training used with juvenile delinquents in residential, community, and school settings. Conclusion: "With considerable reliability [ART] appears to promote skills acquisition and performance, improve anger control, decrease the frequency of acting-out behaviors, and increase the frequency of constructive, prosocial behaviors."

Goldstein, A.P., & Glick, B. (1995). Artful research management: Problems, process and products. In B. Glick & A.P. Goldstein (Eds.), *Managing delinquency programs that work.* Laurel, MD: American Correctional Association.

A review of research on Aggression Replacement Training, with particular emphasis on problems that may arise, and solutions that may work, when one organizes and conducts an extended intervention evaluation program. Considered are matters of program planning, training, monitoring, supervision, maintenance of motivation, coordination of functions, data collection and analysis, and results dissemination.

Goldstein, A.P., Glick, B., Irwin, M.J., Pask-McCartney, C., & Rubama, I. (1989). *Reducing delinquency: Intervention in the community.* New York: Pergamon.

A description of the use of Aggression Replacement Training with 24 juvenile delinquent youth and, for a subsample, their families (parents and siblings). Results of this project indicated that on several criteria, including recidivism, administering the intervention to both the delinquent trainees and their family members yielded significantly greater skill generalization than did working with the youths only or with a wait-list control.

Contents: (1) Community-Based Intervention: A Review; (2) Aggression Replacement Training: Background and Procedures; (3) The Youth Program; (4) The Family Program; (5) Program Evaluation; (6) Administration of Community-Based Programs; (7) Future Perspectives

Goldstein, A.P., & Goedhart, A.W. (1973). The use of Structured Learning for empathy enhancement in paraprofessional psychotherapist training. *Journal of Community Psychology, 1,* 168–173.

<u>EXPERIMENT I</u>

Trainees: Student nurses (N=74)

Skill(s): Empathy

Experimental design: (1) Skillstreaming for empathy (professional trainers), (2) Skillstreaming for empathy (paraprofessional trainers), (3) no-training control

Results: Both Skillstreaming conditions significantly > no-training control on both immediate and generalization measures of empathy

<u>EXPERIMENT II</u>

Trainees: Hospital staff (nurses, attendants, occupational therapists, recreational therapists; N=90)

Skill(s): Empathy

Experimental design: (1) Skillstreaming plus transfer training for empathy, (2) Skillstreaming for empathy, (3) no-training control

Results: Significant Skillstreaming effect for immediate empathy measurement (Groups 1 and 2 > 3); significant transfer effect for generalization empathy measure (Group 1 > 2 and 3)

Goldstein, A.P., Goedhart, A., Hubben, J., Martens, J., Schaaf, W., Van Belle, H., & Wiersema, H. (1973). The use of modeling to increase independent behavior. *Behaviour Research and Therapy, 11,* 21–42.

<u>EXPERIMENT I</u>

Trainees: Psychiatric outpatients (all psychoneurotic or character disorders; N=90)

Skill(s): Independence (assertiveness)

Experimental design: (1) Independence modeling, (2) dependence modeling, (3) no modeling

Results: Warm and no-structuring modeling conditions significantly > cold structuring and control on independence for males and females

EXPERIMENT II

Trainees: Psychiatric outpatients (all psychoneurotic or character disorders; N=60)

Skill(s): Independence (assertiveness)

Experimental design: Independence modeling plus (1) structuring model as warm, (2) structuring model as cold, (3) no structuring of model by male versus female plus a no-structuring/no-modeling control

Results: Warm and no-structuring modeling conditions significantly > cold structuring and control on independence for males and females

EXPERIMENT III

Trainees: Psychiatric inpatients (all schizophrenic; N=54)

Skill(s): Independence (assertiveness)

Experimental design: Presence versus absence of independence modeling by presence versus absence of instructions to behave independently

Results: Significant main and interaction effects for modeling and instructions on independence as compared to no-modeling/no-instructions conditions

Goldstein, A.P., Goedhart, A.W., & Wijngaarden, H.R. (1973). Modeling in de psychotherpie bij patienten uit de lagere sociale klasse. In A.P. Cassee, P.E. Boeke, & J.T. Barendregt (Eds.), *Klinische Psychologie in Nederland.* Deventer: Van Loghum Slaterus.

A presentation (in Dutch) of the origin, rationale, and current status of Skillstreaming. The particular usefulness of this approach with low-income Dutch and American patient populations is stressed.

Goldstein, A.P., Green, D.J., Monti, P.J., & Sardino, T.J. (1977). *Police crisis intervention.* New York: Pergamon.

An applied text oriented toward law enforcement and criminal justice personnel concerned with effective handling of diverse order maintenance and police service matters.

Contents: (1) Introduction; (2) Crisis Intervention Manual for Police; (3) Family Disputes; (4) Mental Disturbance; (5) Drug and Alcohol Intoxication; (6) Rape; (7) Suicide; (8) A Method for Effective Training: Structured Learning; (9) Structured Learning Manual for Police Trainers

Goldstein, A.P., Hoyer, W., & Monti, P.J. (Eds.). (1979). *Police and the elderly.* New York: Pergamon.

The special needs and problems of elderly citizens as related to the role of police is the primary focus of this book. Among the topics addressed are means by which police, other criminal justice personnel, and the elderly themselves can assist in preventing crime against the elderly and minimizing its psychological import when it does occur. Use of Skillstreaming to train police in these roles is systematically presented.

Contents: (1) The Elderly: Who Are They? (2) Fear of Crime and the Elderly; (3) Minority Elderly; (4) Crime Prevention with Elderly Citizens; (5) Police Investigation with Elderly Citizens; (6) Assisting the Elderly Victim; (7) Training the Elderly in Mastery of the Environment; (8) Training Police for Work with the Elderly

Goldstein, A.P., & Pentz, M.A. (1984). Psychological skill training and the aggressive adolescent. *School Psychology Review, 13,* 311–323.

Reviews the history of psychological skills training and the evaluation research reported in the literature focused on the effectiveness of this method. Problems of trainee motivation, prescriptive utilization, and the facilitation of generalization are discussed.

Goldstein, A.P., & Sorcher, M. (1973). Changing managerial behavior by applied learning techniques. *Training and Development Journal, March,* 36–39.

An examination of inadequacies characterizing most managerial training approaches, including the singular focus on attitude change rather than behavior change, unresponsiveness to changing characteristics of the

American work force, and insufficient attention to the implications of research on human learning for managerial training. The manner in which Skillstreaming seeks to correct these inadequacies and provide an effective approach to training managers is presented.

Goldstein, A.P., & Sorcher, M. (1974). *Changing supervisor behavior.* New York: Pergamon.

An applied presentation of Skillstreaming, oriented toward the teaching of supervisory skills, especially in industry. Relevant evaluative research in an industrial context is reported.

Contents: (1) Supervisor Training: Perspectives and Problems; (2) A Focus on Behavior; (3) Modeling; (4) Role-Playing; (5) Social Reinforcement; (6) Transfer Training; (7) Applied Learning: Application and Evidence

Greenleaf, D. (1992). The use of programmed transfer of training and Structured Learning Therapy with disruptive adolescents in a school setting. *Journal of School Psychology, 20,* 122–130.

Trainees: Adolescent boys with history of disruptive behavior (N=43)

Skill(s): Helping others

Experimental design: Skillstreaming versus no Skillstreaming by transfer programming versus no transfer programming plus attention control

Results: Skillstreaming showed significantly greater skill acquisition, minimal generalization, and extended generalization than either no Skillstreaming or attention control. Transfer programming did not augment this significant transfer effect.

Gutride, M.E., Goldstein, A.P., & Hunter, G.F. (1973). The use of modeling and role playing to increase social interaction among schizophrenic patients. *Journal of Counseling and Clinical Psychology, 40,* 408–415.

Trainees: Psychiatric inpatients (all "asocial, withdrawn"; N=133)

Skill(s): Social interaction (an array of conversational and physical approach skill behaviors)

Experimental design: Skillstreaming versus no Skillstreaming by psychotherapy versus no psychotherapy by acute versus chronic

Results: A substantial number of significant interaction and main effects for Skillstreaming across several social interaction behavioral criteria

Gutride, M.E., Goldstein, A.P., & Hunter, G.F. (1974). Structured Learning Therapy with transfer training for chronic inpatients. *Journal of Clinical Psychology, 30,* 277–280.

Trainees: Psychiatric inpatients (all "asocial, withdrawn"; N=106)

Skill(s): Social interaction in a mealtime context

Experimental design: (1) Skillstreaming plus transfer training, (2) Skillstreaming plus additional Skillstreaming, (3) Skillstreaming, (4) companionship control, (5) no-treatment control

Results: A substantial number of significant effects for Skillstreaming across several social interaction behavioral criteria. Significant effects are mainly for Groups 1, 2, and 3 compared to the control conditions, rather than between the Skillstreaming conditions.

Guzzetta, R.A. (1974). *Acquisition and transfer of empathy by the parents of early adolescents through Structured Learning Training.* Unpublished doctoral dissertation, Syracuse University.

Trainees: Mothers of early adolescents (N=37)

Skill(s): Empathy

Experimental design: (1) Skillstreaming for empathy taught to mothers and their children together, (2) Skillstreaming for empathy taught to mothers and their children separately, (3) Skillstreaming for empathy taught to mothers only, (4) no-training control

Results: All three Skillstreaming conditions showed significantly greater acquisition and transfer of empathy than did no-training control mothers. No significant difference existed between Skillstreaming conditions.

Hayman, P.M., & Weiss-Cassady, D.M. (1981). Structured Learning Therapy with mentally ill criminal offenders. *Journal of Offender Counseling, Services and Rehabilitation, 6,* 41–51.

Trainees: Mentally ill incarcerated offenders (N=22)

Skill(s): Social competency subset

Experimental design: A 12-session series of Skillstreaming meetings provided to six trainees. Pre-post changes compared to 16 no-treatment controls

Results: Treatment versus no-treatment significant differences on skill acquisition and on change measure of psychopathology

Healy, J.A. (1975). *Training of hospital staff in accurate effective perception of anger from vocal cues in the context of varying facial cues.* Unpublished master's thesis, Syracuse University.

Trainees: Nurses and attendants (N=44)

Skill(s): Recognition of vocal cues of anger

Experimental design: (1) Skillstreaming for vocal and facial cues, (2) Skillstreaming for vocal cues with exposure to but no training for facial cues, (3) Skillstreaming for vocal cues, (4) no-training control

Results: All Skillstreaming groups significantly > controls on vocal training and test cues; no significant generalization to new (untrained) vocal cues

Healy, J.A. (1979). *Structured Learning Therapy and the promotion of transfer of training through the employment of overlearning and stimulus variability.* Unpublished doctoral dissertation, Syracuse University.

Trainees: Unassertive adolescents in regular junior high school (N=84)

Skill(s): Assertiveness

Experimental design: A 3 × 2 plus control factorial design reflecting the presence versus absence of stimulus variability by three levels of overlearning, plus brief instructions control

Results: Significant effect for overlearning, not for stimulus variability

Hollander, T.G. (1970). *The effects of role playing on attraction, disclosure, and attitude change in a psychotherapy analogue.* Unpublished doctoral dissertation, Syracuse University.

Trainees: V.A. hospital psychiatric inpatients (all males; N=45)

Skill(s): Attraction to the psychotherapist

Experimental design: Role-play versus exposure versus no-treatment control

Results: No significant role-playing effects for attraction or disclosure

Hoyer, W.J., Lopez, M., & Goldstein, A.P. (1982). Predicting social skill acquisition and transfer by psychogeriatric inpatients. *International Journal of Behavioral Geriatrics, 1,* 43–46.

Trainees: Elderly institutionalized psychiatric patients (N=47)

Skill(s): Social competency subset

Experimental design: A multiple regression analysis examining several potential predictors of skill acquisition and competence consequent to participation in a series of Skillstreaming sessions

Results: Mental status measures were the best predictors of skill acquisition. Mental status combined with trait anxiety were the best predictors of skill maintenance.

Hummel, J. (1979). *Session variability and skill content as transfer enhancers in Structured Learning training.* Unpublished doctoral dissertation, Syracuse University.

Trainees: Aggressive preadolescents (N=47)

Skill(s): Self-control, negotiation

Experimental design: Skillstreaming-variable conditions versus Skillstreaming-constant conditions by self-control skill versus negotiation skill versus both

Results: Skillstreaming-variable conditions significantly > Skillstreaming-constant conditions on both acquisition and transfer dependent measures across both skills singly and combined

Jennings, R.L., & Davis, C.G. (1977). Attraction enhancing client behaviors: A structured learning approach for "Non Yavis, Jr." *Journal of Consulting and Clinical Psychology, 45,* 135–144.

Trainees: Emotionally disturbed lower socioeconomic children and adolescents (N=40)

Skill(s): Interviewee behaviors (initiation, terminating silences, elaboration, and expression of affect)

Experimental design: (1) Skillstreaming for interviewee behaviors versus (2) minimal treatment control in a $2 \times 2 \times 4$ factorial design reflecting (a) repeated measures, (b) treatments, and (c) interviewers

Results: Skillstreaming significantly > minimal treatment control on interview initiation and terminating silences. No significant effects on interview elaboration or expression of affect. Skillstreaming significantly > minimal treatment control on attractiveness to interviewer on portion of study measures.

Jones, Y. (1990). *Aggression Replacement Training in a high school setting.* Unpublished manuscript, Center for Learning & Adjustment Difficulties, Brisbane, Australia.

Trainees: Chronically aggressive high-school age male students (N=45)

Skill(s): Self-control and aggression management subset

Experimental design: Compared (1) Aggression Replacement Training, (2) Moral Education, and (3) no-training control

Results: Compared to the two control conditions, students completing the Aggression Replacement Training program showed a significant decrease in aggressive incidents, a significant increase in coping incidents, and acquired more social skills. Students in Condition 1 also improved on self-control and impulsivity.

Lack, D.Z. (1971). *The effect of a model and instructions on psychotherapist self-disclosure.* Unpublished master's thesis, Syracuse University.

Trainees: Mental hospital attendants (N=60)

Skill(s): Self-disclosure

Experimental design: Presence versus absence of modeled self-disclosure by presence versus absence of instructions to self-disclose

Results: Significant modeling and instruction effects for self-disclosure

Lack, D.Z. (1975). *Problem-solving training, Structured Learning training, and didactic instruction in the preparation of paraprofessional mental health personnel for the utilization of contingency management techniques.* Unpublished doctoral dissertation, Syracuse University.

Trainees: Nurses and attendants (N=50)

Skill(s): Contingency management

Experimental design: Skillstreaming for problem solving and contingency management versus Skillstreaming for contingency management by instruction for problem solving and contingency management versus instruction for contingency management plus no-training control

Results: Significant Skillstreaming effects for problem solving

Leeman, L.W., Gibbs, J.C., Fuller, D., & Potter, G. (1991). Evaluation of a multi-component treatment program for juvenile delinquents. *Aggressive Behavior, 19,* 281–292.

Trainees: Incarcerated male juvenile offenders (N=57)

Skill(s): Interpersonal and self-management

Experimental design: Compared (1) EQUIP program (positive peer culture, Aggression Replacement Training, and means to correct disordered criminal thinking), (2) motivational control group, and (3) no-training control group

Results: EQUIP > both control groups on such institutional behaviors as self-reported misconduct, staff-field incident reports, unexcused absences from school, and recidivism rate at both 1-month and 1-year follow-up

Liberman, B. (1970). *The effect of modeling procedures on attraction and disclosure in a psychotherapy analogue.* Unpublished doctoral dissertation, Syracuse University.

Trainees: Alcoholic inpatients (N=84, all males)

Skill(s): Self-disclosure; attraction to the psychotherapist

Experimental design: High versus low modeled self-disclosure by high versus low modeled attraction plus neutral-tape and no-tape controls

Results: Significant modeling effect for self-disclosure; no modeling effect for attraction

Litwak, S.E. (1977). *The use of the helper therapy principle to increase therapeutic effectiveness and reduce therapeutic resistance: Structured Learning Therapy with resistant adolescents.* Unpublished doctoral dissertation, Syracuse University.

Trainees: Junior high school students (N=48)

Skill(s): Following instructions

Experimental design: (1) Skillstreaming for following instructions—trainees anticipate serving as Skillstreaming trainers and (2) Skillstreaming for following instructions—no trainee anticipation of serving as trainers versus (3) no-treatment control by three parallel conditions involving a skill target not concerned with resistance reduction (i.e., expressing a compliment)

Results: Group 1 significantly > Group 2 significantly > Group 3 on both skills on immediate posttest and transfer measures

Lopez, M.A. (1974). *The influence of vocal and facial cue training on the identification of affect communicated via paralinguistic cues.* Unpublished master's thesis, Syracuse University.

Trainees: Nurses and attendants (N=52)

Skill(s): Recognition of vocal cues of depression

Experimental design: (1) Skillstreaming for vocal and facial cues, (2) Skillstreaming for facial cues, (3) Skillstreaming for vocal cues, (4) no-training control.

Results: Skillstreaming for vocal cues plus either facial cue training (Group 1) or Skillstreaming for facial cues (Group 2) significantly > Skillstreaming for vocal cues (Group 3) or no-training control (Group 4) on posttest and generalization criteria

Lopez, M.A., Hoyer, W., & Goldstein, A.P. (1979). *Effects of overlearning and incentive on the acquisition and transfer of interpersonal skills with institutionalized elderly patients.* Unpublished manuscript, Syracuse University.

Trainees: Elderly inpatients in state hospital (N=56)

Skill(s): Starting a conversation

Experimental design: Skillstreaming plus high versus moderate versus low overlearning by presence versus absence of material reinforcement

Results: Significant skill acquisition effect across Skillstreaming conditions; significant transfer enhancement effect for both overlearning and concrete reinforcement

Magaro, P., & West, A.N. (1983). Structured Learning Therapy: A study with chronic psychiatric patients and levels of pathology. *Behavior Modification, 7,* 29–40.

Trainees: Adult, chronic psychiatric patients (N=38)

Skill(s): A graded series of 20 Skillstreaming skills, from starting a conversation to self-control and decision making

Experimental design: Six-month course of Skillstreaming provided to eight patient groups. Grouping based on initial skill levels.

Results: Pre-post comparisons revealed general increase in skill competence across groups, with greatest gains among patients categorized with paranoid or disorganized features.

McGinnis, E. (1985). Skillstreaming: Teaching social skills to children with behavioral disorders. *Teaching Exceptional Children, 17,* 160–167.

A description of the procedures, curriculum, and modifications in the Skillstreaming approach as applied to behavior disordered elementary-age children.

McGinnis, E., & Goldstein, A.P. (1984). *Skillstreaming the elementary school child: A guide for teaching prosocial skills.* Champaign, IL: Research Press.

A practitioner-oriented trainer's manual presenting the background, procedures, materials, and measures necessary to successfully organize and effectively manage Skillstreaming groups for elementary-age children.

Contents: (1) Introduction; (2) Components of Structured Learning; (3) Assessment for Selection and Grouping; (4) Beginning a Structured Learning Group; (5) Conducting a Structured Learning Group; (6) Prosocial Skills; (7) Structured Learning in Use; (8) Suggestions for Use; (9) Managing Behavior Problems

McGinnis, E., & Goldstein, A.P. (1990). *Skillstreaming in early childhood: Teaching prosocial skills to the preschool and kindergarten child.* Champaign, IL: Reseach Press.

A presentation of procedures and materials needed to initiate and carry out successful Skillstreaming instruction with children ages 3 to 6.

Contents: (1) Introduction; (2) Components of Skillstreaming; (3) Identifying and Evaluating Children for Skillstreaming; (4) Planning and Beginning Skillstreaming Instruction; (5) Implementing Skillstreaming Instruction; (6) Prosocial Skills; (7) Managing Behavior Problems

Miller, M.C. (1992). Student and teacher perceptions related to behavior change after Skillstreaming training. *Behavior Disorders, 17,* 271–295.

Trainees: Behavior-disordered adolescents (N=70)

Skill(s): Several Skillstreaming skills

Experimental design: Pre-post comparisons of skill competence as perceived by trainees and by their teachers

Results: Substantial effects as a function of Skillstreaming as rated by the trainees' teachers; absence of such effects in trainee's own ratings

Miron, M., & Goldstein, A.P. (1978). *Hostage.* New York: Pergamon.

An applied presentation oriented toward law enforcement and criminal justice personnel concerned with hostage and terrorism situations.

Contents: (1) Introduction; (2) The Cotton Case; (3) The Kiritsis Case; (4) The Hanafi Muslim Case; (5) The Hearst Case; (6) The Media, "Shrinks," and Other Civilians; (7) Hostage Negotiation Procedures; (8) A Method for Effective Training: Skillstreaming; (9) Skillstreaming Manual for Police Trainers

Moses, J. (May, 1974). *Supervisory relationship training: A new approach to supervisory training, results of evaluation research.* New York: AT&T Human Resources Development Department.

Trainees: Supervisor trainees (N=183)

Skill(s): Effective management of an array of supervisor-supervisee relationship problems involving discrimination, absenteeism, and theft

Experimental design: Skillstreaming for supervisory relationship skills versus no training

Results: Trained supervisors significantly > untrained supervisors on all behavioral and questionnaire criteria

Muris, P., Heldens, H., & Schreurs, L. (1992). Goldstein training for children in special needs education. *Kind en Adolescent, 13,* 193–198.

A case study report of the impressionistically successful use of Skillstreaming with four mentally retarded Dutch adolescents.

O'Brien, D. (1977). *Trainer-trainee FIRO-B compatibility as a determinant of certain process events in Structured Learning Therapy.* Unpublished master's thesis, Syracuse University.

Trainees: Nurses and attendants at state mental hospital (N=60)

Skill(s): Structured Learning trainer group leadership behaviors vis à vis low affection (actor) trainees

Experimental design: Trainers with high versus low originator compatibility for FIRO-B control by compatible or incompatible trainees; also, trainers with high versus low originator compatibility for FIRO-B affection by compatible or incompatible trainees

Results: No significant between-trainer effects. No significant trainer by trainee effects. Trainers more competent but less warm with cold, versus neutral, trainees.

Orenstein, R. (1969). *The influence of self-esteem on modeling behavior in a psychotherapy analogue.* Unpublished master's thesis, Syracuse University.

Trainees: University undergraduates (all females; N=80)

Skill(s): Attraction to the psychotherapist

Experimental design: High versus low modeled attraction by high versus low subject self-esteem

Results: Significant modeling effect for attraction; no modeling effect for self-esteem. Subjects viewing a high attraction model were also significantly more willing to disclose, as were high self-esteem subjects. Low self-esteem subjects were significantly easier to persuade.

Orenstein, R. (1973). *Effect of training patients to focus on their feelings on level of experiencing in a subsequent interview.* Unpublished doctoral dissertation, Syracuse University.

Trainees: Psychiatric inpatients (all female; N=75)

Skill(s): Focusing (ability to be aware of one's own affective experiencing)

Experimental design: (1) Skillstreaming for focusing, (2) focusing manual, (3) brief instruction for focusing, (4) attention control, (5) no-treatment control

Results: No significant between-group differences in focusing ability

Perry, M.A. (1970). *Didactic instructions for and modeling of empathy.* Unpublished doctoral dissertation, Syracuse University.

Trainees: Clergy (all male; N=66)

Skill(s): Empathy

Experimental design: High empathy modeling versus low empathy modeling versus no modeling by presence versus absence of instructions to be empathic

Results: Significant modeling effect for empathy. No significant instructions or interaction effects for empathy.

Perry, M.A. (1976). *Structured Learning Therapy for skill training of mentally retarded children.* Unpublished manuscript, University of Washington, Seattle.

Trainees: Mildly and moderately retarded halfway house residents (N=36)

Skill(s): Social interaction skills

Experimental design: Skillstreaming for social interaction skills versus attention control versus no-treatment control

Results: Skillstreaming significantly > controls on mealtime social interaction skills

Raleigh, R. (1977). *Individual versus group Structured Learning Therapy for assertiveness training with senior and junior high school students.* Unpublished doctoral dissertation, Syracuse University.

Trainees: Senior and junior high school students (N=80)

Skill(s): Assertiveness

Experimental design: Individual versus group Skillstreaming by senior versus junior high school student trainees plus attention control and no-treatment control

Results: Skillstreaming in groups significantly > all other Skillstreaming and control conditions on assertiveness on both acquisition and transfer criteria

Reed, M.K. (1994). Social skills training to reduce depression in adolescents. *Adolescence, 29*, 293–302.

Trainees: Seriously depressed adolescents (N=10)

Skill(s): Social competency, self-evaluation, affective expression

Experimental design: Skillstreaming versus no-training control plus male or female

Results: Both immediate and sustained reduction in depression for male trainees, but not for females

Robertson, B. (1978). *The effects of Structured Learning trainers' need to control on their group leadership behavior with aggressive and withdrawn trainees.* Unpublished master's thesis, Syracuse University.

Trainees: Nurses and attendants at state mental hospital (N=60)

Skill(s): Skillstreaming trainer group leadership behaviors

Experimental design: Trainers high or low on need to control in interpersonal contexts versus controlling or cooperative actor trainees

Results: Trainers high on need to control significantly > competence with actively resistant trainees than trainers low on need to control. High need to control trainers significantly > attraction to actively resistive than to neutral trainees.

Robinson, R. (1973). *Evaluation of a Structured Learning empathy training program for lower socioeconomic status home-aide trainees.* Unpublished master's thesis, Syracuse University.

Trainees: Home-aide trainees (N=29)

Skill(s): Empathy

Experimental design: (1) Skillstreaming for empathy, (2) didactic training of empathy, (3) no-treatment control

Results: Skillstreaming > didactic training or no-treatment control on immediate posttest and generalization measures of empathy

Rosenthal, N. (1975). *Matching counselor trainees' conceptual level and training approaches: A study in the acquisition and enhancement of confrontation skills.* Unpublished doctoral dissertation, Syracuse University.

Trainees: Counselor trainees (N=60)

Skill(s): Confrontation (ability to point out to clients discrepancies in the verbal and/or nonverbal contents of their statements)

Experimental design: Skillstreaming for confrontation, training conducted by a trainer in "standard" Skillstreaming groups versus Skillstreaming for confrontation, self-instructional training format, by high versus low conceptual level trainees, plus attention control

Results: Significant interaction effects on confrontation skill for type of Skillstreaming (leader-led versus self-instructional) by conceptual level (high versus low). Skillstreaming (both types) > attention control on confrontation skill.

Sasso, G.M., Melloy, K.J., & Kavale, K. (1990). Generalization, maintenance, and behavioral covariation associated with social skills training through Structured Learning. *Behavioral Disorders, 16,* 9–22.

Three students with behavior disorders ranging in age from 8 to 13 years old participated in this study. All three were in a self-contained special education classroom (training setting) and were mainstreamed into at least one general education class (generalization setting). Before, during, and after an 8-week course of Skillstreaming, both they and three peers in the regular class were observed across target skill behaviors. All three trainees exhibited increases in three skill behaviors in the training setting during the program. Two of the three maintained these levels over a 10- to 20-week follow-up period in the training setting and in the mainstream setting. The third did so for only one of the trained skills. Despite these successful outcome data, the prosocial behavior of all three subjects remained significantly below that of their peers in the regular class.

Schneiman, R. (1972). *An evaluation of Structured Learning and didactic learning as methods of training behavior modification skills to lower and middle socioeconomic level teacher-aides.* Unpublished doctoral dissertation, Syracuse University.

Trainees: Teacher aides (30 middle class and 30 lower class; N=60)

Skill(s): Disciplining (appropriate use of rules, disapproval, and praise)

Experimental design: (1) Skillstreaming for disciplining, (2) didactic training for disciplining, (3) no-training control by middle class versus lower class aides

Results: Across social-class levels, Skillstreaming > didactic or no-training on immediate and generalization behavioral measures of disciplining

Shaw, L.W. (1978). *A study of empathy training effectiveness: Comparing computer assisted instruction, Structured Learning training and encounter training exercises.* Unpublished doctoral dissertation, Syracuse University.

Trainees: College undergraduates (N=93)

Skill(s): Empathy

Experimental design: Computer assisted instruction versus Skillstreaming versus encounter training versus no-training control for empathy

Results: Computer assisted instruction and Skillstreaming significantly > no-training control on level of empathy

Solomon, E.J. (1978). *Structured Learning Therapy with abusive parents: Training in self-control.* Unpublished doctoral dissertation, Syracuse University.

Trainees: Child-abusing parents (31 female and 9 male; N=40)

Skill(s): Self-control

Experimental design: Skillstreaming with and without structuring into helper role by Skillstreaming with and without mastery training plus brief instruction control

Results: All Skillstreaming groups significantly > controls on self-control on both acquisition and generalization criteria. Skillstreaming plus helper structuring plus mastery training significantly > all other Skillstreaming groups.

Sorcher, M., & Goldstein, A.P. (1973). A behavior modeling approach in training. *Personnel Administration, 35,* 35–41.

An overview of the nature and potential impact of Skillstreaming in an industrial context. Topics examined include the need for a concrete, behavioral training focus; the basis for the choice of modeling, role-playing, social reinforcement, and transfer training as the components of this behavioral approach; and a brief example of how these procedures are utilized.

Sprafkin, R.P., Gershaw, N.J., & Goldstein, A.P. (1978). Teaching interpersonal skills to psychiatric outpatients: Using Structured Learning Therapy in a community-based setting. *Journal of Rehabilitation, 44,* 26–29.

A presentation of the rationale, procedures, and materials of Structured Learning Therapy. Its potential rehabilitative usefulness in fostering effective and satisfying community functioning is stressed.

Sprafkin, R.P., Gershaw, N.J., & Goldstein, A.P. (1980). Skill training for the disruptive adolescent. *Directive Teacher, 13,* 14–19.

Skills training in general, and the Skillstreaming method in particular, is offered as a viable means for reducing the disruptive behaviors displayed by many adolescents in school and other settings.

Sprafkin, R.P., Gershaw, N.J., & Goldstein, A.P. (1981). Structured Learning Therapy: A skill training approach to social competence. In D.P. Rathjen & J. Foreyt (Eds.), *Social competence: Interventions for children and adults.* New York: Pergamon.

A presentation of the Skillstreaming approach to enhancing the social competence of both typical and atypical adolescents. The value of a psychoeducational strategy for this purpose is described, as are the Skillstreaming procedures and curriculum.

Sprafkin, R.P., Gershaw, N.J., & Goldstein, A.P. (1985). Structured Learning: Its cross cultural roots and implications. In P. Pedersen (Ed.), *Handbook of cross cultural counseling.* Fairfield, CT: Greenwood.

A description of the Skillstreaming method, curriculum, and evaluation research, with special emphasis on program relevance for and applicability to low-income trainee populations.

Sprafkin, R.P., Gershaw, N.J., & Goldstein, A.P. (1993). *Social skills for mental health: A Structured Learning approach.* Boston: Allyn & Bacon.

A description of the use of Skillstreaming with chronic adult mental patients, with emphasis on their preparation via this intervention for functional living in the community and in other noninstitutional settings.

Contents: (1) Introduction: The Skill-Deficient Client; (2) Structured Learning: Background and Development; (3) Structured Learning: Implementation Procedures; (4) Structured Learning Skills; (5) Managing Problematic Behaviors; (6) Structured Learning in Use

Sprafkin, R.P., & Goldstein, A.P. (1990). Behavior modeling. In S.S. Dubin (Ed.), *Models of professional updating.* San Francisco: Jossey-Bass.

Describes the Skillstreaming method and the wide range of trainees with whom it has been used. Emphasis in this chapter is on the program's utility in enhancing the competence and range of capabilities of various change agent trainees.

Stumphauzer, J.C. (1985). School programs: Staying in school and learning to learn. *Child and Youth Services, 8,* 137–146.

A review of delinquency prevention programs, including behavioral contracting, truancy control, parent training, vandalism reduction, school consultation, and Skillstreaming.

Sturm, D. (1980). *Therapist aggression tolerance and dependency tolerance under standardized client conditions of hostility and dependency.* Unpublished master's thesis, Syracuse University.

Trainees: Parent aides employed at child abuse agency (N=28)

Skill(s): Skillstreaming leadership skills

Experimental design: Two 2 × 2 factorial analyses: (1) high versus low hostile actor-clients by high versus low aggression tolerance aides, and (2) high versus low dependent actor-clients by high versus low dependency tolerance aides

Results: Significant hostile actor × aide tolerance effect; no dependency effects

Sutton, K. (1970). *Effects of modeled empathy and structured social class upon level of therapist displayed empathy.* Unpublished master's thesis, Syracuse University.

Trainees: Attendants (N=60)

Skill(s): Empathy

Experimental design: High versus low modeled empathy by high versus low structured social class

Results: Significant effect for modeled empathy on immediate but not generalization measurement. No significant social class structuring or interaction effects.

Sutton-Simon, K. (1974). *The effects of two types of modeling and rehearsal procedures upon schizophrenics' social skill behavior.* Unpublished doctoral dissertation, Syracuse University.

Trainees: Psychiatric inpatients (all male, all schizophrenic; N=83)

Skill(s): Social interaction behaviors

Experimental design: (1) Skillstreaming with behavioral and cognitive models, (2) Skillstreaming with behavioral models, (3) Skillstreaming with cognitive models, (4) attention control, (5) no-treatment control

Results: No significant between-condition differences

Swanstrom, C.R. (1978). *An examination of Structured Learning Therapy and the helper therapy principle in teaching a self-control strategy to school children with conduct problems.* Unpublished doctoral dissertation, Syracuse University.

Trainees: Elementary school children with acting-out problems (30 boys, 11 girls; N=41)

Skill(s): Self-control

Experimental design: Skillstreaming versus structured discussion by helper experience versus helper structuring versus no helper role plus brief instructions control

Results: Skillstreaming and structured discussion significantly > control on self-control acquisition. No significant transfer or helper role effects.

Trief, P. (1977). *The reduction of egocentrism in acting-out adolescents by Structured Learning Therapy.* Unpublished doctoral dissertation, Syracuse University.

Trainees: Adolescent boys with history of acting-out behaviors (N=58)

Skill(s): Perspective-taking, cooperation

Experimental design: Presence versus absence of Skillstreaming for affective perspective taking by presence versus absence of Skillstreaming for cognitive perspective taking plus no-treatment control

Results: All Skillstreaming groups significantly > controls on perspective-taking acquisition. Skillstreaming plus both affective and cognitive perspective-taking training significantly > controls on generalization criteria.

Walsh, W.G. (1971). *The effects of conformity pressure and modeling on the attraction of hospitalized patients toward an interviewer.* Unpublished doctoral dissertation, Syracuse University.

Trainees: Psychiatric inpatients (all female, mostly schizophrenic; N=60)

Skill(s): Attraction

Experimental design: Presence versus absence of high attraction modeling by presence versus absence of high attraction conformity pressure plus no-treatment control

Results: Significant main and interaction effects for modeling and conformity pressure on attraction. No significant generalization effect.

Wiken, J.P. (1988). Sheltered homes: A new field for clinical psychologists? *Psycholoog, 23,* 301–304.

Discusses the emerging role of clinical psychologists as diagnosticians and trainers for approaches such as Skillstreaming in sheltered homes, community placement locations increasingly being used for mental patients in the Netherlands.

Wood, M.A. (1977). *Acquisition and transfer of assertiveness in passive and aggressive adolescents through the use of Structured Learning Therapy.* Unpublished doctoral dissertation, Syracuse University.

Trainees: Ninth-grade students (N=74)

Skill(s): Assertiveness

Experimental design: Skillstreaming led by (1) teacher, (2) parent, or (3) student trainers by (1) passive or (2) aggressive trainees plus brief instructions control

Results: All Skillstreaming groups significantly > control on assertiveness criteria and on acquisition and transfer criteria. Skillstreaming-teacher trainer > Skillstreaming-student trainer > Skillstreaming-parent trainer on acquisition and minimal transfer criteria.

APPENDIX B
Skillstreaming Checklists and Grouping Chart

TEACHER/STAFF SKILLSTREAMING CHECKLIST

Student:________________________ Class/age: ______________

Teacher/staff: _______________________ Date: ______________

INSTRUCTIONS: Listed below you will find a number of skills that youngsters are more or less proficient in using. This checklist will help you evaluate how well each youngster uses the various skills. For each youngster, rate his or her use of each skill, based on your observations of the youngster's behavior in various situations.

Circle 1 if the youngster is *almost never* good at using the skill.

Circle 2 if the youngster is *seldom* good at using the skill.

Circle 3 if the youngster is *sometimes* good at using the skill.

Circle 4 if the youngster is *often* good at using the skill.

Circle 5 if the youngster is *almost always* good at using the skill.

Please rate the youngster on all skills listed. If you know of a situation in which the youngster has particular difficulty in using the skill well, please note it briefly in the space marked "Problem situation."

	almost never	seldom	sometimes	often	almost always
1. **Listening:** Does the youngster pay attention to someone who is talking and make an effort to understand what is being said? Problem situation:	1	2	3	4	5
2. **Starting a Conversation:** Does the youngster talk to others about light topics and then lead into more serious topics? Problem situation:	1	2	3	4	5

	almost never	seldom	sometimes	often	almost always
3. **Having a Conversation:** Does the youngster talk to others about things of interest to both of them? Problem situation:	1	2	3	4	5
4. **Asking a Question:** Does the youngster decide what information is needed and ask the right person for that information? Problem situation:	1	2	3	4	5
5. **Saying Thank You:** Does the youngster let others know that he/she is grateful for favors, etc.? Problem situation:	1	2	3	4	5
6. **Introducing Yourself:** Does the youngster become acquainted with new people on his/her own initiative? Problem situation:	1	2	3	4	5
7. **Introducing Other People:** Does the youngster help others become acquainted with one another? Problem situation:	1	2	3	4	5
8. **Giving a Compliment:** Does the youngster tell others that he/she likes something about them or their activities? Problem situation:	1	2	3	4	5

	almost never	seldom	sometimes	often	almost always
9. **Asking for Help:** Does the youngster request assistance when he/she is having difficulty? Problem situation:	1	2	3	4	5
10. **Joining In:** Does the youngster decide on the best way to become part of an ongoing activity or group? Problem situation:	1	2	3	4	5
11. **Giving Instructions:** Does the youngster clearly explain to others how they are to do a specific task? Problem situation:	1	2	3	4	5
12. **Following Instructions:** Does the youngster pay attention to instructions, give his/her reactions, and carry the instructions out adequately? Problem situation:	1	2	3	4	5
13. **Apologizing:** Does the youngster tell others that he/she is sorry after doing something wrong? Problem situation:	1	2	3	4	5

	almost never	seldom	sometimes	often	almost always
14. **Convincing Others:** Does the youngster attempt to persuade others that his/her ideas are better and will be more useful than those of the other person? Problem situation:	1	2	3	4	5
15. **Knowing Your Feelings:** Does the youngster try to recognize which emotions he/she has at different times? Problem situation:	1	2	3	4	5
16. **Expressing Your Feelings:** Does the youngster let others know which emotions he/she is feeling? Problem situation:	1	2	3	4	5
17. **Understanding the Feelings of Others:** Does the youngster try to figure out what other people are feeling? Problem situation:	1	2	3	4	5
18. **Dealing with Someone Else's Anger:** Does the youngster try to understand other people's angry feelings? Problem situation:	1	2	3	4	5

	almost never	seldom	sometimes	often	almost always
19. **Expressing Affection:** Does the youngster let others know that he/she cares about them? Problem situation:	1	2	3	4	5
20. **Dealing with Fear:** Does the youngster figure out why he/she is afraid and do something to reduce the fear? Problem situation:	1	2	3	4	5
21. **Rewarding Yourself:** Does the youngster say and do nice things for himself/herself when the reward is deserved? Problem situation:	1	2	3	4	5
22. **Asking Permission:** Does the youngster figure out when permission is needed to do something and then ask the right person for permission? Problem situation:	1	2	3	4	5
23. **Sharing Something:** Does the youngster offer to share what he/she has with others who might appreciate it? Problem situation:	1	2	3	4	5

	almost never	seldom	sometimes	often	almost always
24. **Helping Others:** Does the youngster give assistance to others who might need or want help? Problem situation:	1	2	3	4	5
25. **Negotiating:** Does the youngster arrive at a plan that satisfies both him/her and others who have taken different positions? Problem situation:	1	2	3	4	5
26. **Using Self-Control:** Does the youngster control his/her temper so that things do not get out of hand? Problem situation:	1	2	3	4	5
27. **Standing Up for Your Rights:** Does the youngster assert his/her rights by letting people know where he/she stands on an issue? Problem situation:	1	2	3	4	5
28. **Responding to Teasing:** Does the youngster deal with being teased by others in ways that allow him/her to remain in control of himself/herself? Problem situation:	1	2	3	4	5

	almost never	seldom	sometimes	often	almost always
29. **Avoiding Trouble with Others:** Does the youngster stay out of situations that might get him/her into trouble? Problem situation:	1	2	3	4	5
30. **Keeping Out of Fights:** Does the youngster figure out ways other than fighting to handle difficult situations? Problem situation:	1	2	3	4	5
31. **Making a Complaint:** Does the youngster tell others when they are responsible for creating a particular problem for him/her and then attempt to find a solution for the problem? Problem situation:	1	2	3	4	5
32. **Answering a Complaint:** Does the youngster try to arrive at a fair solution to someone's justified complaint? Problem situation:	1	2	3	4	5
33. **Being a Good Sport:** Does the youngster express an honest compliment to others about how they played a game? Problem situation:	1	2	3	4	5

	almost never	seldom	sometimes	often	almost always
34. **Dealing with Embarrassment:** Does the youngster do things that help him/her feel less embarrassed or self-conscious? Problem situation:	1	2	3	4	5
35. **Dealing with Being Left Out:** Does the youngster decide whether he/she has been left out of some activity and then do things to feel better about the situation? Problem situation:	1	2	3	4	5
36. **Standing Up for a Friend:** Does the youngster let other people know when a friend has not been treated fairly? Problem situation:	1	2	3	4	5
37. **Responding to Persuasion:** Does the youngster carefully consider the position of another person, comparing it to his/her own, before deciding what to do? Problem situation:	1	2	3	4	5
38. **Responding to Failure:** Does the youngster figure out the reason for failing in a particular situation and what he/she can do about it in order to be more successful in the future? Problem situation:	1	2	3	4	5

	almost never	seldom	sometimes	often	almost always
39. **Dealing with Contradictory Messages:** Does the youngster recognize and deal with the confusion that results when others tell him/her one thing but say or do things that indicate that they mean something else? Problem situation:	1	2	3	4	5
40. **Dealing with an Accusation:** Does the youngster figure out what he/she has been accused of and why, then decide on the best way to deal with the person who made the accusation? Problem situation:	1	2	3	4	5
41. **Getting Ready for a Difficult Conversation:** Does the youngster plan on the best way to present his/her point of view prior to a stressful conversation? Problem situation:	1	2	3	4	5
42. **Dealing with Group Pressure:** Does the youngster decide what he/she wants to do when others want him/her to do something else? Problem situation:	1	2	3	4	5

	almost never	seldom	sometimes	often	almost always
43. **Deciding on Something to Do:** Does the youngster deal with feeling bored by starting an interesting activity? Problem situation:	1	2	3	4	5
44. **Deciding What Caused a Problem:** Does the youngster find out whether an event was caused by something that was within his/her control? Problem situation:	1	2	3	4	5
45. **Setting a Goal:** Does the youngster realistically decide on what he/she can accomplish prior to starting a task? Problem situation:	1	2	3	4	5
46. **Deciding on Your Abilities:** Does the youngster realistically figure out how well he/she might do at a particular task? Problem situation:	1	2	3	4	5
47. **Gathering Information:** Does the youngster decide what he/she needs to know and how to get that information? Problem situation:	1	2	3	4	5

	almost never	seldom	sometimes	often	almost always
48. **Arranging Problems by Importance:** Does the youngster decide realistically which of a number of problems is most important and should be dealt with first? Problem situation:	1	2	3	4	5
49. **Making a Decision:** Does the youngster consider possibilities and make choices that he/she feels will be best? Problem situation:	1	2	3	4	5
50. **Concentrating on a Task:** Does the youngster make those preparations that will help him/her get a job done? Problem situation:	1	2	3	4	5

PARENT SKILLSTREAMING CHECKLIST

Name: ______________________________ Date: ______________

Child's name: ____________________ Birth date: ______________

INSTRUCTIONS: Based on your observations in various situations, rate your child's use of the following skills.

Circle 1 if your child *almost never* uses the skill.

Circle 2 if your child *seldom* uses the skill.

Circle 3 if your child *sometimes* uses the skill.

Circle 4 if your child *often* uses the skill.

Circle 5 if your child *almost always* uses the skill.

	almost never	seldom	sometimes	often	almost always
1. **Listening:** Does your child listen when you or others talk to him/her? Comments:	1	2	3	4	5
2. **Starting a Conversation:** Does your child begin conversations with other people? Comments:	1	2	3	4	5
3. **Having a Conversation:** Does your child talk to others about things of interest to both of them? Comments:	1	2	3	4	5

	almost never	seldom	sometimes	often	almost always
4. **Asking a Question:** Does your child know how and when to ask questions of another person? Comments:	1	2	3	4	5
5. **Saying Thank You:** Does your child let others know that he/she is grateful for favors, etc.? Comments:	1	2	3	4	5
6. **Introducing Yourself:** Does your child become acquainted with new people on his/her own? Comments:	1	2	3	4	5
7. **Introducing Other People:** Does your child help others become acquainted with one another? Comments:	1	2	3	4	5
8. **Giving a Compliment:** Does your child tell others that he/she likes something about them or something they have done? Comments:	1	2	3	4	5
9. **Asking for Help:** Does your child request assistance when he/she is having difficulty? Comments:	1	2	3	4	5

	almost never	seldom	sometimes	often	almost always
10. **Joining In:** Does your child take steps to become part of an ongoing activity or group? Comments:	1	2	3	4	5
11. **Giving Instructions:** Does your child clearly explain to others how and why they should do something? Comments:	1	2	3	4	5
12. **Following Instructions:** Does your child carry out instructions from others quickly and correctly? Comments:	1	2	3	4	5
13. **Apologizing:** Does your child tell others he/she is sorry after doing something wrong? Comments:	1	2	3	4	5
14. **Convincing Others:** Does your child attempt to persuade others that his/her ideas are better than theirs? Comments:	1	2	3	4	5
15. **Knowing Your Feelings:** Does your child recognize which emotions he or she has at different times? Comments:	1	2	3	4	5

	almost never	seldom	sometimes	often	almost always
16. **Expressing Your Feelings:** Does your child let others know which emotions he/she is feeling? Comments:	1	2	3	4	5
17. **Understanding the Feelings of Others:** Does your child understand what other people are feeling? Comments:	1	2	3	4	5
18. **Dealing with Someone Else's Anger:** Does your child try to understand someone else's anger without getting angry himself/herself? Comments:	1	2	3	4	5
19. **Expressing Affection:** Does your child let others know that he/she cares about them? Comments:	1	2	3	4	5
20. **Dealing with Fear:** Does your child figure out why he/she is afraid and do something to reduce the fear? Comments:	1	2	3	4	5
21. **Rewarding Yourself:** Does your child say and do nice things for himself/herself when it is deserved? Comments:	1	2	3	4	5

	almost never	seldom	sometimes	often	almost always
22. **Asking Permission:** Does your child understand when permission is needed and ask the right person for it? Comments:	1	2	3	4	5
23. **Sharing Something:** Does your child offer to share what he/she has with others? Comments:	1	2	3	4	5
24. **Helping Others:** Does your child give assistance to others who might need or want it? Comments:	1	2	3	4	5
25. **Negotiating:** Does your child help arrive at a plan that satisfies both himself/herself and others who have taken different positions? Comments:	1	2	3	4	5
26. **Using Self-Control:** Does your child control his/her temper so things do not get out of hand? Comments:	1	2	3	4	5
27. **Standing Up for Your Rights:** Does your child assert his/her rights by letting other people know where he/she stands on an issue? Comments:	1	2	3	4	5

	almost never	seldom	sometimes	often	almost always
28. **Responding to Teasing:** Does your child deal in a constructive way with being teased? Comments:	1	2	3	4	5
29. **Avoiding Trouble with Others:** Does your child stay out of situations that might get him/her in trouble? Comments:	1	2	3	4	5
30. **Keeping Out of Fights:** Does your child figure out ways other than fighting to handle difficult situations? Comments:	1	2	3	4	5
31. **Making a Complaint:** Does your child disagree with others in acceptable ways? Comments:	1	2	3	4	5
32. **Answering a Complaint:** Does your child try to arrive at a fair solution to someone else's justified complaint? Comments:	1	2	3	4	5
33. **Being a Good Sport:** Does your child express an honest compliment to others about how they played a game? Comments:	1	2	3	4	5

	almost never	seldom	sometimes	often	almost always
34. **Dealing with Embarrassment:** Does your child do things that help him/her feel less embarrassed or self-conscious? Comments:	1	2	3	4	5
35. **Dealing with Being Left Out:** Does your child deal positively with being left out of some activity? Comments:	1	2	3	4	5
36. **Standing Up for a Friend:** Does your child let other people know when a friend has not been treated fairly? Comments:	1	2	3	4	5
37. **Responding to Persuasion:** Does your child think alternatives through before responding to persuasion from others? Comments:	1	2	3	4	5
38. **Responding to Failure:** Does your child figure out the reasons he/she failed at something and how to correct the failure? Comments:	1	2	3	4	5

	almost never	seldom	sometimes	often	almost always
39. **Dealing with Contradictory Messages:** Does your child recognize and deal with it when others say or do one thing but also indicate they mean something else? Comments:	1	2	3	4	5
40. **Dealing with an Accusation:** Does your child figure out what he/she has been accused of, then use constructive ways of dealing with it? Comments:	1	2	3	4	5
41. **Getting Ready for a Difficult Conversation:** Does your child plan on the best way to present his/her own point of view before a stressful conversation? Comments:	1	2	3	4	5
42. **Dealing with Group Pressure:** Does your child decide what he/she wants to do when others are urging him/her to do something else? Comments:	1	2	3	4	5
43. **Deciding on Something to Do:** Does your child deal with feeling bored by starting an interesting activity? Comments:	1	2	3	4	5

	almost never	seldom	sometimes	often	almost always
44. **Deciding What Caused a Problem:** Does your child try to find out whether an event was caused by something under his/her control? Comments:	1	2	3	4	5
45. **Setting a Goal:** Does your child realistically plan on what he/she would like to accomplish before starting a task? Comments:	1	2	3	4	5
46. **Deciding on Your Abilities:** Does your child accurately figure out how well he/she might do at a particular task? Comments:	1	2	3	4	5
47. **Gathering Information:** Does your child decide what he/she needs to know and how to get that information? Comments:	1	2	3	4	5
48. **Arranging Problems by Importance:** Does your child realistically decide which of a number of problems is most important and should be dealt with first? Comments:	1	2	3	4	5

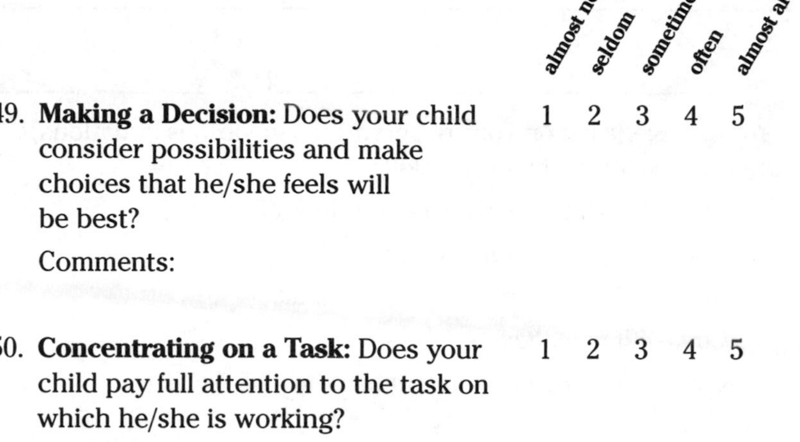

49. **Making a Decision:** Does your child consider possibilities and make choices that he/she feels will be best? 1 2 3 4 5

Comments:

50. **Concentrating on a Task:** Does your child pay full attention to the task on which he/she is working? 1 2 3 4 5

Comments:

STUDENT SKILLSTREAMING CHECKLIST

Name:______________________________ Date ______________

INSTRUCTIONS: Based on your observations in various situations, rate your use of the following skills.

Circle 1 if you *almost never* use the skill.

Circle 2 if you *seldom* use the skill.

Circle 3 if you *sometimes* use the skill.

Circle 4 if you *often* use the skill.

Circle 5 if you *almost always* use the skill.

	almost never	seldom	sometimes	often	almost always
1. Do I listen to someone who is talking to me?	1	2	3	4	5
2. Do I start conversations with other people?	1	2	3	4	5
3. Do I talk with other people about things that interest both of us?	1	2	3	4	5
4. Do I ask questions when I need or want to know something?	1	2	3	4	5
5. Do I say thank you when someone does something for me?	1	2	3	4	5
6. Do I introduce myself to new people?	1	2	3	4	5
7. Do I introduce people who haven't met before to each other?	1	2	3	4	5
8. Do I tell other people when I like how they are or something they have done?	1	2	3	4	5
9. Do I ask for help when I am having difficulty doing something?	1	2	3	4	5

	almost never	seldom	sometimes	often	almost always
10. Do I try to join in when others are doing something I'd like to be part of?	1	2	3	4	5
11. Do I clearly explain to others how and why they should do something?	1	2	3	4	5
12. Do I carry out instructions from other people quickly and correctly?	1	2	3	4	5
13. Do I apologize to others when I have done something wrong?	1	2	3	4	5
14. Do I try to convince others that my ideas are better than theirs?	1	2	3	4	5
15. Do I recognize the feelings I have at different times?	1	2	3	4	5
16. Do I let others know what I am feeling and do it in a good way?	1	2	3	4	5
17. Do I understand what other people are feeling?	1	2	3	4	5
18. Do I try to understand, and not get angry, when someone else is angry?	1	2	3	4	5
19. Do I let others know when I care about them?	1	2	3	4	5
20. Do I know what makes me afraid and do things so that I don't stay that way?	1	2	3	4	5
21. Do I say and do nice things for myself when I have earned it?	1	2	3	4	5
22. Do I understand when permission is needed to do something and ask the right person for it?	1	2	3	4	5
23. Do I offer to share what I have with others?	1	2	3	4	5

	almost never	seldom	sometimes	often	almost always
24. Do I help others who might need or want help?	1	2	3	4	5
25. Do I try to make both of us satisfied with the result when someone and I disagree?	1	2	3	4	5
26. Do I control my temper when I feel upset?	1	2	3	4	5
27. Do I stand up for my rights to let other people know what I think or feel?	1	2	3	4	5
28. Do I stay in control when someone teases me?	1	2	3	4	5
29. Do I try to stay out of situations that might get me in trouble?	1	2	3	4	5
30. Do I figure out ways other than fighting to handle difficult situations?	1	2	3	4	5
31. Do I make complaints I have about others in a fair way?	1	2	3	4	5
32. Do I handle complaints made against me in a fair way?	1	2	3	4	5
33. Do I say nice things to others after a game about how they played?	1	2	3	4	5
34. Do I do things that help me feel less embarrassed when difficulties happen?	1	2	3	4	5
35. Do I deal positively with being left out of some activity?	1	2	3	4	5
36. Do I let people know when I feel a friend has not been treated fairly?	1	2	3	4	5
37. Do I think choices through before answering when someone is trying to convince me about something?	1	2	3	4	5

	almost never	seldom	sometimes	often	almost always
38. Do I try to figure out the reasons it happened when I fail at something?	1	2	3	4	5
39. Do I deal with it well when someone says or does one thing but means something else?	1	2	3	4	5
40. Do I deal with it well when someone accuses me of doing something?	1	2	3	4	5
41. Do I plan ahead the best ways to handle it before I have a difficult conversation?	1	2	3	4	5
42. Do I decide what I want to do when others pressure me to do something else?	1	2	3	4	5
43. Do I think of good things to do and then do them when I feel bored?	1	2	3	4	5
44. Do I, when there is a problem, try to find out what caused it?	1	2	3	4	5
45. Do I think about what I would like to do before I start a new task?	1	2	3	4	5
46. Do I think about what I am really able to do before I start a new task?	1	2	3	4	5
47. Do I decide, before doing something, what I need to know and how to find out?	1	2	3	4	5
48. Do I decide which problem is most important and should be handled first?	1	2	3	4	5
49. Do I think about different possibilities and choose the one that is best?	1	2	3	4	5
50. Do I pay full attention to whatever I am working on?	1	2	3	4	5

SKILLSTREAMING GROUPING CHART

GROUP I **Beginning Social Skills**	student names								
1. Listening									
2. Starting a Conversation									
3. Having a Conversation									
4. Asking a Question									
5. Saying Thank You									
6. Introducing Yourself									
7. Introducing Other People									
8. Giving a Compliment									

GROUP II **Advanced Social Skills**	student names								
9. Asking for Help									
10. Joining In									
11. Giving Instructions									
12. Following Instructions									
13. Apologizing									
14. Convincing Others									

GROUP III Skills for Dealing with Feelings	student names								
15. Knowing Your Feelings									
16. Expressing Your Feelings									
17. Understanding the Feelings of Others									
18. Dealing with Someone Else's Anger									
19. Expressing Affection									
20. Dealing with Fear									
21. Rewarding Yourself									

GROUP IV Skill Alternatives to Aggression	student names								
22. Asking Permission									
23. Sharing Something									
24. Helping Others									
25. Negotiating									
26. Using Self-Control									
27. Standing Up for Your Rights									
28. Responding to Teasing									
29. Avoiding Trouble with Others									
30. Keeping Out of Fights									

GROUP V Skills for Dealing with Stress	student names								
31. Making a Complaint									
32. Answering a Complaint									
33. Being a Good Sport									
34. Dealing with Embarrassment									
35. Dealing with Being Left Out									
36. Standing Up for a Friend									
37. Responding to Persuasion									
38. Responding to Failure									
39. Dealing with Contradictory Messages									
40. Dealing with an Accusation									
41. Getting Ready for a Difficult Conversation									
42. Dealing with Group Pressure									

GROUP VI Planning Skills	student names								
43. Deciding on Something to Do									
44. Deciding What Caused a Problem									
45. Setting a Goal									
46. Deciding on Your Abilities									
47. Gathering Information									
48. Arranging Problems by Importance									
49. Making a Decision									
50. Concentrating on a Task									

APPENDIX C
Supplementary Skillstreaming Components

All that is truly needed to implement a Skillstreaming program for adolescents is this program text. However, a number of other Skillstreaming materials, both print and video, will make the task easier. Supplementary Skillstreaming components for adolescents are described in this appendix. Skillstreaming components for young children and elementary-age children are listed in Appendix D.

For current prices and ordering information
write, call, or fax:

Research Press
2612 North Mattis Avenue
Champaign, Illinois 61821
Phone: 217-352-3273
Toll-Free: 1-800-519-2707
Fax: 217-352-1221

Print Components

Program Forms

Skillstreaming the Adolescent: New Strategies and Perspectives for Teaching Prosocial Skills—Program Forms, by Dr. Arnold P. Goldstein and Dr. Ellen McGinnis, 1997 (papercover, 8½ × 11–inch format, 48 pages, ISBN 0–87822–371–1).

CONTENTS

- Teacher/Staff, Parent, and Student Skillstreaming Checklists
- Skillstreaming Grouping Chart
- Homework Reports
- Skill Contract
- Skill Sheet
- Self-Recording Forms
- School-Home Note
- Parent/Staff Skill Rating Form

Student Manual

Skillstreaming the Adolescent—Student Manual, by Dr. Arnold P. Goldstein and Dr. Ellen McGinnis, 1997 (papercover, 8½ × 11–inch format, 64 pages, ISBN 0–87822–370–3).

A clear, concise guide for students, designed to promote active involvement in the Skillstreaming group. Serves as a reference and organizer.

CONTENTS

1: Introduction to Skillstreaming. Introduces Skillstreaming and discusses its main purposes. Students can read this section as a group and then complete the Student Skill Checklist included to help them identify their skill strengths and weaknesses.

2: Skillstreaming Methods. Briefly describes Skillstreaming's four instructional methods: modeling, role-playing, feedback, and transfer (homework). This overview prepares students for the next section, which applies these methods to specific skill learning.

3: Skillstreaming in Action. Gives step-by-step guidance through the modeling, role-playing, and feedback process for one skill—Responding to Teasing. Clarifies the roles of main actor, co-actor, and observers during the role-play.

4: Skill Homework. Gives detailed instructions for completing skill homework assignments. Includes sample homework reports filled out by a student learning the skill of Responding to Teasing.

5: Skillstreaming Skills. Lists the 50 Skillstreaming skills according to their six categories: Beginning Social Skills, Advanced Social Skills, Skills for Dealing with Feelings, Skill Alternatives to Aggression, Skills for Dealing with Stress, and Planning Skills. Gives a brief rationale for skill learning in each category in order to help students identify which skills they would most like to learn.

6: Making It All Work. Offers suggestions to improve skill performance and success. Topics include nonverbal communication; what to do when a skill does not bring about a desired outcome; adjusting skills relative to people, places, and situations; and skill shifting and skill combinations.

Skill Cards

Skillstreaming the Adolescent—Skill Cards, by Dr. Arnold P. Goldstein and Dr. Ellen McGinnis, 1997.

Convenient 3 × 5–inch cards designed for student use during Skillstreaming sessions and homework assignments. Cards list the behavioral steps for each of the 50 adolescent Skillstreaming skills. Eight cards are provided for each skill (400 cards in all).

Video Components

People Skills: Doing 'em Right! (Adolescent Level), by Dr. Arnold P. Goldstein and Dr. Ellen McGinnis, 1997 (17 minutes).

Shows a Skillstreaming group in progress to help prospective group members learn what is expected in the group, understand how skill learning can help them, and motivate them to participate. Group leaders model the skill of Dealing with Group Pressure; students role-play the skill, receive feedback from other group members, then choose their real-life homework assignments.

The Skillstreaming Video: How to Teach Students Prosocial Skills, by Dr. Arnold P. Goldstein and Dr. Ellen McGinnis, 1988 (26 minutes).

Designed for teachers and other staff, this videotape shows Drs. Goldstein and McGinnis in actual training sessions with educators and small groups of adolescents and elementary-age children. Clearly demonstrates the Skillstreaming teaching model and the program's four main components—modeling, role-playing, performance feedback, and transfer training.

APPENDIX D
Skillstreaming Materials for Other Instructional Levels

Young Children

Program Text

Skillstreaming in Early Childhood: Teaching Prosocial Skills to the Preschool and Kindergarten Child, by Dr. Ellen McGinnis and Dr. Arnold P. Goldstein, 1990 (papercover, 200 pages, ISBN 0–87822–320–7).

Program Forms

Skillstreaming in Early Childhood: Teaching Prosocial Skills to the Preschool and Kindergarten Child—Program Forms, by Dr. Ellen McGinnis and Dr. Arnold P. Goldstein, 1990 (papercover, 8½ × 11–inch format, 80 pages, ISBN 0–87822–321–5).

Elementary-Age Children

Program Text

Skillstreaming the Elementary School Child: New Strategies and Perspectives for Teaching Prosocial Skills (rev. ed.), by Dr. Ellen McGinnis and Dr. Arnold P. Goldstein, 1997 (papercover, 352 pages, ISBN 0–87822–372–X).

Program Forms

Skillstreaming the Elementary School Child: New Strategies and Perspectives for Teaching Prosocial Skills—Program Forms (rev. ed.), by Dr. Ellen McGinnis and Dr. Arnold P. Goldstein, 1997 (papercover, 8½ × 11–inch format, 64 pages, ISBN 0–87822–374–6).

Student Manual

Skillstreaming the Elementary School Child—Student Manual, by Dr. Ellen McGinnis and Dr. Arnold P. Goldstein, 1997 (papercover, 8½ × 11–inch format, 80 pages, ISBN 0–87822–373–8).

Student Video

People Skills: Doing 'em Right! (Elementary Level), by Dr. Ellen McGinnis and Dr. Arnold P. Goldstein, 1997 (17 minutes).

Skill Cards

Skillstreaming the Elementary School Child—Skill Cards, by Dr. Ellen McGinnis and Dr. Arnold P. Goldstein, 1997.

Professional Training

The Skillstreaming Video: How to Teach Students Prosocial Skills, by Dr. Arnold P. Goldstein and Dr. Ellen McGinnis, 1988 (26 minutes).

References

Adler, A. (1924). *The practice and theory of individual psychology.* New York: Harcourt Brace Jovanovich.

Alberto, P.A., & Troutman, A.C. (1982). *Applied behavior analysis for teachers: Influencing student performance.* Columbus, OH: Charles E. Merrill.

American School Health Association. (1989). *National adolescent student health survey.* Oakland, CA: Third Party Publishing.

Anderson, R.A. (1978). *Stress power.* New York: Human Sciences.

Arbuthnot, J., & Gordon, D.A. (1983). Moral reasoning development in correctional intervention. *Journal of Correctional Education, 34,* 133–138.

Argyle, M. (1981). The experimental study of the basic features of situations. In D. Magnusson (Ed.), *Toward a psychology of situations: An interactional perspective.* Hillsdale, NJ: Erlbaum.

Arkowitz, H. (1977). Measurement and modification of minimal dating behavior. In M. Hersen, R.M. Eisler, & P.M. Miller (Eds.), *Progress in behavior modification* (Vol. 5). New York: Academic.

Aronson, E., Blaney, N., Stephan, C., Sikes, J., & Snapp, M. (1978). *The Jigsaw classroom.* Beverly Hills, CA: Sage.

Assagioli, R. (1973). *The act of will.* New York: Viking.

Aukstakalnis, S., & Blatner, D. (1992). *Silicon mirage: The art and science of virtual reality.* Berkeley, CA: Peachpit Press.

Axelrod, S., & Apsche, J. (Eds.). (1982). *The effects and side effects of punishment on human behavior.* New York: Academic.

Ayllon, T., & Azrin, N.H. (1968). *The token economy: A motivational system for therapy rehabilitation.* New York: Appleton-Century-Crofts.

Azrin, N.H., & Holz, W.C. (1966). Punishment. In W.K. Honig (Ed.), *Operant behavior: Areas of research and application.* New York: Appleton-Century-Crofts.

Backman, C. (1979). Epilogue: A new paradigm. In G. Ginsburg (Ed.), *Emerging strategies in social psychological research.* Chichester, England: Wiley.

Ban, J.R., & Ciminillo, L.M. (1977). *Violence and vandalism in public education.* Danville, IL: Interstate.

Bandura, A. (1973). *Aggression: A social learning analysis.* Englewood Cliffs, NJ: Prentice Hall.

Baumrind, D. (1975). Early socialization and adolescent competence. In S.E. Dragastin & G.H. Elder (Eds.), *Adolescence in the life cycle.* Washington, DC: Hemisphere.

Bayh, B. (1975, April). *Our nation's school—A report card: "A" in school violence and vandalism* (Preliminary report of the Subcommittee to Investigate Juvenile Delinquency). Washington, DC: U.S. Senate.

Benson, H. (1975). *The relaxation response.* New York: Avon.

Bergin, A.E., & Lambert, M.J. (1978). The evaluation of therapeutic outcomes. In S.L. Garfield & A.E. Bergin (Eds.), *Handbook of psychotherapy and behavior change.* New York: Wiley.

Block, A. (1977). The battered teacher. *Today's Education, 66,* 58–62.

Bradley, C.E. (1967). Vandalism and protective devices: Studies, conclusions, recommendations. *Proceedings of the Association of School Business Officials, 53,* 236–245.

Brown, P., & Fraser, C. (1979). Speech as a marker of situations. In K. Scherer & H. Giles (Eds.), *Social markers in speech.* Cambridge, England: Cambridge University Press.

Bryan, J.H., & Test, M.A. (1967). Models and helping: Naturalistic studies in aiding behavior. *Journal of Personality and Social Psychology, 6,* 400–407.

California Department of Education. (1990). *School crime in California for the 1988–1989 school year.* Sacramento, CA: Author.

Canale, J.R. (1977). The effect of modeling and length of ownership on sharing behavior of children. *Social Behavior and Personality, 5,* 187–191.

Carr, E.G. (1981). Contingency management. In A.P. Goldstein, E.G. Carr, W. Davidson, & P. Wehr (Eds.), *In response to aggression.* New York: Pergamon.

Cartledge, G., & Johnson, S. (1997). Cultural sensitivity. In A.P. Goldstein & J.C. Conoley (Eds.), *School violence intervention: A practical handbook.* New York: Guilford.

Cartledge, G., & Milburn, J.F. (1995). *Teaching social skills to children and youth.* Boston: Allyn & Bacon.

Casserly, M.D., Bass, S.A., & Garrett, J.R. (1980). *School vandalism: Strategies for prevention.* Lexington, MA: Lexington Books.

Center to Prevent Handgun Violence. (1990). *Caught in the crossfire: A report on gun violence in our nation's schools.* Washington, DC: Author.

Chandler, M., Greenspan, S., & Barenboim, C. (1974). Assessment and training of role-taking and referential communication skills in institutionalized emotionally disturbed children. *Developmental Psychology, 10,* 546–553.

Csikszentmihalyi, M., & Larsen, R. (1978). *Intrinsic rewards in school crime.* Hackensack, NJ: National Council on Crime and Delinquency.

Curran, J.P. (1977). Skills training as an approach to the treatment of heterosexual-social anxiety: A review. *Psychological Bulletin, 84,* 140–157.

Davis, A. (1967). Language and social class perspectives. In B. Goldstein (Ed.), *Low income youth in urban areas.* New York: Holt.

DeLange, J.M., Lanham, S.L., & Barton, J.A. (1981). Social skills training for juvenile delinquents: Behavioral skill training and cognitive techniques. In D. Upper & S. Ross (Eds.), *Behavioral group therapy, 1981: An annual review.* Champaign, IL: Research Press.

Dil, N. (1972). *Sensitivity of emotionally disturbed and emotionally non-disturbed elementary school children to emotional meanings of facial expressions.* Unpublished doctoral dissertation, Indiana University, Bloomington.

Dryfoos, J.G. (1994). *Full-service schools.* San Francisco: Jossey-Bass.

Ellis, H. (1965). *The transfer of learning.* New York: Macmillan.

Emery, J.E. (1975). *Social perception processes in normal and learning disabled children.* Unpublished doctoral dissertation, New York University.

Epps, S., Thompson, B.J., & Lane, M.P. (1985). *Procedures for incorporating generalization programming into interventions for behaviorally disordered students.* Unpublished manuscript, Iowa State University, Ames.

Evers, W.L., & Schwartz, J.C. (1973). Modifying social withdrawal in preschoolers: The effects of filmed modeling and teacher praise. *Journal of Abnormal Child Psychology, 1,* 248–256.

Feindler, E.L. (1979). *Cognitive and behavioral approaches to anger control training in explosive adolescents.* Unpublished doctoral dissertation, West Virginia University, Morgantown.

Feindler, E.L., & Ecton, R.B. (1986). *Adolescent anger control: Cognitive-behavioral techniques.* New York: Pergamon.

Ferster, C.B., & Skinner, B.F. (1957). *Schedules of reinforcement.* New York: Appleton-Century-Crofts.

Field, T. (1981). Early peer relations. In P.S. Strain (Ed.), *The utilization of classroom peers as behavior change agents.* New York: Plenum.

Firestone, P. (1976). The effects and side effects of time out on an aggressive nursery school child. *Journal of Behavior Therapy and Experimental Psychiatry, 6,* 79–81.

Fluegelman, A. (1981). *More new games.* Garden City, NY: Dolphin.

Ford, D.H., & Urban, H.B. (1963). *Systems of psychotherapy.* New York: Wiley.

Foxx, R.M., & Azrin, N.H. (1973). A method of eliminating aggressive-disruptive behavior for retarded and brain-damaged patients. *Behaviour Research and Therapy, 10,* 15–27.

Galassi, J.P., & Galassi, M.D. (1984). Promoting transfer and maintenance of counseling outcomes. In S.D. Brown & R.W. Lent (Eds.), *Handbook of counseling psychology.* New York: Wiley.

Garbarino, J. (1973). High school size and adolescent social development. *Human Ecology Forum, 4,* 26–29.

Gibbs, J.C. , Potter, G., & Goldstein, A.P. (1995). *The EQUIP program: Teaching youth to think and act responsibly through a peer-helping approach.* Champaign, IL: Research Press.

Giebink, J.W., Stover, D.S., & Fahl, M.A. (1968). Teaching adaptive responses in frustration to emotionally disturbed boys. *Journal of Consulting and Clinical Psychology, 32,* 336–368.

Goldstein, A.P. (1973). *Structured Learning Therapy: Toward a psychotherapy for the poor.* New York: Academic.

Goldstein, A.P. (1981). *Psychological skill training.* New York: Pergamon.

Goldstein, A.P. (1988). *The Prepare Curriculum: Teaching prosocial competencies.* Champaign, IL: Research Press.

Goldstein, A.P. (1990). *The refusal skills video.* Champaign, IL: Research Press.

Goldstein, A.P. (1992). *School violence: Its community context and potential solutions* (Testimony presented to the Subcommittee on Elementary, Secondary and Vocational Education, Committee on Education and Labor). Washington, DC: U.S. House of Representatives.

Goldstein, A.P., Glick, B., Carthan, W., & Blancero, D. (1994). *The prosocial gang.* Thousand Oaks, CA: Sage.

Goldstein, A.P., Glick, B., Irwin, M.J., Pask-McCartney, C., & Rubama, I. (1989). *Reducing delinquency: Intervention in the community.* New York: Pergamon.

Goldstein, A.P., Glick, B., Reiner, S., Zimmerman, D., & Coultry, T. (1986). *Aggression Replacement Training: A comprehensive program for aggressive youth.* Champaign, IL: Research Press.

Goldstein, A.P., Harootunian, B., & Conoley, J.C. (1994). *Student aggression: Prevention, control, replacement.* New York: Guilford.

Goldstein, A.P., Heller, K., & Sechrest, L.B. (1966). *Psychotherapy and the psychology of behavior change.* New York: Wiley.

Goldstein, A.P., & Kanfer, F.H. (1979). *Maximizing treatment gains.* New York: Academic.

Goldstein, A.P., & McGinnis, E. (1988). *The Skillstreaming video.* Champaign, IL: Research Press.

Goldstein, A.P., & Michaels, G.Y. (1985). *Empathy: Development, training and consequences.* Hillsdale, NJ: Erlbaum.

Goldstein, A.P., Palumbo, J., Striepling, S., & Voutsinas, A.M. (1995). *Break it up: A teacher's guide to managing student aggression.* Champaign, IL: Research Press.

Goldstein, A.P., Sprafkin, R.P., & Gershaw, N.J. (1976). *Skill training for community living: Applying Structured Learning Therapy.* New York: Pergamon.

Goldstein, A.P., Sprafkin, R.P., Gershaw, N.J., & Klein, P. (1980). *Skillstreaming the adolescent: A structured learning approach to teaching prosocial skills.* Champaign, IL: Research Press.

Gordon, S.B., & Asher, M.J. (1994). *Meeting the ADD challenge: A practical guide for teachers.* Champaign, IL: Research Press.

Grant, J.E. (1987). *Problem solving intervention for aggressive adolescent males: A preliminary investigation.* Unpublished doctoral dissertation, Syracuse University.

Greenwood, C.R., Hops, H., Delquadri, J., & Guild, J. (1974). Group contingencies for group consequences in classroom management: A further analysis. *Journal of Applied Behavior Analysis, 7,* 413–425.

Guralnick, M.J. (1981). Peer influences on the development of communicative competence. In P. Strain (Eds.), *The utilization of classroom peers as behavior change agents.* New York: Plenum.

Guzzetta, R.A. (1974). *Acquisition and transfer of empathy by the parents of early adolescents through structured learning training.* Unpublished doctoral dissertation, Syracuse University.

Hess, R.D., & Shipman, V.C. (1965). Early experience and the socialization of cognitive modes in children. *Child Development, 36,* 869–886.

Homme, L., Csanyi, A.P., Gonzales, M.A., & Rechs, J.R. (1969). *How to use contingency contracting in the classroom.* Champaign, IL: Research Press.

Horney, K. (1939). *New ways in psychoanalyses.* New York: Norton.

Ianni, F.A.J. (1978). The social organization of the high school: School-specific aspects of school crime. In E. Wenk & N. Harlow (Eds.), *School crime and disruption.* Davis, CA: Responsible Action.

Jacobson, E. (1938). *Progressive relaxation.* University of Chicago Press.

Jensen, A.R. (1967). Social class and verbal learning. In J.P. DeCecco (Ed.), *The psychology of language, thought and instruction.* New York: Holt.

Kagan, S. (1985). Learning to cooperate. In R. Slavin, S. Sharan, S. Kagan, R. Hertz-Lazarowitz, C. Webb, & R. Schmuck (Eds.), *Learning to cooperate, cooperating to learn.* New York: Plenum.

Kanfer, F.H., & Karoly, P. (1972). Self-control: A behavioristic excursion into the lion's den. *Behavior Therapy, 3,* 398–416.

Karoly, P. (1980). Operant methods. In E. Kanfer & A.P. Goldstein (Eds.), *Helping people change.* New York: Pergamon.

Karoly, P., & Steffen, J.J. (Eds.). (1980). *Improving the long term effects of psychotherapy.* New York: Gardner.

Kazdin, A.E. (1975). *Behavior modification in applied settings.* Homewood, IL: Dorsey.

Keeley, S.M., Shemberg, K.M., & Carbonell, J. (1976). Operant clinical intervention: Behavior management or beyond? Where are the data? *Behavior Therapy, 7,* 292–305.

Knight, B.J., & West, D.J. (1975). Temporary and continuing delinquency. *British Journal of Criminology, 15,* 43–50.

Kohlberg, L. (1969). Stage and sequence: The cognitive-developmental approach to socialization. In D.A. Goslin (Ed.), *Handbook of socialization theory and research.* Chicago: Rand McNally.

Kohlberg, L. (Ed.). (1973). *Collected papers on moral development and moral education.* Cambridge, MA: Harvard University, Center for Moral Education.

Kohn, A. (1986). *No contest.* Boston: Houghton Mifflin.

Kounin, J. (1970). *Discipline and group management in classrooms.* New York: Holt, Rinehart and Winston.

Ladd, G.W., & Mize, J. (1983). A cognitive-social learning model of social skill training. *Psychological Review, 90,* 127–157.

Loeber, R., & Dishion, T. (1983). Early predictors of male delinquency: A review. *Psychological Bulletin, 94,* 68–99.

Maller, J.B. (1929). *Cooperation and competition: An experimental study in innovation.* New York: Columbia University, Teachers College.

Manaster, G.J. (1977). *Adolescent development and the life tasks.* Boston: Allyn & Bacon.

McDermott, M.J. (1979). *Criminal victimization in urban schools.* Albany, NY: Criminal Justice Research Center.

McGinnis, E., & Goldstein, A.P. (1984). *Skillstreaming the elementary school child: A guide for teaching prosocial skills.* Champaign, IL: Research Press.

Metropolitan Life Insurance Co. (1993). *Violence in America's public schools.* New York: Author.

Miller, G., & Prinz, R.J. (1991). Designing interventions for stealing. In G. Stoner, M.R. Shinn, & H.M. Walker (Eds.), *Interventions for achievement and behavior problems.* Silver Springs, MD: National Association of School Psychologists.

Moriarty, A.E., & Toussieng, P.W. (1976). *Adolescent coping.* New York: Grune & Stratton.

Morris, R.J. (1976). *Behavior modification with children.* Cambridge, MA: Winthrop.

Morrison, R.L., & Bellack, A.S. (1981). The role of social perception in social skills. *Behavior Therapy, 12,* 69–70.

Muscott, H., & Gifford, T. (1994). Virtual reality and social skills training for students with behavior disorders: Applications, challenges and promising practice. *Education and Treatment of Children, 17,* 417–434.

Naranjo, C., & Ornstein, R.E. (1971). *On the psychology of mediation.* New York: Viking.

National Association of School Security Directors. (1975). *Crime in schools: 1974.* Washington, DC: Author.

National Center for Education Statistics. (1991). *Public school principal survey on safe, disciplined, and drug-free schools.* Washington, DC: U.S. Department of Education.

National Education Association. (1956). Teacher opinion on pupil behavior, 1955–1956. *Research Bulletin on the National Education Association, 34*(2).

Neilans, T.H., & Israel, A.C. (1981). Towards maintenance and generalization of behavior change: Teaching children self-regulation and self-instructional skills. *Cognitive Therapy and Research, 5,* 189–195.

Newsom, C., Favell, J.E., & Rincover, A. (1982). The side effects of punishment. In S. Axelrod & J. Apsche (Eds.), *The effects and side effects of punishment on human behavior.* New York: Academic.

Orlick, T. (1978). *The cooperative sports and games book.* New York: Pantheon.

Osgood, C.E. (1953). *Method and theory in experimental psychology.* New York: Oxford University Press.

Pablant, P., & Baxter, J.C. (1975). Environmental correlates of school vandalism. *Journal of the American Institute of Planners, 41,* 270–279.

Patterson, G.R., Reid, J.B., Jones, R.R., & Conger, R.E. (1975). *A social learning approach to family intervention* (Vol. 1). Eugene, OR: Castalia.

Pfeiffer, J.W., & Jones, J.E. (1974). *A handbook of structured experiences for human relations training* (Vols. 1–5). LaJolla, CA: University Associates.

Rachman, S.J., & Wilson, G.T. (1980). *The effects of psychological therapy.* New York: Pergamon.

Rank, O. (1945). *Will therapy.* New York: Knopf.

Remboldt, C. (1994). *Violence in schools: The enabling factor.* Minneapolis: Johnson Institute.

Robins, L.N., West, P.A., & Herjanic, B.L. (1975). Arrests and delinquency in two generations: A study of black urban families and their children. *Journal of Child Psychology and Psychiatry, 16,* 125–140.

Rogers, C.R. (1951). *Client-centered therapy: Its current practice, implications, and theory.* Boston: Houghton Mifflin.

Rosenberg, M. (1975). The dissonant context and adolescent self-concept. In S.E. Dragastin & G.H. Elder (Eds.), *Adolescence in the life cycle.* Washington, DC: Hemisphere.

Rothenberg, B.B. (1970). Children's social sensitivity and the relationship to interpersonal competence, interpersonal comfort, and intellectual level. *Developmental Psychology, 2,* 335–350.

Rubel, R.J. (1977). *Unruly school: Disorders, disruptions, and crimes.* Lexington, MA: D.C. Heath.

Sarason, I.G., Glaser, E.M., & Fargo, G.A. (1972). *Reinforcing productive classroom behavior.* New York: Behavioral Publications.

Schofield, W. (1964). *Psychotherapy, the purchase of friendship.* Englewood Cliffs, NJ: Prentice Hall.

School Safety Council. (1989). *Weapons in school.* Washington, DC: U.S. Department of Justice.

Selman, R.L. (1980). *The growth of interpersonal understanding.* New York: Academic.

Sharon, S., & Sharon, Y. (1976). *Small-group teaching.* Englewood Cliffs, NJ: Prentice Hall.

Siegel, L.M., & Senna, J.J. (1991). *Juvenile delinquency: Theory, practice & law.* St. Paul: West.

Skinner, B.F. (1938). *The behavior of organisms: An experimental analysis.* New York: Appleton-Century-Crofts.

Skinner, B.F. (1953). *Science and human behavior.* New York: Macmillan.

Slavin, R.E. (1980). *Using Student Team Learning* (rev. ed.). Baltimore, MD: Johns Hopkins University, Center for Social Organization of Schools.

Smith, M.L., & Glass, G.V. (1977). Meta-analysis of psychotherapy outcome studies. *American Psychologist, 32,* 752–760.

Spivack, G., Platt, J.J., & Shure, M.B. (1976). *The problem-solving approach to adjustment.* San Francisco: Jossey-Bass.

Stefanko, M.S. (1989). *Rates of secondary school vandalism and violence: Trends, demographic differences and the effects of the attitudes and behaviors of principals.* Unpublished doctoral dissertation, Claremont College.

Stokes, T.F., & Baer, D.M. (1977). An implicit technology of generalization. *Journal of Applied Behavior Analysis, 10,* 349–367.

Sullivan, H.S. (1953). *Conceptions of modern psychiatry.* New York: Norton.

Sulzer-Azaroff, B., & Mayer, G.R. (1977). *Applying behavior analysis procedures with children and youth.* New York: Holt, Rinehart and Winston.

Tharp, R.G., & Wetzel, R.J. (1969). *Behavior modification in the natural environment.* New York: Academic.

Thayer, L., & Beeler, K.D. (1975). *Activities and exercises for affective education.* Washington, DC: American Educational Research Associates.

Thorndike, E.L., & Woodworth, R.S. (1901). The influence of improvement in one mental function upon the efficiency of other functions. *Psychological Review, 8,* 247–261.

Turner, C.W., & Thrasher, M. (1970). *School size does make a difference.* San Diego: Institute for Educational Management.

Tygart, C. (1988). Public school vandalism: Toward a synthesis of theories and transition to paradigm analysis. *Adolescence, 23,* 187–199.

U.S. Department of Justice. (1988). *Report to the nation on crime and justice.* Washington, DC: U.S. Government Printing Office.

U.S. Department of Justice. (1993). *Bureau of Justice news release.* Washington, DC: Author.

Van Houten, R. (1982). Punishment: From the animal laboratory to the applied setting. In S. Axelrod & J. Apsche (Eds.), *The effects and side effects of punishment on human behavior.* New York: Academic.

Vestermark, S.D., & Blauvelt, P.D. (1978). *Controlling crime in the school: A complete security handbook for administrators.* West Nyack, NY: Parker.

Walker, H.M. (1979). *The acting-out child: Coping with classroom disruption.* Boston: Allyn & Bacon.

Werner, E.E., & Smith, R.S. (1982). *Vulnerable but invincible.* New York: McGraw-Hill.

White, G.D., Nielson, G., & Johnson, S.M. (1972). Time out duration and the suppression of deviant behavior in children. *Journal of Applied Behavior Analysis, 5,* 111–120.

Yamamoto, J., & Goin, M.K. (1965). On the treatment of the poor. *American Journal of Psychiatry, 122,* 267–271.

Zimmerman, D. (1983). Moral education. In A.P. Goldstein (Ed.), *Prevention and control of aggression.* New York: Pergamon.

NAME INDEX

Subject Index

About the Authors

Arnold P. Goldstein joined the clinical psychology section of Syracuse University's Psychology Department in 1963 and both taught there and directed its Psychotherapy Center until 1980. In 1981, he founded the Center for Research on Aggression, which he currently directs. He joined Syracuse University's Division of Special Education in 1985 and in 1990 helped organize and codirect the New York State Task Force on Juvenile Gangs. Dr. Goldstein has a career-long interest, as both researcher and practitioner, in difficult-to-reach clients. Since 1980, his main research and psychoeducational focus has been youth violence. He is the developer of psychoeducational programs and curricula designed to teach prosocial behaviors to chronically antisocial persons. Dr. Goldstein's many books include, among others, *Aggression Replacement Training: A Comprehensive Intervention for Aggressive Youth, The Prepare Curriculum: Teaching Prosocial Competencies, Delinquents on Delinquency, The Gang Intervention Handbook,* and *Break It Up: A Teacher's Guide to Managing Student Aggression.*

Ellen McGinnis earned her PhD from the University of Iowa in 1986. She holds degrees in elementary education, special education, and school administration. She has taught elementary and secondary students in the public schools in Minnesota, Iowa, and Arizona. In addition, she has served as a special education consultant in both public and hospital schools and as assistant professor of special education at the University of Wisconsin–Eau Claire. For the past 5 years, Dr. McGinnis has served with the Des Moines Public Schools as the principal of the education program at Orchard Place, a residential and day treatment facility for children and adolescents with emotional/behavioral disorders. The author of numerous articles on identifying and teaching youth with emotional/behavioral disorders, Dr. McGinnis is coauthor with Dr. Arnold P. Goldstein of *Skillstreaming in Early Childhood* and first author of the newly revised edition of *Skillstreaming the Elementary School Child.* She and her husband, Carl Smith, are the parents of Sara, age 14, and Alex, age 10.